Henry Wadsworth Longfellow

Prose Works

With Bibliographical and Critical Notes

Henry Wadsworth Longfellow

Prose Works
With Bibliographical and Critical Notes

ISBN/EAN: 9783744685368

Printed in Europe, USA, Canada, Australia, Japan

Cover: Foto ©Thomas Meinert / pixelio.de

More available books at **www.hansebooks.com**

HYPERION
AND KAVANAGH

BY

HENRY WADSWORTH LONGFELLOW

BOSTON AND NEW YORK
HOUGHTON, MIFFLIN AND COMPANY
The Riverside Press, Cambridge
M DCCC XC

The Riverside Press, Cambridge, Mass., U. S. A.
Electrotyped and Printed by H. O. Houghton & Company.

CONTENTS

6 CONTENTS

HYPERION

INTRODUCTORY NOTE.

Hyperion as a book was begun in September, 1838, pursued vigorously during the fall, worked at more slowly through the winter, and finally put into the printer's hands in June, 1839. It was finished by the end of July, and published the second week in August. The material, however, out of which the book was made took shape earlier. The basis of it was the experience of Mr. Longfellow in Europe in 1835 and 1836. He left New York in the spring of 1835, accompanied by his wife and two friends ; spent the summer in England and Northern Europe, but went to Rotterdam in the fall. There his wife died at the end of November. He travelled thence alone to Heidelberg, where he passed the winter, and in the following summer was in the Tyrol and Switzerland, returning to America in October, 1836. His recently published *Life* enables us to trace his journey step by step, and the route from Rotterdam to Heidelberg is precisely that of Paul Flemming, while the studies of his hero in Heidelberg, his friendships and his excursions in the coming summer, correspond substantially with Mr. Longfellow's own course, as indicated in his diary and letters.

Mr. Samuel Longfellow points out the identity of characters in the book with certain persons whom the author fell in with, and the whole tale is a rescript, only slightly disguised, of the poet's spiritual as well as external experience. He himself clearly indicated the relation which he held to his work in a letter to Mr. George Washington Greene, in which he says : —

" I have written a Romance during this past year. The *feelings* of the book are true ; the *events* of the story mostly fictitious. The heroine, of course, bears a resemblance to the lady, without being an exact portrait. There is no betrayal of confidence, *no real scene* described. *Hyperion* is the name of the book, not of the hero. It merely indicates that here is the life of one who in his feelings and purposes is a ' son of Heaven and Earth,' and who, though obscured by clouds, yet ' moves on high.' Further than this the name has nothing to do with the book, and in fact is mentioned only once in the course of it. I expect to be mightily abused. People will say that I am the hero of my own romance, and compare myself to the sun, to Hyperion Apollo. This is not so. I wish only to embody certain feelings which are mine, not to magnify myself."

In writing *Hyperion* Mr. Longfellow easily wrought into the fabric material which he had previously used in other forms. In the summer before he began the active preparation of the book, he delivered before his classes at Cambridge a course of lectures upon the Lives of Literary Men, and from these he took the chapters on Jean Paul, on the Lives of Scholars, and on Literary Fame in the first Book; the sketch of an artist's life in

Rome and the picture of the Middle Ages, given in the third Book ; and the chapter on Hoffmann and his writings, in the fourth Book. From *The Blank Book of a Country Schoolmaster*, also, which he contributed to *The Knickerbocker* in 1834 and 1835, he drew some passages.

His diary indicates the eagerness with which he set about the book, the impatience with which he bore interruptions, and the severity of the criticism to which he subjected his work. He had at first intended to name his hero Hyperion, then he gave him the name of St. Clair, and finally abandoned that for Paul Flemming. The occasional notes in his diary intimate the hold which the book had upon his mind : —

" *October* 18, 1838. Wrote a chapter in Hyperion. Thus slowly goes on the work. Well, or ill, I must work right on, and wait for no happier moments.

" *October* 23. Worked at Hyperion again. Wrote chapter six of Book IV., — a touch at philosophical *dreamery*. But I have so many interruptions ! No matter, — onward ! If it be but one chapter a week, it would complete the book within a year. That 's too long.

" *November* 5. A rainy day, and now a rainy night, — for a chapter in Hyperion ! Let me see what I can do at a dash ! Come out of thy drawer, thou thin, marbled portfolio ! Open thy lips, and speak of Heidelberg and the Baron ! And out of this flourish came nothing but revision of my work and meditation. And as I sat and meditated deep into the night, I resolved to suppress one entire book ; namely, St. Clair's Day-Book.

" *November* 8. A rainy day. Passed the greater part

of it at work on Hyperion, retouching and writing. Wrote a new chapter one to Book III.; namely, the short chapter on Spring.

"*December* 10. Company till noon. . . . After they had gone, sat down to Hyperion. Went without my dinner and wrote till dark; the Baron and Heidelberg; and the arrangement of the last chapter of Book I. The first volume is now ready for the press.

"*December* 18. Contrived to write a short chapter in Hyperion, chapter eight, Book IV. Hope to get into train again soon, and go on gallantly as before. So much for breaks.

"*April* 5, 1839. Confined to my chamber with a bad cold and feverish unrest. Worked at Hyperion like a hero.

"*April* 6. An exact counterpart of yesterday; and I at work upon my Romance, — changing and arranging and writing out various portions. Wrote the last chapter, though others remain to be written."

He wrote to his father, under date of June 16, 1839 : —

" I have begun to print Hyperion, and have three men at work upon it, setting type. I hope to have it out in about a month; and shall, unless Colman delays. As to the *money* part of the business, he is to pay me three hundred and seventy-five dollars, by his notes, on the day of publication; said notes payable in three and six months. . . . At all events, I get the book very handsomely printed and widely circulated; and this is a great point. As to its success, I am very sanguine. I look upon the work of my hands with a very complacent smile; and it will take a great deal of persuasion to convince me that the book is not good. This is my candid opinion."

After the book had been out a few weeks he wrote again to his father : —

" Hyperion attracts great attention, and excites very strong and opposite feelings. Some praise, and others condemn in no measured terms ; and the book sells with a rapidity far beyond my expectations. I hear that a new edition will soon be called for ; which, if so, will be a triumph, considering the nature of the book. People seem to be much puzzled about it, and some are quite angry because they cannot see through it as easily as their *a b c.* But I have the approbation of those whose approbation I most desire, and of course do not much care how others abuse. What delights me is that it calls forth very *strong* and decided opinions. I am free for once from the *laudatur et alget.*"

" See what ill-luck with Hyperion " [he wrote to Mr. Greene, January 2, 1840]. " The publisher fails ; half the edition (that is, twelve hundred copies) is seized by creditors and locked up ; and the book has been out of the market for four months. No matter. I had the glorious satisfaction of writing it. . . . I called it *Hyperion*, because it *moves on high*, among clouds and stars, and expresses the various aspirations of the soul of man. It is all modelled on this idea, style and all. It contains my cherished thoughts for three years. Pardon my saying so much. In offset, I will send you the ' horrible dispraise' I spoke of, though the papers that uttered it have since nearly come round, and have even praised some parts of it. How victorious is silence ! "

The publisher who failed was Samuel Colman, of New York. The book came out in two volumes in boards, with pale olive-colored paper sides. The author's name was not printed on the title-page, but the book was announced as by the author of

Outre-Mer. Mr. Longfellow took the opportunity
afforded by subsequent editions to revise the text,
but the structure of the work remains unchanged.
The motto, which in the first edition was placed on
the title-page, is a translation from an inscription
which he read upon a funeral tablet in the church-
yard of St. Gilgen in the Tyrol, as described
in Book IV., chapter viii. It is curious that
ten years later, in 1849, when he had completed
Kavanagh, he meditated a continuation of *Hype-
rion,* intending in it to bring his hero to America.

These two works were not the only contribu-
tions which Mr. Longfellow made to fiction in
prose, but they were the only ones which he cared
to preserve. He mentions in a letter to Mr.
Greene that he has published a tale in *The Token*
for 1832, and another in the same annual for 1833.
The former of these was entitled *The Indian
Summer;* the latter was *The Bald Eagle,* and
may have been the accomplishment of a design,
mentioned in his note-book in 1829, of a sketch
based on the reception of Lafayette in a country
village.

HYPERION

A ROMANCE

Look not mournfully into the Past. It comes not back again. Wisely improve the Present. It is thine. Go forth to meet the shadowy Future, without fear, and with a manly heart.

BOOK THE FIRST.

CHAPTER I.

THE HERO.

In John Lyly's " Endymion," Sir Topas is made to say : " Dost thou know what a poet is ? Why, fool, a poet is as much as one should say, — a poet ! " And thou, reader, dost thou know what a hero is ? Why, a hero is as much as one should say, — a hero ! Some romance-writers, however, say much more than this. Nay, the old Lombard, Matteo Maria Bojardo, set all the church-bells in Scandiano ringing, merely because he had found a name for one of his heroes. Here, also, shall church-bells be rung, but more solemnly.

The setting of a great hope is like the setting of the sun. The brightness of our life is gone. Shadows of evening fall around us, and the world seems but a dim reflection, — itself a broader shadow. We look forward into the coming lonely

night. The soul withdraws into itself. Then
stars arise, and the night is holy.

Paul Flemming had experienced this, though
still young. The friend of his youth was dead.
The bough had broken " under the burden of the
unripe fruit." And when, after a season, he looked
up again from the blindness of his sorrow, all
things seemed unreal. Like the man whose sight
had been restored by miracle, he beheld men, as
trees, walking. His household gods were broken.
He had no home. His sympathies cried aloud
from his desolate soul, and there came no answer
from the busy, turbulent world around him. He
did not willingly give way to grief. He struggled
to be cheerful, — to be strong. But he could no
longer look into the familiar faces of his friends.
He could no longer live alone, where he had lived
with her. He went abroad, that the sea might be
between him and the grave. Alas! between him
and his sorrow there could be no sea, but that of
time.

He had already passed many months in lonely
wandering, and was now pursuing his way along
the Rhine, to the South of Germany. He had
journeyed the same way before, in brighter days
and a brighter season of the year, in the May of
life and in the month of May. He knew the beau-
tiful river all by heart, — every rock and ruin,
every echo, every legend. The ancient castles,
grim and hoar, that had taken root as it were on
the cliffs, — they were all his ; for his thoughts
dwelt in them, and the wind told him tales.

He had passed a sleepless night at Rolandseck,

and had risen before daybreak. He opened the
window of the balcony to hear the rushing of the
Rhine. It was a damp December morning; and
clouds were passing over the sky, — thin, vapory
clouds, whose snow-white skirts were "often spotted
with golden tears, which men call stars." The day
dawned slowly; and, in the mingling of daylight
and starlight, the island and cloister of Nonnen-
werth made together but one broad, dark shadow
on the silver breast of the river. Beyond, rose the
summits of the Siebengebirg. Solemn and dark,
like a monk, stood the Drachenfels, in his hood of
mist; and rearward extended the curtain of moun-
tains, back to the Wolkenburg, — the Castle of
Clouds.

But Flemming thought not of the scene before
him. · Sorrow unspeakable was upon his spirit in
that lonely hour; and, hiding his face in his hands,
he exclaimed aloud : —

"Spirit of the past! look not so mournfully at
me with thy great tearful eyes! Touch me not
with thy cold hand! Breathe not upon me with
the icy breath of the grave! Chant no more that
dirge of sorrow, through the long and silent watches
of the night!"

Mournful voices from afar seemed to answer,
"Treuenfels!" and he remembered how others had
suffered, and his heart grew still.

Slowly the landscape brightened. Down the
rushing stream came a boat, with its white wings
spread, and darted like a swallow through the nar-
row pass of God's-Help. The boatmen were sing-
ing, — but not the song of Roland the Brave,

which was heard of old by the weeping Hildegund,
as she sat within the walls of that cloister which
now looked forth in the pale morning from amid
the leafless linden-trees. The dim traditions of
those gray old times rose in the traveller's memory ;
for the ruined tower of Rolandseck was still look-
ing down upon the Kloster Nonnenwerth, as if the
sound of the funeral bell had changed the faithful
paladin to stone and he were watching still to see
the form of his beloved one come forth, not from
her cloister, but from her grave. Thus the brazen
clasps of the book of legends were opened, and, on
the page illuminated by the misty rays of the rising
sun, he read again the tales of Liba, and the mourn-
ful bride of Argenfels, and Siegfried, the mighty
slayer of the dragon. Meanwhile the mists had
risen from the Rhine, and the whole air was filled
with golden vapor, through which he beheld the
sun, hanging in heaven like a drop of blood.
Even thus shone the sun within him, amid the
wintry vapors uprising from the valley of the
shadow of death, through which flowed the stream
of his life, — sighing, sighing !

CHAPTER II.

THE CHRIST OF ANDERNACH.

Paul Flemming resumed his solitary journey.
The morning was still misty, but not cold. Across
the Rhine the sun came wading through the red-
dish vapors ; and soft and silver-white outspread
the broad river, without a ripple upon its surface

or visible motion of the ever-moving current. A little vessel, with one loose sail, was riding at anchor, keel to keel with another that lay beneath it, its own apparition, — and all was silent, and calm, and beautiful.

The road was for the most part solitary; for there are but few travellers upon the Rhine in winter. Peasant-women were at work in the vineyards, climbing up the slippery hillsides, like beasts of burden, with large baskets upon their backs. And once during the morning a band of apprentices, with knapsacks, passed by, singing, " The Rhine ! the Rhine ! a blessing on the Rhine ! "

Oh, the pride of the German heart in this noble river ! And right it is ; for, of all the rivers of this beautiful earth, there is none so beautiful as this. There is hardly a league of its whole course, from its cradle in the snowy Alps to its grave in the sands of Holland, which boasts not its peculiar charms. By heavens ! If I were a German, I would be proud of it too; and of the clustering grapes that hang about its temples, as it reels onward through vineyards in a triumphal march, like Bacchus crowned and drunken.

But I will not attempt to describe the Rhine ; it would make this chapter much too long. And to do it well, one should write like a god ; and his language flow onward royally with breaks and dashes, like the waters of that royal river, and antique, quaint, and Gothic times be reflected in it. Alas ! this evening mine flows not at all. Flow, then, into this smoke-colored goblet, thou blood of the Rhine ! out of thy prison-house, —

out of thy long-necked, tapering flask, in shape
not unlike a church-spire among thy native hills ;
and from the crystal belfry loud ring the merry
tinkling bells, while I drink a health to my hero,
in whose heart is sadness, and in whose ears the
bells of Andernach are ringing noon.

He is threading his way along through a narrow
alley, and now up a flight of stone steps, and along
the city wall, towards that old round tower built
by the Archbishop Frederick of Cologne, in the
twelfth century. It has a romantic interest in his
eyes ; for he has still in his mind and heart that
beautiful sketch of Carové, in which is described a
day on the tower of Andernach. He finds the old
keeper and his wife still there ; and the old keeper
closes the door behind him slowly, as of yore, lest
he should jam too hard the poor souls in purgatory,
whose fate it is to suffer in the cracks of doors and
hinges. But, alas ! alas ! the daughter, the maiden
with long, dark eyelashes ! she is asleep in her
little grave, under the linden-trees of Feldkirche,
with rosemary in her folded hands !

Flemming returned to the hotel disappointed.
As he passed along the narrow streets, he was
dreaming of many things ; but mostly of the
keeper's daughter, asleep in the churchyard of
Feldkirche. Suddenly, on turning the corner of
an ancient, gloomy church, his attention was ar-
rested by a little chapel in an angle of the wall.
It was only a small thatched roof, like a bird's
nest ; under which stood a rude wooden image of
the Saviour on the cross. A real crown of thorns
was upon his head, which was bowed downward, as

if in the death agony; and drops of blood were
falling down his cheeks, and from his hands and
feet and side. The face was haggard and ghastly
beyond expression, and wore a look of unutterable
bodily anguish. The rude sculptor had given it
this, but his art could go no further. The sub-
limity of death in a dying Saviour, the expiring
God-likeness of Jesus of Nazareth, was not there.
The artist had caught no heavenly inspiration from
his theme. All was coarse, harsh, and revolting
to a sensitive mind; and Flemming turned away
with a shudder, as he saw this fearful image gazing
at him, with its fixed and half-shut eyes.

He soon reached the hotel, but that face of
agony still haunted him. He could not refrain
from speaking of it to a very old woman, who sat
knitting by the window of the dining-room, in a
high-backed, old-fashioned arm-chair. I believe
she was the inn-keeper's grandmother. At all
events, she was old enough to be so. She took off
her owl-eyed spectacles, and, as she wiped the
glasses with her handkerchief, said: —

"Thou dear Heaven! Is it possible? Did
you never hear of the Christ of Andernach?"

Flemming answered in the negative.

"Thou dear Heaven!" continued the old wo-
man. "It is a very wonderful story; and a true
one, as every good Christian in Andernach will
tell you. And it all happened before the death
of my blessed man, four years ago; let me see,
— yes, four years ago, come Christmas."

Here the old woman stopped speaking, but went
on with her knitting. Other thoughts seemed to

occupy her mind. She was thinking, no doubt, of her blessed man, as German widows call their dead husbands. But Flemming having expressed an ardent wish to hear the wonderful story, she told it, in nearly the following words.

" There was once a poor old woman in Andernach whose name was Frau Martha, and she lived all alone in a house by herself, and loved all the Saints and the Blessed Virgin, and was as good as an angel, and sold tarts down by the Rheinkrahn. But her house was very old, and the roof-tiles were broken, and she was too poor to get new ones, and the rain kept coming in, and no Christian soul in Andernach would help her. But the Frau Martha was a good woman, and never did anybody any harm, but went to mass every morning, and sold tarts down by the Rheinkrahn. Now one dark, windy night, when all the good Christians in Andernach were asleep in the feathers, Frau Martha, who lay under the roof, heard a great noise over her head, and in her chamber, drip! drip! drip! as if the rain were dropping down through the broken tiles. Dear soul! and, sure enough, it was. And then there was a pounding and hammering overhead, as if somebody were at work on the roof; and she thought it was Pelz-Nickel tearing the tiles off, because she had not been to confession often enough. So she began to pray; and the faster she said her Pater-noster and her Ave Maria, the faster Pelz-Nickel pounded and pulled; and drip! drip! drip! it went all round her in the dark chamber, till the poor woman was frightened out of her wits, and ran to

the window to call for help. Then in a moment all was still, — death-still. But she saw a light streaming through the mist and rain, and a great shadow on the house opposite. And then somebody came down from the top of her house by a ladder, and had a lantern in his hand; and he took the ladder on his shoulder and passed down the street. But she could not see clearly, because the window was streaked with rain. And in the morning the old broken tiles were found scattered about the street, and there were new ones on the roof, and the old house has never leaked to this blessed day.

"As soon as mass was over, Frau Martha told the priest what had happened, and he said it was not Pelz-Nickel, but, without doubt, St. Castor or St. Florian. Then she went to the market and told Frau Bridget all about it; and Frau Bridget said, that, two nights before, Hans Claus, the cooper, had heard a great pounding in his shop, and in the morning found new hoops on all his hogsheads; and that a man with a lantern and a ladder had been seen riding out of town at midnight on a donkey; and that the same night the old windmill, at Kloster St. Thomas, had been mended, and the old gate of the churchyard at Feldkirche made as good as new, though nobody knew how the man got across the river. Then Frau Martha went down to the Rheinkrahn and told all these stories over again; and the old ferryman of Fahr said he could tell something about it; for, the very night that the churchyard-gate was mended, he was lying awake in his bed, be-

cause he could not sleep, and he heard a loud knocking at the door, and somebody calling to him to get up and set him over the river. And when he got up, he saw a man down by the river with a lantern and a ladder; but as he was going down to him, the man blew out the light, and it was so dark he could not see who he was; and his boat was old and leaky, and he was afraid to set him over in the dark; but the man said he must be in Andernach that night; and so he set him over. And after they had crossed the river, he watched the man, till he came to an image of the Holy Virgin, and saw him put the ladder against the wall, and go up and light his lamp, and then walk along the street. And in the morning he found his old boat all calked, and tight, and painted red, and he could not for his blessed life tell who did it, unless it were the man with the lantern. Dear soul! how strange it was!

"And so it went on for some time; and whenever the man with the lantern had been seen walking through the street at night, so sure as the morning came, some work had been done for the sake of some good soul; and everybody knew he did it; and yet nobody could find out who he was, nor where he lived; — for, whenever anybody came near him, he blew out his light, turned down another street, and suddenly disappeared, nobody could tell how. And some said it was Rübezahl; and some, Pelz-Nickel; and some, St. Anthony-on-the-Heath.

"Now one stormy night, a poor, sinful creature was wandering about the streets, with her babe in

her arms, and she was hungry, and cold, and no
soul in Andernach would take her in. And when
she came to the church, where the great crucifix
stands, she saw no light in the little chapel at the
corner; but she sat down on a stone at the foot of
the cross and began to pray, and prayed till she
fell asleep, with her poor little babe on her bosom.
But she did not sleep long; for a bright light
shone full in her face; and when she opened her
eyes, she saw a pale man, with a lantern, standing
right before her. He was almost naked; and
there was blood upon his hands and body, and
great tears in his beautiful eyes, and his face was
like the face of the Saviour on the cross. Not a
single word did he say to the poor woman; but
looked at her compassionately, and gave her a loaf
of bread, and took the little babe in his arms, and
kissed it. Then the mother looked up to the great
crucifix, but there was no image there; and she
shrieked and fell down as if she were dead. And
there she was found with her child; and a few
days after, they both died, and were buried to-
gether in one grave. And nobody would have be-
lieved her story, if a woman, who lived at the cor-
ner, had not gone to the window when she heard
the scream, and seen the figure hang the lantern
up in its place, and then set the ladder against the
wall, and go up and nail itself to the cross. Since
that night it has never moved again. Ach! Herr
Je!"

Such was the legend of the Christ of Ander-
nach, as the old woman in spectacles told it to
Flemming. It made a painful impression on his

sick and morbid soul; and he felt now for the first time how great is the power of popular superstition.

The post-chaise being already at the door, Flemming was soon on the road to Coblentz, a town which stands upon the Rhine, at the mouth of the Mosel, opposite Ehrenbreitstein. It is by no means a long drive from Andernach to Coblentz; and the only incident which occurred to enliven the way was the appearance of a fat, red-faced man on horseback, trotting slowly towards Andernach. As they met, the mad little postilion gave him a friendly cut with his whip, and broke out into an exclamation, which showed he was from Münster : —

"Jesmariosp! my friend! How is the Man in the Kaufhaus?"

Now to any candid mind this would seem a fair question enough; but not so thought the red-faced man on horseback; for he waxed exceedingly angry, and replied, as the chaise whirled by : —

"The devil take you, and your Westphalian ham, and pumpernickel!"

Flemming called to his servant, and the servant to the postilion, for an explanation of this short dialogue; and the explanation was, that on the belfry of the Kaufhaus in Coblentz is a huge head with a brazen helmet and a beard; and whenever the clock strikes, at each stroke of the hammer, this giant's head opens its great jaws and smites its teeth together, as if, like the brazen head of Friar Bacon, it would say, "Time was; Time is; Time is past." This figure is known through all the

country round-about as " The Man in the Kauf-
haus ; " and when a friend in the country meets a
friend from Coblentz, instead of saying, " How
are all the good people in Coblentz ? " — he says,
" How is the Man in the Kaufhaus ? " Thus the
giant has a great part to play in the town. And
thus ended the first day of Flemming's Rhine-
journey ; and the only good deed he had done was
to give an alms to a poor beggar woman, who lifted
up her trembling hands and exclaimed : —

" Thou blessed babe ! "

CHAPTER III.

HOMUNCULUS.

After all, a journey up the Rhine, in the mists
and solitude of December, is not so unpleasant as
the reader may imagine. You have the whole
road and river to yourself. Nobody is on the
wing; hardly a single traveller. The ruins are the
same ; and the river, and the outlines of the hills ;
and there are few living figures in the landscape
to wake you from your musings, distract your
thoughts, and cover you with dust.

Thus likewise thought our traveller, as he con-
tinued his journey ön the morrow. The day is
overcast, and the clouds threaten rain or snow.
Why does he stop at the little village of Capellen?
Because, right above him on the high cliff, the
glorious ruin of Stolzenfels is looking at him with
its hollow eyes, and beckoning to him with its
gigantic finger, as if to say, " Come up hither, and

I will tell thee an old tale." Therefore he alights, and goes up the narrow village lane, and up the stone steps, and up the steep pathway, and throws himself into the arms of that ancient ruin, and holds his breath, to hear the quick footsteps of the falling snow, like the footsteps of angels descending upon earth. And that ancient ruin speaks to him with its hollow voice, and says : —

" Beware of dreams ! Beware of the illusions of fancy ! Beware of the solemn deceivings of thy vast desires ! Beneath me flows the Rhine, and, like the stream of Time, it flows amid the ruins of the Past. I see myself therein, and I know that I am old. Thou, too, shalt be old. Be wise in season. Like the stream of thy life runs the stream beneath us. Down from the distant Alps, — out into the wide world, it bursts away, like a youth from the house of his fathers. Broad-breasted and strong, and with earnest endeavors, like manhood, it makes itself a way through these difficult mountain-passes. And at length, in its old age, it falters, and its steps are weary and slow, and it sinks into the sand, and, through its grave, passes into the great ocean, which is its eternity. Thus shall it be with thee.

" In ancient times, there dwelt within these halls a follower of Jesus of Jerusalem, — an Archbishop in the Church of Christ. He gave himself up to dreams, to the illusions of fancy, to the vast desires of the human soul. He sought after the impossible. He sought after the Elixir of Life, — the Philosopher's Stone. The wealth that should

have fed the poor was melted in his crucibles. Within these walls the Eagle of the clouds sucked the blood of the Red Lion, and received the spiritual love of the Green Dragon; but, alas! was childless. In solitude and utter silence did the disciple of the Hermetic Philosophy toil from day to day, from night to night. From the place where thou standest, he gazed at evening upon hills, and vales, and waters spread beneath him; and saw how the setting sun had changed them all to gold, by an alchemy more cunning than his own. He saw the world beneath his feet; and said in his heart, that he alone was wise. Alas! he read more willingly in the book of Paracelsus than in the book of Nature; and, believing that ' where reason hath experience, faith hath no mind,' would fain have made unto himself a child, as the Philosopher taught, — a poor homunculus, in a glass bottle. And he died poor and childless! "

Whether it were worth while to climb the Stolzenfels to hear such a homily as this, some persons may perhaps doubt. But Paul Flemming doubted not. He laid the lesson to heart; and it would have saved him many an hour of sorrow, if he had learned that lesson better, and remembered it longer.

In ancient times, there stood in the citadel of Athens three statues of Minerva. The first was of olive-wood, and, according to popular tradition, had fallen from heaven. The second was of bronze, commemorating the victory of Marathon; and the third of gold and ivory, — a great miracle of art, in the age of Pericles. And thus in the citadel of

Time stands Man himself. In childhood, shaped of soft and delicate wood, just fallen from heaven; in manhood, a statue of bronze, commemorating struggle and victory; and, lastly, in the maturity of age, perfectly shaped in gold and ivory,— a miracle of art!

Flemming had already lived through the olive age. He was passing into the age of bronze, into his early manhood; and in his hands the flowers of Paradise were changing to the sword and shield.

And this reminds me that I have not yet described my hero. I will do it now, as he stands looking down on the glorious landscape;— but in few words. Both in person and character he resembled Harold the Fair-Hair of Norway, who is described, in the old Icelandic Death-Song of Regner Hairy-Breeches, as "the young chief so proud of his flowing locks; he who spent his mornings among the young maidens; he who loved to converse with the handsome widows." This was an amiable weakness, and it sometimes led him into mischief. Imagination was the ruling power of his mind. His thoughts were twin-born; the thought itself, and its figurative semblance in the outer world. Thus, through the quiet, still waters of his soul each image floated double, "swan and shadow."

These traits of character, a good heart, and a poetic imagination, made his life joyous and the world beautiful; till at length Death cut down the sweet blue flower that bloomed beside him, and wounded him with that sharp sickle, so that he bowed his head, and would fain have been bound

up in the same sheaf with the sweet blue flower. Then the world seemed to him less beautiful, and life became earnest. It would have been well, if he could have forgotten the past; that he might not so mournfully have lived in it, but might have enjoyed and improved the present. But this his heart refused to do; and ever, as he floated upon the great sea of life, he looked down through the transparent waters, checkered with sunshine and shade, into the vast chambers of the mighty deep in which his happier days had sunk, and wherein they were lying still visible, like golden sands, and precious stones, and pearls; and, half in despair, half in hope, he grasped downward after them again, and drew back his hand, filled only with sea-weed, and dripping with briny tears! And between him and those golden sands a radiant image floated, like the spirit in Dante's Paradise, singing, " Ave Maria ! " and while it sang, down-sinking, and slowly vanishing away.

In all things he acted more from impulse than from fixed principle, as is the case with most young men. Indeed, his principles hardly had time to take root; for he pulled them all up, every now and then, as children do the flowers they have planted, — to see if they are growing. Yet there was much in him which was good; for underneath the flowers and greensward of poetry, and the good principles which would have taken root had he given them time, there lay a strong and healthy soil of common sense, — freshened by living springs of feeling, and enriched by many faded hopes, that had fallen upon it like dead leaves.

CHAPTER IV.

THE LANDLADY'S DAUGHTER.

" Allez, Fuchs ! allez, lustig ! " cried the impatient postilion to his horses, in accents which, like the wild echo of the Lurley Felsen, came first from one side of the river and then from the other, — that is to say, in words alternately French and German. The truth is, he was tired of waiting ; and when Flemming had at length resumed his seat in the post-chaise, the poor horses had to make up the time he had lost in dreams on the mountain. This is far oftener the case than most people imagine. One half of the world must sweat and groan, that the other half may dream. It would have been a difficult task for the traveller or his postilion to persuade the horses that these dreams were all for their good.

The next stopping-place was the little tavern of the Star, an out-of-the-way corner in the town of Salzig. It stands on the banks of the Rhine ; and, directly in front of it, sheer from the water's edge, rise the mountains of Liebenstein and Sternenfels, each with its ruined castle. These are the Brothers of the old tradition, still gazing at each other face to face ; and beneath them, in the valley, stands a cloister, — meet emblem of that orphan child they both so passionately loved.

In a small flat-bottomed boat did the landlady's daughter row Flemming " over the Rhine-stream, rapid and roaring wide." She was a beautiful girl of sixteen ; with black hair, and dark, lovely eyes,

and a face that had a story to tell. How different faces are in this particular! Some of them speak not. They are books in which not a line is written, save perhaps a date. Others are great Family Bibles, with both the Old and the New Testament written in them. Others are Mother Goose and nursery tales; others, bad tragedies, or pickle-herring farces; and others, like that of the land-lady's daughter at the Star, sweet love-anthologies, and songs of the affections. It was on that account that Flemming said to her, as they glided out into the swift stream, "My dear child! do you know the story of the Liebenstein?"

"The story of the Liebenstein," she answered, "I knew by heart when I was a little child."

And here her large, dark, passionate eyes looked into Flemming's, and he doubted not that she had learned the story far too soon and far too well. That story he longed to hear, as if it were un-known to him; for he knew that the girl, who had got it by heart when a child, would tell it as it should be told. So he begged her to repeat the story, which she was but too glad to do; for she loved and believed it, as if it had all been writ-ten in the Bible. But before she began, she rested a moment on her oars, and, taking the crucifix which hung suspended from her neck, kissed it, and then let it sink down into her bosom, as if it were an anchor she was dropping into her heart. Meanwhile, her moist, dark eyes were turned to heaven. Perhaps her soul was walking with the souls of Cunizza, and Rahab, and Mary Magdalen. Or perhaps she was thinking of that nun, of whom

St. Gregory says, in his Dialogues, that, having greedily eaten a lettuce in a garden without making the sign of the cross, she found herself soon after possessed with a devil.

The probability, however, is that she was looking at the ruined castles only, and not to heaven, for she soon began her story and told Flemming how, "a great, great many years ago, an old man lived in the Liebenstein with his two sons; and how both the young men loved the Lady Geraldine, an orphan, under their father's care; and how the elder brother went away in despair, and the younger was betrothed to the Lady Geraldine; and how they were as happy as Aschenputtel and the Prince. And then the holy St. Bernard came and carried away all the young men to the war, just as Napoleon did afterwards; and the young lord went to the Holy Land, and the Lady Geraldine sat in her tower and wept, and waited for her lover's return, while the old father built the Sternenfels for them to live in when they were married. And when it was finished, the old man died; and the elder brother came back and lived in the Liebenstein, and took care of the gentle lady. Erelong there came news from the Holy Land that the war was over; and the heart of the gentle lady beat with joy, till she heard that her faithless lover was coming back with a Greek wife, — the wicked man! — and then she went into a convent and became a holy nun. So the young lord of Sternenfels came home, and lived in his castle in great splendor with the Greek woman, who was a wicked woman, and did what

she ought not to do. But the elder brother was angry for the wrong done the gentle lady, and challenged the lord of Sternenfels to single combat. And while they were fighting with their great swords in the valley of Bornhofen behind the castle, the convent bells began to ring, and the Lady Geraldine came forth with a train of nuns all dressed in white, and made the brothers friends again, and told them she was the bride of Heaven, and happier in her convent than she could have been in the Liebenstein or the Sternenfels. And when the brothers returned, they found that the false Greek wife had gone away with another knight. So they lived together in peace, and were never married. And when they died " —

" Lisbeth ! Lisbeth ! " cried a sharp voice from the shore, " Lisbeth ! where are you taking the gentleman ? "

This recalled the poor girl to her senses; and she saw how fast they were floating down stream. For, in telling the story, she had forgotten everything else, and the swift current had swept them down to the tall walnut-trees of Kamp. They landed in front of the Capuchin monastery. Lisbeth led the way through the little village, and, turning to the right, pointed up the romantic, lonely valley which leads to the Liebenstein, and even offered to go with him. But Flemming patted her cheek, and shook his head. He went up the valley alone.

CHAPTER V.

JEAN PAUL, THE ONLY-ONE.

It was already night when Flemming crossed the Roman bridge over the Nahe, and entered the town of Bingen. He stopped at the White Horse; and, before going to bed, looked out into the dim starlight from his window towards the Rhine, and his heart leaped within him to behold the bold outline of the neighboring hills crested with Gothic ruins; — which in the morning proved to be only a high slated roof, with fantastic chimneys.

The morning was bright and frosty, and the river tinged with gay colors by the rising sun. A soft, thin vapor floated in the air. In the sunbeams flashed the hoar-frost like silver stars, and through a long avenue of trees, whose dripping branches bent and scattered pearls before him, Paul Flemming journeyed on in triumph.

The man in the play who wished for " some forty pounds of lovely beef, placed in a Mediterranean Sea of brewis," might have seen his ample desires almost realized at the table d'hôte of the Rheinischen Hof, in Mayence, where Flemming dined that day. At the head of the table sat a gentleman with a smooth, broad forehead and large, intelligent eyes. He was from Baireuth in Franconia; and talked about poetry and Jean Paul to a pale, romantic-looking lady on his right. There was music all dinner-time, at the other end of the hall, — a harp and a horn and a voice, — so that a great part of the fat gentleman's conversation with

the pale lady was lost to Flemming, who sat opposite to her, and could look right into her large, melancholy eyes. But what he heard so much interested him, — indeed, the very name of the beloved Jean Paul would have been enough for this, — that he ventured to join in the conversation, and asked the German if he had known the poet personally.

"Yes, I knew him well," replied the stranger. "I am a native of Baireuth, where he passed the best years of his life. In my mind, the man and the author are closely united. I never read a page of his writings without hearing his voice, and seeing his form before me. There he sits, with his majestic, mountainous forehead, his mild blue eyes, and finely cut nose and mouth ; his massive frame clad loosely and carelessly in an old green frock, from the pockets of which the corners of books project, and perhaps the end of a loaf of bread and the nose of a bottle ; a straw hat, lined with green, lying near him ; a huge walking-stick in his hand, and at his feet a white poodle, with pink eyes, and a string round his neck. You would sooner have taken him for a master-carpenter than for a poet. Is he a favorite author of yours ?" Flemming answered in the affirmative.

"But a foreigner must find it exceedingly difficult to understand him," said the gentleman. "It is by no means an easy task for us Germans."

"I have always observed," replied Flemming, "that the true understanding and appreciation of a poet depend more upon individual than upon national character. If there be a sympathy be-

tween the minds of writer and reader, the bounds and barriers of a foreign tongue are soon over-leaped. If you once understand an author's character, the comprehension of his writings becomes easy."

" Very true," replied the German ; " and the character of Richter is too marked to be easily misunderstood. Its prominent traits are tenderness and manliness, — qualities which are seldom found united in so high a degree as in him. Over all he sees, over all he writes, are spread the sunbeams of a cheerful spirit, — the light of inexhaustible human love. Every sound of human joy and of human sorrow finds a deep-resounding echo in his bosom. In every man, he loves his humanity only, not his superiority. The avowed object of all his literary labors was to raise up again the down-sunken faith in God, Virtue, and Immortality; and, in an egotistical, revolutionary age, to warm again our human sympathies, which have now grown cold. And not less boundless is his love for Nature, — for this outward, beautiful world. He embraces it all in his arms."

" Yes," answered Flemming, almost taking the words out of the stranger's mouth, " for in his mind all things become idealized. He seems to describe himself when he describes the hero of his Titan, as a child, rocking in a high wind upon the branches of a full-blossomed apple-tree, and as its summit, blown abroad by the wind, now sunk him in deep green, and now tossed him aloft in deep blue and glancing sunshine, — in his imagination stood that tree gigantic; — it grew alone in the

universe, as if it were the tree of eternal life; its roots struck down into the abyss; the white and red clouds hung as blossoms upon it; the moon as fruit; the little stars sparkled like dew, and Albano reposed in its measureless summit; and a storm swayed the summit out of Day into Night, · and out of Night into Day."

" Yet the spirit of love," interrupted the Franconian, " was not weakness, but strength. It was united in him with great manliness. The sword of his spirit had been forged and beaten by poverty. Its temper had been tried by a thirty years' war. It was not broken, not even blunted, but rather strengthened and sharpened, by the blows it gave and received. And, possessing this noble spirit of humanity, endurance, and self-denial, he made literature his profession; as if he had been divinely commissioned to write. He seems to have cared for nothing else, to have thought of nothing else, than living quietly and making books. He says that he felt it his duty, not to enjoy, nor to acquire, but to write; and boasted that he had made as many books as he had lived years."

" And what do you Germans consider the prominent characteristics of his genius? "

" Most undoubtedly, his wild imagination and his playfulness. He throws over all things a strange and magic coloring. You are startled at the boldness and beauty of his figures and illustrations, which are scattered everywhere with a reckless prodigality; multitudinous, like the blossoms of early summer, and as fragrant and beautiful. With a thousand extravagances are mingled

ten thousand beauties of thought and expression,
which kindle the reader's imagination, and lead
it onward in a bold flight, through the glow of
sunrise and sunset, and the dewy coldness and
starlight of summer nights. He is difficult to
understand, intricate, strange, drawing his illus-
trations from every by-corner of science, art, and
nature, — a comet among the bright stars of Ger-
man literature. When you read his works, it is
as if you were climbing a high mountain, in merry
company, to see the sun rise. At times you are
enveloped in mist, the morning wind sweeps by
you with a shout, you hear the far-off muttering
thunders. Wide beneath you spreads the land-
scape, — field, meadow, town, and winding river.
The ringing of distant church-bells, or the sound
of solemn village clock, reaches you; then arises
the sweet and manifold fragrance of flowers, the
birds begin to sing, the vapors roll away, up
comes the glorious sun, you revel like a lark in
the sunshine and bright blue heaven, and all is a
delirious dream of soul and sense, when suddenly
a friend at your elbow laughs aloud, and offers
you a piece of Bologna sausage. As in real life,
so in his writings: the serious and the comic, the
sublime and the grotesque, the pathetic and the
ludicrous, are mingled together. At times he is
sententious, energetic, simple; then, again, obscure
and diffuse. His thoughts are like mummies em-
balmed in spices, and wrapped about with curious
envelopments; but within these the thoughts them-
selves are kings. At times glad, beautiful images,
airy forms, move by you, graceful, harmonious;

at times the glaring, wild-looking fancies, chained together by hyphens, brackets, and dashes, brave and base, high and low, all in their motley dresses, go sweeping down the dusty page, like the galley-slaves that sweep the streets of Rome, where you may chance to see the nobleman and the peasant manacled together."

Flemming smiled at the German's warmth, to which the presence of the lady and the Lauben-heimer wine seemed each to have contributed some-thing, and then said : —

" Better an outlaw than not free ! — These are his own words. And thus he changes at his will. Like the God Thor, of the old Northern my-thology, he now holds forth the seven stars in the bright heaven above us, and now hides himself in clouds, and pounds away with his great hammer."

" And yet this is not affectation in him," re-joined the German. " It is his nature, — it is Jean Paul. And the figures and ornaments of his style, wild, fantastic, and ofttimes startling, like those in Gothic cathedrals, are not merely what they seem, but massive coignes and buttresses, which support the fabric. Remove them, and the roof and walls fall in. And through these gar-goyles, these wild faces, these images of beasts and men carved upon spouts and gutters, flow out, like gathered rain, the bright, abundant thoughts that have fallen from heaven. And all he does is done with a kind of serious playfulness. He is a sea-monster, disporting himself on the broad ocean ; his very sport is earnest; there is something majestic and serious about it. In everything there

is strength, a rough good-nature, all sunshine over-
head, and underneath the heavy moaning of the
sea. Well may he be called ' Jean Paul, the
Only-One.' "

With such discourse the hour of dinner passed ;
and after dinner Flemming went to the cathedral.
They were singing vespers. A beadle, dressed in
blue, with a cocked hat and a crimson sash and
collar, was strutting, like a turkey, along the aisles.
This important gentleman conducted Flemming
through the church, and showed him the choir,
with its heavy-sculptured stalls of oak, and the
beautiful figures in brown stone over the bishops'
tombs. He then led him, by a side-door, into the
old and ruined cloisters of St. Willigis. Through
the low Gothic arches the sunshine streamed upon
the pavement of tombstones, whose images and in-
scriptions are mostly effaced by the footsteps of
many generations. There stands the tomb of Frau-
enlob, the Minnesinger. His face is sculptured on
an entablature in the wall ; a fine, strongly-marked,
and serious countenance. Below it is a bas-relief,
representing the poet's funeral. He is carried to
his grave by ladies, whose praise he sang, and
thereby won the name of Frauenlob.

"This, then," said Flemming, " is the grave,
not of Praise-God Bare-bones, but of Praise-the-
Ladies Meissen, who wrote songs 'somewhat of
lust, and somewhat of love.' But where sleeps the
dust of his rival and foe, sweet Master Bartholo-
mew Rainbow ? "

He meant this for an aside ; but the turkey-cock
picked it up, and answered : —

"I do not know. He did not belong to this parish."

I will not prolong this journey, for I am weary and way-worn, and would fain be at Heidelberg with my readers and my hero. It was already night when he reached the Manheim gate, and drove down the long Hauptstrasse so slowly, that it seemed to him endless. The shops were lighted on each side of the street, and he saw faces at the windows here and there, and figures passing in the lamplight, visible for a moment, and then swallowed up in the darkness. The thoughts that filled his mind were strange, as are always the thoughts of a traveller who enters for the first time a strange city. This little world had been going on for centuries before he came, and would go on for centuries after he was gone. Of all the thousands who inhabited it, he knew nothing ; and what knew they, or thought, of the stranger, who, in that close post-chaise, weary with travel, and chilled by the evening wind, was slowly rumbling over the paved street? Truly, this world can go on without us, if we would but think so. If it had been a hearse instead of a post-chaise, it would have been all the same to the people of Heidelberg, though by no means the same to Paul Flemming.

But at the farther end of the city, near the Castle and the Carls-Thor, one warm heart was waiting to receive him ; and this was the German heart of his friend, the Baron of Hohenfels, with whom he was to pass the winter in Heidelberg. No sooner had the carriage stopped at the iron-grated gate, and the postilion blown his horn, to announce

the arrival of a traveller, than the Baron was seen among the servants at the door; and, a few moments afterwards, the two long-absent friends were in each other's arms, and Flemming received a kiss upon each cheek, and another on the mouth, as a pledge and seal of the German's friendship. They held each other long by the hand, and looked into each other's face, and saw themselves in each other's eyes, both literally and figuratively; literally, inasmuch as the images were there, and figuratively, inasmuch as each was imagining what the other thought of him, after the lapse of some years. In friendly hopes and questionings and answers, the evening glided away at the supper-table, where many more things were discussed than the roasted hare and the Johannisberger; and they sat late into the night, conversing of the thoughts and feelings and delights which fill the hearts of young men who have already enjoyed and suffered, and hoped and been disappointed.

CHAPTER VI.

HEIDELBERG AND THE BARON.

High and hoar on the forehead of the Jetten-bühl stands the Castle of Heidelberg. Behind it rise the oak-crested hills of the Geissberg and the Kaiserstuhl; and in front, from the wide terrace of masonry, you can almost throw a stone upon the roofs of the town, so close do they lie beneath. Above this terrace rises the broad front of the chapel of Saint Udalrich. On the left stands the

slender octagon tower of the horologe; and on
the right, a huge round tower, battered and shat-
tered by the mace of war, shores up with its broad
shoulders the beautiful palace and garden-terrace
of Elizabeth, wife of the Count Palatine Freder-
ick. In the rear are older palaces and towers,
forming a vast, irregular quadrangle; — Rodolph's
ancient castle, with its Gothic gloriette and fantas-
tic gables; the Giant's Tower, guarding the draw-
bridge over the moat; the Rent Tower, with the
linden-trees growing on its summit; and the mag-
nificent Rittersaal of Otho-Henry, Count Palatine
of the Rhine and Grand Seneschal of the Holy
Roman Empire. From the gardens behind the
castle, you pass under the archway of the Giant's
Tower into the great courtyard. The diverse ar-
chitecture of different ages strikes the eye, and
curious sculptures. In niches on the wall of Saint
Udalrich's chapel stand rows of knights in armor,
broken and dismembered; and on the front of
Otho's Rittersaal, the heroes of Jewish history and
classic fable. You enter the open and desolate
chambers of the ruin, and on every side are me-
dallions and family arms; the Globe of the Em-
pire and the Golden Fleece, or the Eagle of the
Cæsars, resting on the escutcheons of Bavaria and
the Palatinate. Over the windows and doorways
and chimney-pieces are sculptures and mouldings
of exquisite workmanship; and the eye is bewil-
dered by the profusion of caryatides, and ara-
besques, and rosettes, and fan-like flutings, and .
garlands of fruits and flowers and acorns, and bul-
locks' heads with draperies of foliage, and muzzles

of lions, holding rings in their teeth. The cun-
ning hand of Art was busy for six centuries in
raising and adorning these walls; the mailed hands
of Time and War have defaced and overthrown
them in less than two. Next to the Alhambra of
Granada, the Castle of Heidelberg is the most
magnificent ruin of the Middle Ages.

In the valley below flows the rushing stream
of the Neckar. Close from its margin, on the
opposite side, rises the Mountain of All-Saints,
crowned with the ruins of a convent, and up the
valley stretches the mountain-curtain of the Oden-
wald. So close and many are the hills which east-
ward shut the valley in, that the river seems a
lake. But westward it opens upon the broad
plain of the Rhine, like the mouth of a trumpet,
and like the blast of a trumpet is at times the
wintry wind through this narrow mountain-pass.
The blue Alsatian hills rise beyond, and on a
platform or strip of level land, between the Neckar
and the mountains, right under the castle, stands
the town of Heidelberg; as the old song says, " a
pleasant town, when it has done raining."

Something of this did Paul Flemming behold,
when he rose the next morning and looked from
his window. It was a warm, vapory morning, and
a struggle was going on between the mist and the
rising sun. The sun had taken the hill-tops, but
the mist still kept possession of the valley and
the town. The steeple of the great church rose
through a dense mass of snow-white clouds, and
on the hills the dim vapors were rolling across the
windows of the ruined castle, like the fiery smoke

of a fierce conflagration. It seemed to him an image of the rising of the sun of Truth on a benighted world; its light streamed through the ruins of centuries; and, down in the Valley of Time, the cross on the Christian church caught its rays, though the priests were singing in mist and darkness below.

In the warm breakfast-room he found the Baron waiting for him. He was lying upon a sofa, in morning gown and purple-velvet slippers, both with flowers upon them. He had a guitar in his hand, and a pipe in his mouth, at the same time smoking, playing, and humming his favorite song from Goethe : —

> The water rushed, the water swelled,
> A fisher sat thereby.

Flemming could hardly refrain from laughing at the sight of his friend, and told him it reminded him of a street-musician he once saw in Aix-la-Chapelle, who was playing upon six instruments at once ; having a helmet with bells on his head, a Pan's-reed in his cravat, a violin in his hand, a triangle on his knee, cymbals on his heels, and on his back a bass-drum, which he played with his elbows. To tell the truth, the Baron of Hohenfels was rather a miscellaneous youth, rather a universal genius. He pursued all things with eagerness, but for a short time only : music, poetry, painting, pleasure, even the study of the Pandects. His feelings were keenly alive to the enjoyment of life. His great defect was, that he was too much in love with human nature. But by the power of imagination, in him, the bearded goat was changed to a

bright Capricornus; no longer an animal on earth,
but a constellation in heaven. An easy and indo-
lent disposition made him gentle and childlike in
his manners, and, in short, the beauty of his char-
acter, like that of the precious opal, was owing to
a defect in its organization. His person was tall
and slightly built; his hair light; and his eyes
blue, and as beautiful as those of a girl. In the
tones of his voice there was something indescriba-
bly gentle and winning, and he spoke the Ger-
man language with the soft, musical accent of his
native province of Kurland. In his manners, if
he had not " Antinous' easy sway," he had at least
an easy sway of his own. Such, in few words,
was the friend of Flemming.

"And what do you think of Heidelberg and the
old castle?" said he, as they seated themselves at
the breakfast-table.

"Last night the town seemed very long to me,"
replied Flemming; "and as to the castle, I have
as yet had but a glimpse of it through the mist.
They tell me there is nothing finer in its way than
this magnificent ruin, and I have no doubt I shall
find it so. Only I wish the stone were gray, and
not red. But, red or gray, I foresee that I shall
waste many a long hour in its desolate halls.
Pray, does anybody live there nowadays?"

"Nobody," answered the Baron, " but the man
who shows the Heidelberg Tun, and a Frenchman,
who has been there sketching ever since the year
eighteen hundred and ten. He has, moreover,
written a super-magnificent description of the ruin,
in which he says, that during the day only birds

of prey disturb it with their piercing cries, and at night, screech owls, and other fallow deer. You must buy his book and his sketches."

"Yes, the quotation and the tone of your voice will certainly persuade me so to do."

"Take his or none, my friend, for you will find no others. And seriously, his sketches are very good. There is one on the wall there, which is beautiful, save and except that straddle-bug figure among the bushes in the corner."

"But is there no ghost, no haunted chamber in the old castle?" asked Flemming, after casting a hasty glance at the picture.

"Oh, certainly," replied the Baron; "there are two. There is the ghost of the Virgin Mary in Ruprecht's Tower, and the Devil in the Dungeon."

"Ha! that is grand!" exclaimed Flemming, with evident delight. "Tell me the whole story, quickly! I am as curious as a child."

"It is a tale of the times of Louis le Débonnaire," said the Baron, with a smile; "a mouldy tradition of a credulous age. His brother Frederick lived here in the castle with him, and had a flirtation with Leonore von Luzelstein, a lady of the court, whom he afterwards despised, and was consequently most cordially hated by her. From political motives, he was equally hateful to certain petty German tyrants, who, in order to effect his ruin, accused him of heresy. But his brother Louis would not deliver him up to their fury, and they resolved to effect by stratagem what they could not by intrigue. Accordingly, Leonore von Luzelstein, disguised as the Virgin

Mary, and the father confessor of the Elector, in
the costume of Satan, made their appearance in
the Elector's bedchamber at midnight, and fright-
ened him so horribly, that he consented to deliver
up his brother into the hands of two Black
Knights, who pretended to be ambassadors from
the Vehm-Gericht. They proceeded together to
Frederick's chamber, where, luckily, old Gemmin-
gen, a brave soldier, kept guard behind the arras.
The monk went foremost in his Satanic garb, but
no sooner had he set foot in the prince's bedcham-
ber, than the brave Gemmingen drew his sword,
and said quaintly, ' Die, wretch ! ' and so he died.
The rest took to their heels, and were heard of no
more. And now the souls of Leonore and the
monk haunt the scene of their midnight crime.
You will find the story in the Frenchman's book,
worked up with a kind of red-morocco and burnt-
cork sublimity, and great melodramatic clanking
of chains, and hooting of owls, and other fallow
deer ! "

" After breakfast," said Flemming, " we will go
up to the castle. I must get acquainted with this
mirror of owls, this modern Till Eulenspiegel.
See what a glorious morning we have ! It is truly
a wondrous winter ! what summer sunshine ! what
soft Venetian fogs ! How the wanton, treacherous
air coquets with the old graybeard trees ! Such
weather makes the grass and our beards grow
apace ! But we have an old saying in English,
that winter never rots in the sky. So he will come
down at last in his old-fashioned mealy coat. We
shall have snow in spring ; and the blossoms will

be all snow-flakes. And afterwards a summer, which will be no summer, but, as Jean Paul says, only a winter painted green. Is it not so ? "

" Unless I am much deceived in the climate of Heidelberg," replied the Baron, " we shall not have to wait long for snow. We have sudden changes here, and I should not marvel much if it snowed before night."

" The greater reason for making good use of the morning sunshine, then. Let us hasten to the castle, after which my heart yearns."

CHAPTER VII.

LIVES OF SCHOLARS.

The forebodings of the Baron proved true. In the afternoon the weather changed. The western wind began to blow, and drew a cloud-veil over the face of Heaven, as a breath does over the human face in a mirror. Soon the snow began to fall. Athwart the distant landscape it swept like a white mist. The storm-wind came from the Alsatian hills, and struck the dense clouds aslant through the air. And ever faster fell the snow, a roaring torrent from those mountainous clouds. The setting sun glared wildly from the summit of the hills, and sank like a burning ship at sea, wrecked in the tempest. Thus the evening set in ; and winter stood at the gate wagging his white and shaggy beard, like an old harper chanting an old rhyme : " How cold it is ! how cold it is ! "

" I like such a storm as this," said Flemming,

who stood at the window, looking out into the
tempest and the gathering darkness. " The silent
falling of snow is to me one of the most solemn
things in nature. The fall of autumnal leaves does
not so much affect me. But the driving storm is
grand. It startles me ; it awakens me. It is wild
and woful, like my own soul. I cannot help think-
ing of the sea ; how the waves run and toss their
arms about, — and the wind plays on those great
sonorous harps, the shrouds and masts of ships.
Winter is here in earnest ! How the old churl
whistles and threshes the snow ! Sleet and rain
are falling too. Already the trees are bearded
with icicles, and the two broad branches of yon-
der pine look like the white mustache of some old
German baron."

" And to-morrow it will look more wintry still,"
said his friend. " We shall wake up and find that
the frost-spirit has been at work all night building
Gothic cathedrals on our windows, just as the Devil
built the Cathedral of Cologne. So draw the cur-
tains, and come, sit here by the warm fire."

" And now," said Flemming, having done as his
friend desired, " tell me something of Heidelberg
and its University. I suppose we shall lead about
as solitary and studious a life here as we did of
yore in little Göttingen, with nothing to amuse us,
save our own day-dreams."

" Pretty much so," replied the Baron ; " which
cannot fail to please you, since you are in pursuit
of tranquillity. As to the University, it is, as you
know, one of the oldest in Germany. It was
founded in the fourteenth century by the Count

Palatine Ruprecht, and had in the first year more
than five hundred students, all busily committing
to memory, after the old scholastic wise, the rules
of grammar versified by Alexander de Villa Dei,
and the extracts made by Peter the Spaniard from
Michel Psellus's Synopsis of Aristotle's Organon,
and the Categories, with Porphyry's Commentaries.
Truly, I do not much wonder that Erigena Scotus
should have been put to death by his scholars with
their penknives. They must have been pushed to
the very verge of despair."

" What a strange picture a university presents
to the imagination ! The lives of scholars in their
cloistered stillness ; — literary men of retired
habits, and professors who study sixteen hours a
day, and never see the world but on a Sunday.
Nature has, no doubt for some wise purpose, placed
in their hearts this love of literary labor and se-
clusion. Otherwise, who would feed the undying
lamp of thought ? But for such men as these, a
blast of wind through the chinks and crannies of
this old world, or the flapping of a conqueror's
banner, would blow it out forever. The light of
the soul is easily extinguished. And whenever I
reflect upon these things, I become aware of the
great importance, in a nation's history, of the in-
dividual fame of scholars and literary men. I fear
that it is far greater than the world is willing to
acknowledge, or, perhaps I should say, than the
world has thought of acknowledging. Blot out
from England's history the names of Chaucer,
Shakespeare, Spenser, and Milton only, and how
much of her glory would you blot out with them !

Take from Italy such names as Dante, Petrarch, Boccaccio, Michel Angelo, and Raphael, and how much would be wanting to the completeness of her glory! How would the history of Spain look, if the leaves were torn out on which are written the names of Cervantes, Lope de Vega, and Calderon? What would be the fame of Portugal, without her Camoens; of France, without her Racine, and Rabelais, and Voltaire; or of Germany, without her Martin Luther, her Goethe, and her Schiller? Nay, what were the nations of old, without their philosophers, poets, and historians? Tell me, do not these men, in all ages and in all places, emblazon with bright colors the armorial bearings of their country? Yes, and far more than this; for in all ages and in all places they give humanity assurance of its greatness, and say, 'Call not this time or people wholly barbarous; for thus much, even then and there, could the human mind achieve!' But the boisterous world has hardly thought of acknowledging all this. Therein it has shown itself somewhat ungrateful. Else, whence the great reproach, the general scorn, the loud derision, with which, to take a familiar example, the monks of the Middle Ages are regarded? That they slept their lives away is most untrue. For in an age when books were few, — so few, so precious, that they were often chained to their oaken shelves with iron chains, like galley-slaves to their benches, — these men, with their laborious hands, copied upon parchment all the lore and wisdom of the past, and transmitted it to us. Perhaps it is not too much to say, that, but for these monks, not

one line of the classics would have reached our day. Surely, then, we can pardon something to those superstitious ages, perhaps even the mysticism of the scholastic philosophy ; since, after all, we can find no harm in it, only the mistaking of the possible for the real, and the high aspirings of the human mind after a long-sought and unknown somewhat. I think the name of Martin Luther, the monk of Wittenberg, alone sufficient to redeem all monkhood from the reproach of laziness. If this will not, perhaps the vast folios of Thomas Aquinas will ; or the countless manuscripts, still treasured in old libraries, whose yellow and wrinkled pages remind one of the hands that wrote them and the faces that once bent over them."

"An eloquent homily," said the Baron, laughing ; "a most touching appeal in behalf of suffering humanity! For my part, I am no friend of this entire seclusion from the world. It has a very injurious effect on the mind of a scholar. The Chinese proverb is true : a single conversation across the table with a wise man is better than ten years' mere study of books. I have known some of these literary men who thus shut themselves up from the world. Their minds never come in contact with those of their fellow-men. They read little. They think much. They are mere dreamers. They know not what is new nor what is old. They often strike upon trains of thought, which stand written in good authors some century or so back, and are even current in the mouths of men around them. But they know it not, and imagine

they are bringing forward something very original, when they publish their thoughts."

"It reminds me," replied Flemming, "of what Dr. Johnson said of Goldsmith, when he proposed to travel abroad in order to bring home improvements: 'He will bring home a wheelbarrow, and call that an improvement.' It is unfortunately the same with some of these scholars."

"And the worst of it is," said the Baron, "that, in solitude, some fixed idea will often take root in the mind, and grow till it overshadow all one's thoughts. To this must all opinions come; no thought can enter there, which shall not be wedded to the fixed idea. There it remains and grows. It is like the watchman's wife, in the Tower of Waiblingen, who grew to such a size, that she could not get down the narrow staircase, and when her husband died, his successor was forced to marry the fat widow in the Tower."

"I remember an old English comedy," said Flemming, laughing, "in which a scholar is described as a creature that can strike fire in the morning at his tinder-box, — put on a pair of lined slippers, — sit ruminating till dinner, and then go to his meat when the bell rings ; — one that hath a peculiar gift in a cough, and a license to spit ; — or, if you will have him defined by negatives, he is one that cannot make a good leg, — one that cannot eat a mess of broth cleanly. What think you of that ? "

"That is just as people are always represented in English comedy," said the Baron. "The portrait is overcharged, — caricatured."

" And yet," continued Flemming, " no longer ago than yesterday, in the preface of a work by a Professor of Philosophy in the University of Halle, I read this passage."

He opened a book and read : —

" Here in Halle, where we have no public garden and no Tivoli, no London Exchange, no Paris Chamber of Deputies, no Berlin nor Vienna theatres, no Strasburg Minster nor Salzburg Alps, no Grecian ruins nor fantastic Catholicism, — in fine, nothing, which, after one's daily task is finished, can divert and refresh him, without his knowing or caring how, — I consider the sight of a proof-sheet quite as delightful as a walk in the Prater of Vienna. I fill my pipe very quietly, take out my inkstand and pens, seat myself in the corner of my sofa, read, correct, and now for the first time really set about thinking what I have written. To see this origin of a book, this metamorphosis of manuscript into print, is a delight to which I give myself up entirely. Look you, — this melancholy pleasure, which would have furnished the departed Voss with worthy matter for more than one blessed Idyl (the more so, as on such occasions I am generally arrayed in a morning gown, though, I am sorry to say, not a calamanco one, with great flowers), — this melancholy pleasure has already grown here in Halle to a sweet, pedantic habit. Since I began my hermit's life here, I have been printing ; and so long as I remain here, I shall keep on printing. In all probability, I shall die with a proof-sheet in my hand."

" This," said Flemming, closing the book, " is no

caricature by a writer of comedy, but a portrait by
a man's own hand. We can see by it how easily,
under certain circumstances, one may glide into
habits of seclusion, and in a kind of undress, slip-
shod hardihood, with a pipe and a proof-sheet,
defy the world. Into this state scholars have too
often fallen, thus giving some ground for the
prevalent opinion that scholarship and rusticity
are inseparable. To me, I confess, it is painful to
see the scholar and the world assume so often a
hostile attitude, and set each other at defiance.
Surely, it is a characteristic trait of a great and
liberal mind, that it recognizes humanity in all its
forms and conditions. I am a student and always,
when I sit alone at night, I recognize the divin-
ity of the student, as she reveals herself to me in
the flame of the midnight lamp. But, because
solitude and books are not unpleasant to me, —
nay, wished for, sought after, — shall I say to my
brother, Thou fool! Shall I take the world by
the beard, and say, Thou art old, and mad! Shall
I look society in the face, and say, Thou art heart-
less! — Heartless! Beware of that word! The
good Jean Paul says very wisely that 'Life in
every shape should be precious to us, for the same
reason that the Turks carefully collect every scrap
of paper that comes in their way, because the name
of God may be written upon it.' Nothing is more
true than this, yet nothing more neglected."

 "If it be painful to see this misunderstanding
between scholars and the world," said the Baron,
"I think it is still more painful to see the pri-
vate sufferings of authors by profession. How

many have languished in poverty, how many died
broken-hearted, how many gone mad with over-
excitement and disappointed hopes! How in-
structive and painfully interesting are their lives!
with so many weaknesses, so much to pardon, so
much to pity, so much to admire! I think he was
not so far out of the way who said that, next to
the Newgate Calendar, the Biography of Authors
is the most sickening chapter in the history of
man."

"It is indeed enough to make one's heart ache!"
interrupted Flemming. "Only think of Johnson
and Savage, rambling about the streets of London
at midnight, without a place to sleep in; Otway
starved to death; Collins mad, and howling like a
dog, through the aisles of Chichester Cathedral, at
the sound of church music! and Goldsmith, strut-
ting up Fleet Street in his peach-blossom coat, to
knock a bookseller over the pate with one of his
own volumes; and then, in his poverty, about to
marry his landlady in Green Arbor Court."

"A life of sorrow and privation, a hard life in-
deed, do these poor devil authors have of it,"
replied the Baron; "and then at last must get
them to the workhouse, or creep away into some
hospital to die."

"After all," said Flemming, with a sigh, "pov-
erty is not a crime."

"But something worse," interrupted the Baron;
"as Dufresny said, when he married his laundress,
because he could not pay her bill. He was the
author, as you know, of the opera of Lot, at whose
representation the great pun was made; — I say

the great pun, as we say the great Tun of Heidel-
berg. As one of the performers was singing the
line, ' *L'amour a vaincu Loth,*' (*vingt culottes*)
a voice from the pit cried out, ' *Qu'il en donne
une à l'auteur !* ' "

Flemming laughed at the unseasonable jest;
and then, after a short pause, continued : —

" And yet, if you look closely at the causes of
these calamities of authors, you will find that many
of them spring from false and exaggerated ideas
of poetry and the poetic character ; and from dis-
dain of common sense, upon which all character
worth having is founded. This comes from keep-
ing aloof from the world, apart from our fellow-
men, disdainful of society, as frivolous. By too
much sitting still the body becomes unhealthy, and
soon the mind. This is Nature's law. She will
never see her children wronged. If the mind,
which rules the body, ever forgets itself so far as
to trample upon its slave, the slave is never gen-
erous enough to forgive the injury, but will rise
and smite its oppressor. Thus has many a mon-
arch mind been dethroned."

" After all," said the Baron, " we must pardon
much to men of genius. A delicate organization
renders them keenly susceptible to pain and pleas-
ure. And then they idealize everything ; and, in
the moonlight of fancy, even the deformity of vice
seems beautiful."

" And this you think should be forgiven ? "

" At all events, it is forgiven. The world loves
a spice of wickedness. Talk as you will about
principle, impulse is more attractive, even when it

goes too far. The passions of youth, like unhooded hawks, fly high, with musical bells upon their jesses, and we forget the cruelty of the sport in the dauntless bearing of the gallant bird."

" And thus do the world and society corrupt the scholar ! " exclaimed Flemming.

Here the Baron rang, and ordered a bottle of Prince Metternich. He then very slowly filled his pipe, and began to smoke. Flemming was lost in a day-dream.

CHAPTER VIII.

LITERARY FAME.

Time has a Doomsday-Book, upon whose pages he is continually recording illustrious names. But as often as a new name is written there, an old one disappears. Only a few stand in illuminated characters, never to be effaced. These are the high nobility of Nature, — Lords of the Public Domain of Thought. Posterity shall never question their titles. But those whose fame lives only in the indiscreet opinion of unwise men must soon be as well forgotten as if they had never been. To this great oblivion must most men come. It is better, therefore, that they should soon make up their minds to this, — well knowing that, as their bodies must erelong be resolved into dust again, and their graves tell no tales of them, so must their names likewise be utterly forgotten, and their most cherished thoughts, purposes, and opinions have no longer an individual being among men, but be

resolved and incorporated into the universe of thought. If, then, the imagination can trace the noble dust of heroes, till we find it stopping a beer-barrel, and know that

Imperial Cæsar, dead and turned to clay,
May stop a hole to keep the wind away, —

not less can it trace the noble thoughts of great men, till it finds them mouldered into the common dust of conversation, and used to stop men's mouths, and patch up theories, to keep out the flaws of opinion. Such, for example, are all popular adages and wise proverbs, which are now resolved into the common mass of thought; their authors forgotten, and having no more an individual being among men.

It is better, therefore, that men should soon make up their minds to be forgotten, and look about them, or within them, for some higher motive, in what they do, than the approbation of men, which is Fame, — namely, their duty; that they should be constantly and quietly at work, each in his sphere, regardless of effects, and leaving their fame to take care of itself. Difficult must this indeed be, in our imperfection; impossible, perhaps, to achieve it wholly. Yet the resolute, the indomitable will of man can achieve much, — at times, even this victory over himself; being persuaded that fame comes only when deserved, and then is as inevitable as destiny, for it is destiny.

It has become a common saying that men of genius are always in advance of their age; which is true. There is something equally true, yet not so common; namely, that, of these men of genius,

the best and bravest are in advance not only of their own age, but of every age. As the German prose-poet says, every possible future is behind them. We cannot suppose that a period of time will ever arrive, when the world, or any considerable portion of it, shall have come up abreast with these great minds, so as fully to comprehend them.

And, oh, how majestically they walk in history! some like the sun, " with all his travelling glories round him; " others wrapped in gloom, yet glorious as a night with stars. Through the else silent darkness of the past, the spirit hears their slow and solemn footsteps. Onward they pass, like those hoary elders seen in the vision of an earthly paradise, attendant angels bearing golden lights before them, and, above and behind, the whole air painted with seven listed colors, as from the trail of pennons!

And yet, on earth these men were not happy, — not all happy, in the outward circumstance of their lives. They were in want and in pain, and familiar with prison bars and the damp, weeping walls of dungeons! Oh, I have looked with wonder upon those who, in sorrow and privation, and bodily discomfort, and sickness, which is the shadow of death, have worked right on to the accomplishment of their great purposes, toiling much, enduring much, fulfilling much, — and then, with shattered nerves, and sinews all unstrung, have laid themselves down in the grave, and slept the sleep of death, — and the world talks of them, while they sleep!

It would seem, indeed, as if all their sufferings

had but sanctified them; as if the death-angel, in passing, had touched them with the hem of his garment, and made them holy; as if the hand of disease had been stretched out over them only to make the sign of the cross upon their souls! And as in the sun's eclipse we can behold the great stars shining in the heavens, so in this life-eclipse have these men beheld the lights of the great eternity, burning solemnly and forever!

This was Flemming's reverie. It was broken by the voice of the Baron, suddenly exclaiming: —

"An angel is flying over the house! — Here, in this goblet, fragrant as the honey of Hymettus, fragrant as the wild-flowers in the Angel's Meadow, I drink to the divinity of thy dreams."

"This is all sunshine," said Flemming, as he drank. "The wine of the Prince, and the Prince of wines. By the way, did you ever read that brilliant Italian dithyrambic, Redi's Bacchus in Tuscany? an ode which seems to have been poured out of the author's soul, as from a golden pitcher,

> Filled with the wine
> Of the vine
> Benign,
> That flames so red in Sansovine.

He calls the Montepulciano the king of all wines."

"Prince Metternich," said the Baron, "is greater than any king in Italy, and I wonder that this precious wine has never inspired a German poet to write a Bacchus on the Rhine. Many little songs we have on this theme, but none very extraordinary. The best are Max Schenkendorf's Song of the Rhine, and the Song of Rhine-Wine, by

Claudius, a poet who never drank Rhenish without sugar. We will drink for him a blessing on the Rhine."

And again the crystal lips of the goblets kissed each other, with a musical chime, as of evening bells at vintage-time from the villages on the Rhine. Of a truth, I do not much wonder that the German poet Schiller loved to write by candle-light with a bottle of Rhine-wine upon the table. Nor do I wonder at the worthy schoolmaster, Roger Ascham, when he says, in one of his letters from Germany to Mr. John Raven, of John's College: " Tell Mr. Maden I will drink with him now a carouse of wine ; and would to God he had a vessel of Rhenish wine ; and perchance, when I come to Cambridge, I will so provide here, that every year I will have a little piece of Rhenish wine." Nor, in fine, do I wonder at the German emperor of whom he speaks in another letter to the same John Raven, and says, " The emperor drank the best that I ever saw ; he had his head in the glass five times as long as any of us, and never drank less than a good quart at once of Rhenish wine."

" But to resume our old theme of scholars and their whereabout," said the Baron, with an unusual glow, caught, no doubt, from the golden sunshine, imprisoned, like the student Anselmus, in the glass bottle ; " where should the scholar live ? In solitude, or in society ? in the green stillness of the country, where he can hear the heart of Nature beat, or in the dark, gray town, where he can hear and feel the throbbing heart of man ? I will make

answer for him, and say, in the dark, gray town. Oh, they do greatly err who think that the stars are all the poetry which cities have; and therefore that the poet's only dwelling should be in sylvan solitudes, under the green roof of trees. Beautiful, no doubt, are all the forms of Nature, when transfigured by the miraculous power of poetry; hamlets and harvest-fields, and nut-brown waters, flowing ever under the forest, vast and shadowy, with all the sights and sounds of rural life. But after all, what are these but the decorations and painted scenery in the great theatre of human life? What are they but the coarse materials of the poet's song? Glorious indeed is the world of God around us, but more glorious the world of God within us. There lies the Land of Song; there lies the poet's native land. The river of life, that flows through streets tumultuous, bearing along so many gallant hearts, so many wrecks of humanity; — the many homes and households, each a little world in itself, revolving round its fireside, as a central sun; all forms of human joy and suffering, brought into that narrow compass; — and to be in this, and be a part of this; acting, thinking, rejoicing, sorrowing, with his fellow-men; — such, such should be the poet's life. If he would describe the world, he should live in the world. The mind of the scholar, if you would have it large and liberal, should come in contact with other minds. It is better that his armor should be somewhat bruised by rude encounters, even, than hang forever rusting on the wall. Nor will his themes be few or trivial, because apparently

shut in between the walls of houses, and having merely the decorations of street scenery. A ruined character is as picturesque as a ruined castle. There are dark abysses and yawning gulfs in the human heart, which can be rendered passable only by bridging them over with iron nerves and sinews, as Challey bridged the Sarine in Switzerland, and Telford the sea between Anglesea and England, with chain bridges. These are the great themes of human thought; not green grass, and flowers, and moonlight. Besides, the mere external forms of Nature we make our own, and carry with us everywhere, by the power of memory."

"I fear, however," interrupted Flemming, "that in towns the soul of man grows proud. He needs at times to be sent forth, like the Assyrian monarch, into green fields, 'a wondrous wretch and weedless,' to eat green herbs, and be wakened and chastised by the rain shower and winter's bitter weather. Moreover, in cities there is danger of the soul's becoming wed to pleasure, and forgetful of its high vocation. There have been souls dedicated to heaven from childhood, and guarded by good angels as sweet seclusions for holy thoughts, and prayers, and all good purposes; wherein pious wishes dwelt like nuns, and every image was a saint; and yet in life's vicissitudes, by the treachery of occasion, by the thronging passions of great cities, have become soiled and sinful. They resemble those convents on the river Rhine, which have been changed to taverns; from whose chambers the pious inmates have long departed, and in whose cloisters the footsteps of travellers have ef-

faced the images of buried saints, and whose walls are written over with ribaldry and the names of strangers, and resound no more with holy hymns, but with revelry and loud voices."

"Both town and country have their dangers," said the Baron; "and therefore, wherever the scholar lives, he must never forget his high vocation. Other artists give themselves up wholly to the study of their art. It becomes with them almost religion. For the most part, and in their youth at least, they dwell in lands where the whole atmosphere of the soul is beauty; laden with it, as the air may be with vapor, till their very nature is saturated with the genius of their art. Such, for example, is the artist's life in Italy."

"I agree with you," exclaimed Flemming; "and such should be the poet's everywhere; for he has his Rome, his Florence, his whole glowing Italy, within the four walls of his library. He has in his books the ruins of an antique world, — and the glories of a modern one, — his Apollo and Transfiguration. He must neither forget nor undervalue his vocation, but thank God that he is a poet; and everywhere be true to himself, and to ' the vision and the faculty divine ' he recognizes within him."

"But, at any rate, a town life is most eventful," continued the Baron. "The men who make, or take, the lives of poets and scholars, always complain that these lives are barren of incidents. Hardly a literary biography begins without some such apology, unwisely made. I confess, however, that it is not made without some show of truth, if

by incidents we mean only those startling events which suddenly turn aside the stream of time, and change the world's history in an hour. There is certainly a uniformity, pleasing or unpleasing, in literary life, which for the most part makes to-day seem twin-born with yesterday. But if by incidents you mean events in the history of the human mind, (and why not?) noiseless events, that do not scar the forehead of the world as battles do, yet change it not the less, then surely the lives of literary men are most eventful. The complaint and the apology are both foolish. I do not see why a successful book is not as great an event as a successful campaign ; only different in kind, and not easily compared."

" Indeed," interrupted Flemming, " in no sense is the complaint strictly true, though at times apparently so. Events enough there are, were they all set down. A life that is worth writing at all is worth writing minutely. Besides, all literary men have not lived in silence and solitude ; — not all in stillness, not all in shadow. For many have lived in troubled times, in the rude and adverse fortunes of the state and age, and could say, with Wallenstein,

> Our life was but a battle and a march ;
> And, like the wind's blast, never resting, homeless,
> We stormed across the war-convulsed earth.

Many such examples has history recorded, — Dante, Cervantes, Byron, and others ; men of iron, — men who have dared to breast the strong breath of public opinion, and, like spectre-ships, come sailing right against the wind. Others have been

puffed out · by the first adverse wind that blew ;
disgraced and sorrowful, because they could not
please others. Had they been men, they would
have made these disappointments their best
friends, and learned from them the needful lesson
of self-reliance."

" To confess the truth," added the Baron, " the
lives of literary men, with their hopes and disap-
pointments, and quarrels and calamities, present a
melancholy picture of man's strength and weakness.
On that very account the scholar can make them
profitable for encouragement; consolation, warn-
ing."

" And after all," continued Flemming, " perhaps
the greatest lesson which the lives of literary men
teach us is told in a single word : Wait ! Every
man must patiently bide his time. He must wait.
More particularly in lands like my native land,
where the pulse of life beats with such feverish
and impatient throbs, is the lesson needful. Our
national character wants the dignity of repose.
We seem to live in the midst of a battle, — there
is such a din, such a hurrying to and fro. In the
streets of a crowded city it is difficult to walk
slowly. You feel the rushing of the crowd, and
rush with it onward. In the press of our life it is
difficult to be calm. In this stress of wind and
tide, all professions seem to drag their anchors, and
are swept out into the main. The voices of the
Present say, ' Come ! ' But the voices of the Past
say, ' Wait ! ' With calm and solemn footsteps
the rising tide bears against the rushing torrent
up stream, and pushes back the hurrying waters.

With no less calm and solemn footsteps, nor less
certainty, does a great mind bear up against public
opinion, and push back its hurrying stream.
Therefore should every man wait, — should bide
his time. Not in listless idleness, not in useless
pastime, not in querulous dejection, but in con-
stant, steady, cheerful endeavors, always willing
and fulfilling, and accomplishing his task, that,
when the occasion comes, he may be equal to the
occasion. And if it never comes, what matters it?
What matters it to the world, whether I, or you,
or another man did such a deed, or wrote such a
book, so be it the deed and book were well done?
It is the part of an indiscreet and troublesome am-
bition to care too much about fame, about what
the world says of us; to be always looking into
the faces of others for approval; to be always anx-
ious for the effect of what we do and say; to be al-
ways shouting to hear the echo of our own voices.
If you look about you, you will see men who are
wearing life away in feverish anxiety of fame, and
the last we shall ever hear of them will be the
funeral bell that tolls them to their early graves!
Unhappy men, and unsuccessful! because their
purpose is, not to accomplish well their task, but
to clutch the 'fantasy and trick of fame;' and
they go to their graves with purposes unaccom-
plished and wishes unfulfilled. Better for them,
and for the world in their example, had they
known how to wait! Believe me, the talent of
success is nothing more than doing what you can
do well; and doing well whatever you do, — with-
out a thought of fame. If it come at all, it will

come because it is deserved, not because it is
sought after. And, moreover, there will be no
misgivings, no disappointment, no hasty, feverish,
exhausting excitement."

———

Thus endeth the First Book of Hyperion. I
make no record of the winter. Paul Flemming
buried himself in books, — in old, dusty books.
He worked his way diligently through the ancient
poetic lore of Germany, from Frankish Legends
of Saint George, and Saxon Rhyme-Chronicles,
and Nibelungen-Lieds, and Helden-Buchs, and
Songs of the Minnesingers and Meistersingers, and
Ships of Fools, and Reynard the Foxes, and Death-
Dances, and Lamentations of Damned Souls, into
the bright, sunny land of harvests, where, amid
the golden grain and the blue corn-flowers, walk
the modern bards, and sing.

BOOK THE SECOND

Something the heart must have to cherish,
Must love, and joy, and sorrow learn;
Something with passion clasp, or perish,
And in itself to ashes burn.

CHAPTER I.

SPRING.

It was a sweet carol which the Rhodian children sang of old in Spring, bearing in their hands, from door to door, a swallow, as herald of the season:—

The Swallow is come!
The Swallow is come!
Oh, fair are the seasons, and light
Are the days that she brings,
With her dusky wings,
And her bosom snowy white!

A pretty carol, too, is that which the Hungarian boys, on the islands of the Danube, sing to the returning stork in Spring:—

Stork! Stork! poor Stork!
Why is thy foot so bloody?
A Turkish boy hath torn it;
Hungarian boy will heal it,
With fiddle, fife, and drum.

But what child has a heart to sing in this capricious clime of ours, where Spring comes sailing in from the sea, with wet and heavy cloud-sails, and

the misty pennon of the east-wind nailed to the mast? Yet even here, and in the stormy month of March even, there are bright, warm mornings, when we open our windows to inhale the balmy air. The pigeons fly to and fro, and we hear the whirring sound of wings. Old flies crawl out of the cracks, to sun themselves, and think it is Summer. They die in their conceit; and so do our hearts within us, when the cold sea-breath comes from the eastern sea, and again

> The driving hail
> Upon the window beats with icy flail.

The red-flowering maple is first in blossom, its beautiful purple flowers unfolding a fortnight before the leaves. The moose-wood follows, with rose-colored buds and leaves, and the dog-wood, robed in the white of its own pure blossoms. Then comes the sudden rain-storm; and the birds fly to and fro, and shriek. Where do they hide themselves in such storms? at what firesides dry their feathery cloaks? At the fireside of the great, hospitable sun, — to-morrow, not before; — they must sit in wet garments until then.

In all climates Spring is beautiful. In the South it is intoxicating, and sets a poet beside himself. The birds begin to sing; they utter a few rapturous notes, and then wait for an answer in the silent woods. Those green-coated musicians, the frogs, make holiday in the neighboring marshes. They, too, belong to the orchestra of Nature, whose vast theatre is again opened, though the doors have been so long bolted with icicles, and the scenery hung with snow and frost like cobwebs. This is the prelude which announces

the opening of the scene. Already the grass shoots forth. The waters leap with thrilling pulse through the veins of the earth; the sap through the veins of the plants and trees; and the blood through the veins of man. What a thrill of delight in Spring-time! What a joy in being and moving! Men are at work in gardens; and in the air there is an odor of the fresh earth. The leaf-buds begin to swell and blush. The white blossoms of the cherry hang upon the boughs like snow-flakes, and erelong our next-door neighbors will be completely hidden from us by the dense green foliage. The May-flowers open their soft blue eyes. Children are let loose in the fields and gardens. They hold buttercups under each other's chins, to see if they love butter. And the little girls adorn themselves with chains and curls of dandelions; pull out the yellow leaves, to see if the school-boy loves them, and blow the down from the leafless stalk, to find out if their mothers want them at home.

And at night so cloudless and so still! Not a voice of living thing, — not a whisper of leaf or waving bough, — not a breath of wind, — not a sound upon the earth nor in the air! And overhead bends the blue sky, dewy and soft, and radiant with innumerable stars, like the inverted bell of some blue flower, sprinkled with golden dust, and breathing fragrance. Or if the heavens are overcast, it is no wild storm of wind and rain, but clouds that melt and fall in showers. One does not wish to sleep, but lies awake to hear the pleasant sound of the dropping rain.

It was thus the Spring began in Heidelberg.

CHAPTER II.

A COLLOQUY.

" And what think you of Tiedge's Urania ? " said the Baron, smiling, as Paul Flemming closed the book, and laid it upon the table.

" I think," said Flemming, " that it is very much like Jean Paul's grandfather, — in the highest degree poor and pious."

" Bravo ! " exclaimed the Baron. " That is the best criticism I have heard upon the book. For my part, I dislike it as much as Goethe did. It was once very popular, and lay about in every parlor and bedroom. This annoyed the old gentleman exceedingly ; and I do not wonder at it. He complains that at one time nothing was sung or said but this Urania. He believed in Immortality ; but wished to cherish his belief in quietness. He once told a friend of his, that he had, however, learned one thing from all this talk about Tiedge and his Urania ; which was, that the saints, as well as the nobility, constitute an aristocracy. He said he found stupid women who were proud because they believed in Immortality with Tiedge, and had to submit himself to not a few mysterious catechizings and tea-table lectures on this point ; and that he cut them short by saying, that he had no objection whatever to enter into another state of existence hereafter, but prayed only that he might be spared the honor of meeting there any of those who had believed in it here, — for, if he did, they would flock around him on all sides,

exclaiming, ' Were we not in the right? Did we not tell you so? Has it not all turned out just as we said?' "

" How shocked the good old ladies must have been! " said Flemming.

" No doubt their nerves suffered a little; but the young women loved him all the better for being witty and wicked, and thought, if they could only marry him, how they would reform him."

" Bettina Brentano, for instance."

" Oh, no! That happened long afterwards. Goethe was then an old man of sixty. She had never seen him, and knew him only by his writings : a romantic girl of seventeen."

" And yet much in love with the sexagenarian. And surely, a more wild, fantastic passion never sprang up in woman's breast. She was a flower that worshipped the sun."

" She afterwards married Achim von Arnim, and is now a widow. And not the least singular part of the affair is that, having grown older, and I hope colder, she should herself publish the letters which passed between her and Goethe."

" Particularly the letter in which she describes her first visit to Weimar, and her interview with the hitherto invisible divinity of her dreams. The old gentleman took her upon his knees, and she fell asleep with her head upon his shoulder. Oberon must have touched her eyes with the juice of Love - in - idleness. However, this book of Goethe's Correspondence with a Child is a very singular and valuable revelation of the feelings which he excited in female hearts. You say she afterwards married Achim von Arnim? "

" Yes; and he and her brother, Clemens Bren-
tano, published that wondrous book, the Boy's
Wonder-Horn."

" The Boy's Wonder-Horn!" said Flemming,
after a short pause, for the name seemed to have
thrown him into a reverie; — " I know the book
almost by heart. Of all your German books, it
is the one which produces upon my imagination
the most wild and magic influence. I have a pas-
sion for ballads!"

" And who has not?" said the Baron, with a
smile. "They are the gypsy-children of song, born
under green hedgerows, in the leafy lanes and by-
paths of literature, — in the genial Summer-time."

" Why do you say Summer-time, and not Sum-
mer?" inquired Flemming. "The expression re-
minds me of your old Minnesingers; — of Hein-
rich von Ofterdingen, and Walther von der
Vogelweide, and Count Kraft von Toggenburg,
and your own ancestor, I dare say, Burkhart von
Hohenfels. They were always singing of the
gentle Summer-time. They seemed to have lived
poetry, as well as sung it; like the birds who make
their marriage-beds in the voluptuous trees."

" Is that from Shakespeare?"

" No; from Lope de Vega."

" You are deeply read in the lore of antiquity,
and the Aubades and Watch-Songs of the old
Minnesingers. What do you think of the shoe-
maker poets that came after them, — with their
guilds and singing-schools? It makes me laugh
to think how the great streams of your German
Helicon, shrunk to small rivulets, go bubbling and

gurgling over the pebbly names of Zwinger, Wur-
gendrussel, Buchenlin, Hellfire, Old Stoll, Young
Stoll, Strong Bopp, Dang Brotscheim, Batt Spie-
gel, Peter Pfort, and Martin Gumpel. And then
the Corporation of the Twelve Wise Masters, with
their stumpfe-reime and klingende-reime, and their
Hans Tindeisen's rosemary - weise, and Joseph
Schmierer's flowery - paradise - weise, and Frauen-
lob's yellow-weise, and blue-weise, and frog-weise,
and looking-glass-weise ! "

" Oh, I entreat you," exclaimed Flemming,
laughing, " do not call those men poets ! You
transport me to quaint old Nuremberg, and I see
Hans Sachs making shoes, and Hans Folz shaving
the burgomaster."

" By the way," interrupted the Baron, " did you
ever read Hoffmann's beautiful story of Master
Martin, the Cooper of Nuremberg ? I will read
it to you this very night. It is the most delightful
picture of that age which you can conceive. But
look ! the sun has already set behind the Alsatian
hills. Let us go up to the castle and look for the
ghost in Prince Ruprecht's tower. Oh, what a
glorious sunset ! "

Flemming looked at the evening sky, and a
shade of sadness stole over his countenance. He
told not to his friend the sorrow with which his
heart was heavy, but kept it for himself alone.
He knew that the time, which comes to all men, —
the time to suffer and be silent, — had come to him
likewise, and he spake no word. Oh, well has it
been said, that there is no grief like the grief which
does not speak !

CHAPTER III.

OWL-TOWERS.

" There sits the old Frau Himmelauen, perched up in her owl-tower," said the Baron to Flemming, as they passed along the Hauptstrasse. " She looks down through her round-eyed spectacles from her nest there, and watches every one that goes by. I wonder what mischief she is hatching now. Do you know she has nearly ruined your character in town? She says you have a rakish look, because you carry a cane, and your hair curls. Your gloves, also, are a shade too light for a strictly virtuous man."

" It is very kind in her to take such good care of my character, particularly as I am a stranger in town. She is doubtless learned in the Clothes-Philosophy."

" And ignorant of everything else. She asked a friend of mine, the other day, whether Christ was a Catholic or a Protestant."

" That is really too absurd ! "

" Not too absurd to be true. And, ignorant as she is, she contrives to do a good deal of mischief in the course of the year. Why, the women already call you Wilhelm Meister."

" They are at liberty to call me what they please. But you, who know me better, know that I am something more than they would imply by the name."

" She says, moreover, that the American women sit with their feet out of the window, and have no pocket-handkerchiefs."

" Excellent ! "

They crossed the market-place, and went up be-
neath the grand terrace into the court-yard of the
castle.

" Let us go and sit under the great linden-trees,
that grow on the summit of the Rent Tower," said
Flemming. " From that point as from a watch-
tower, we can look down into the garden, and see
the crowd below us."

" And amuse ourselves, as old Frau Himmelauen
does at her window in the Hauptstrasse," added
the Baron.

The keeper's daughter unlocked for them the
door of the tower, and, climbing the steep stair-
case, they seated themselves on a wooden bench
under the linden-trees.

" How beautifully these trees overgrow the old
tower ! And see what a solid mass of masonry
lies in the great fosse down there, toppled from its
base by the explosion of a mine ! It is like a rusty
helmet cleft in twain, but still crested with tower-
ing plumes ! "

" And what a motley crowd in the garden !
Philisters and Sons of the Muses ! And there
goes the venerable Thibaut, taking his evening
stroll. Do you see him there, with his silver hair
flowing over his shoulders, and that friendly face,
which has for so many years pored over the Pan-
dects ? I assure you, he inspires me with awe.
And yet he is a merry old man, and loves his joke,
particularly at the expense of Moses and other
ancient lawgivers."

Here their attention was diverted by a wild-look-

ing person, who passed with long strides under the archway in the fosse, right beneath them, and disappeared among the bushes. He was ill-dressed, his hair flying in the wind, his movements hurried and nervous, and the expression of his broad countenance wild, strange, and earnest.

" Who can that be ? " asked Flemming. " He strides away indignantly, like one of Ossian's ghosts ! "

" A great philosopher, whose name I have forgotten. Truly, a strange owl ! "

" He looks like a lion with a hat on."

" He is a mystic, who reads Schubert's History of the Soul, and lives, for the most part, in the clouds of the Middle Ages. To him the spirit-world is still open. He believes in the transmigration of souls ; and I dare say is now following the spirit of some departed friend, who has taken the form of yonder pigeon."

" What a strange hallucination ! He lives, I suppose, in the land of cloud-shadows. And, as St. Thomas Aquinas was said to be lifted up from the ground by the fervor of his prayers, so, no doubt, is he by the fervor of his visions."

" He certainly appears to neglect all sublunary things ; and, to judge from certain appearances, since you seem fond of holy similitudes, one would say, that, like St. Serapion the Sindonite, he had but one shirt. Yet what cares he ? he lives in that poetic dream-land of his thoughts, and clothes himself in poetry."

" He is a poet, then, as well as a philosopher ? "

" Yes ; but a poet who never writes. There is
nothing in nature to which his imagination does
not give a poetic hue. But the power to make
others see these objects in the same poetic light is
wanting. Still he is a man of fine powers and
feelings ; for next to being a great poet is the
power of understanding one, — of finding one's
self in him, as we Germans say."

Three figures, dressed in black, now came from
one of the green alleys, and stopped on the brink
of a fountain that was playing among the gay flow-
ers in the garden. The eldest of the three was
a woman in that season of life when the early au-
tumn gives to the summer leaves a warmer glow,
yet fades them not. Though the mother of many
children, she was still beautiful ; resembling those
trees which blossom in October, when the leaves
are changing, and whose fruit and blossom are on
the branch at once. At her side was a girl of some
sixteen years, who seemed to lean upon her arm
for support. Her figure was slight ; her coun-
tenance beautiful, though deadly white ; and her
meek eyes like the flower of the nightshade, pale
and blue, but sending forth golden rays. They
were attended by a tall youth of foreign aspect,
who seemed a young Antinous, with a mustache
and a nose *à la Kosciusko.* In other respects a
perfect hero of romance.

" Unless mine eyes deceive me," said the Baron,
" there is the Frau von Ilmenau, with her pale
daughter Emma, and that eternal Polish count.
He is always hovering about them, playing the un-
happy exile, merely to excite that poor girl's sym-

pathies ; and as wretched as genius and wantonness can make him."

" Why, he is already married, you know," replied Flemming. " And his wife is young and beautiful."

" That does not prevent him from being in love with some one else. That question was decided in the Courts of Love in the Middle Ages. Accordingly he has sent his fair wife to Warsaw. But how pale the poor child looks ! "

" She has just recovered from severe illness. In the winter, you know, it was thought she would not live from hour to hour."

" And she has hardly recovered from that disease, before she seems threatened with a worse one ; namely, a hopeless passion. However, people do not die of love nowadays."

" Seldom, perhaps," said Flemming. " And yet it is folly to pretend that one ever wholly recovers from a disappointed passion. Such wounds always leave a scar. There are faces I can never look upon without emotion. There are names I can never hear spoken without almost starting."

" But whom have we here ? "

" That is the French poet Quinet, with his fair German wife ; one of the most interesting women I ever knew. He is the author of a very wild Mystery, or dramatic prose-poem, in which the Ocean, Mont Blanc, and the Cathedral of Strasburg have parts to play ; and the saints on the stained windows of the minster speak, and the statues and dead kings enact the Dance of Death. It is entitled Ahasuerus, or the Wandering Jew."

" Or, as the Danes would translate it, the Shoe-maker of Jerusalem. That would be a still more fantastic title for his fantastic book. You know I am no great admirer of the modern French school of writers. The tales of Paul de Kock seem to me like obscene stories told at dinner-tables. It has been truly said of him that he is not only *popu-laire*, but *populacier;* and rather harshly of George Sand and Victor Hugo, that their works stand like fortifications, well built and well supplied with warlike munitions, but ineffectual against the Grand Army of God, which marches onward, as if nothing had happened. In surveying a na-tional literature, the point you must start from is national character. That lets you into many a secret. The most prominent trait in the French character is love of amusement and excitement ; and " —

" I should say, rather, the fear of ennui," inter-rupted Flemming. " Some one has said, with a great deal of truth, that the gentry of France rush into Paris to escape from ennui, as, in the noble days of chivalry, the defenceless inhabitants of the champaign fled into the castles at the approach of some plundering knight or lawless baron, forsak-ing the inspired twilight of their native groves for the luxurious shades of the royal gardens. What do you think of that ? "

The Baron replied, with a smile : —

" There is only one Paris ; and out of Paris there is no salvation for decent people."

Thus conversing of many things sat the two friends under the linden-trees on the Rent Tower,

till gradually the crowd disappeared from the garden, and the objects around them grew indistinct, in the fading twilight. Between them and the amber-colored western sky, the dense foliage of the trees looked heavy and hard as if cast in bronze; and already the evening stars hung like silver lamps in the towering branches of that Tree of Life, brought more than two centuries ago from its primeval paradise in America, to beautify the gardens of the Palatinate.

" I take a mournful pleasure in gazing at that tree," said Flemming, as they rose to depart. " It stands there so straight and tall, with iron bands around its noble trunk and limbs, in silent majesty, or whispering only in its native tongue, and freighting the homeward wind with sighs! It reminds me of some captive monarch of a savage tribe, brought over the vast ocean for a show, and chained in the public market-place of the city, disdainfully silent, or breathing only in melancholy accents a prayer for his native forest, a longing to be free."

" Magnificent! " cried the Baron. " I always experience something of the same feeling, when I walk through a conservatory. The luxuriant plants of the tropics — those illustrious exotics, with their gorgeous flamingo - colored blossoms, and great flapping leaves, like elephants' ears — have a singular working upon my imagination, and remind me of a menagerie and wild beasts kept in cages. But your illustration is finer, indeed, a grand figure. Put it down for an epic poem."

CHAPTER IV.

A BEER-SCANDAL.

On their way homeward, Flemming and the Baron passed through a narrow lane, in which was a well-known Studenten-Kneipe. At the door stood a young man, whom the Baron at once recognized as his friend Von Kleist. He was a student, and universally acknowledged, among his young acquaintance, as a " devilish handsome fellow," notwithstanding a tremendous scar on his cheek, and a cream-colored mustache as soft as the silk of Indian corn. In short, he was a renowner and a duellist.

" What are you doing here, Von Kleist ? "

" Ah, my dear Baron! Is it you? Come in ; come in. You shall see some sport. A Fox-Commerce is on foot, and a regular Beer-Scandal."

" Shall we go in, Flemming ? "

" Certainly. I should like to see how these things are managed in Heidelberg. You are a baron, and I am a stranger. It is of no consequence what you and I do, as the king's fool Angeli said to the poet Bautra, urging him to put on his hat at the royal dinner-table."

William Lilly, the Astrologer, says, in his Autobiography, that, when he was committed to the guard-room in Whitehall, he thought himself in hell; for " some were sleeping, others swearing, others smoking tobacco, and in the chimney of the room there were two bushels of broken tobacco-pipes, and almost half a load of ashes."

What he would have thought, if he had peeped
into this Heidelberg Studenten-Kneipe, I know
not. He certainly would not have thought himself
in heaven, unless it were a Scandinavian heaven.
The windows were open, and yet so dense was the
atmosphere with the smoke of tobacco and the
fumes of beer, that the tallow candles burned
but dimly. A crowd of students were sitting at
three long tables, in the large hall — a medley of
fellows, known at German universities under the
cant names of Old-Ones, Mossy-Heads, Princes
of Twilight, and Pomatum-Stallions. They were
smoking, drinking, singing, screaming, and dis-
cussing the great Laws of the Broad-Stone and
the Gutter. They had a great deal to say, like-
wise, about Besens, and Zobels, and Poussades;
and, if they had been charged for the noise they
made, as travellers used to be in the old Dutch
taverns, they would have a longer bill to pay for
that than for their beer.

In a large arm-chair, upon the middle table,
sat one of those distinguished individuals known
among German students as a Senior, or Leader of
a Landsmannschaft. He was booted and spurred,
and wore a very small crimson cap, and a very
tight blue jacket, and very long hair, and a very
dirty shirt. He was President of the night; and,
as Flemming entered the hall with the Baron and
his friend, striking upon the table with a mighty
broad-sword, he cried in a loud voice : —

"Silentium!"

At the same moment, a door at the end of the
hall was thrown open, and a procession of new-

comers, or Nasty-Foxes, as they are called in the
collcge dialect, entered two by two, looking wild,
and green, and foolish. As they came forward,
they were obliged to pass under a pair of naked
swords, held crosswise by two Old-Ones, who, with
pieces of burnt cork, made an enormous pair of
mustaches on the smooth rosy cheeks of each, as
he passed beneath this arch of triumph. While
the procession was entering the hall, the President
lifted up his voice again, and began to sing the
well-known Fox-song, in the chorus of which all
present joined lustily.

What comes there from the hill ?
What comes there from the hill ?
What comes there from the leathery hill ?
 Sa! Sa!
 Leathery hill !
What comes there from the hill ?

It is a postilion!
It is a postilion!
It is a leathery postilion!
 Sa! Sa!
 Postilion !
It is a postilion !

What brings the postilion ?
What brings the postilion ?
What brings the leathery postilion ?
 Sa! Sa!
 Postilion!
What brings the postilion ?

He bringeth us a Fox!
He bringeth us a Fox !
He bringeth us a leathery Fox !
 Sa! Sa!
 Leathery Fox!
He bringeth us a Fox!

Your servant, Masters mine!
Your servant, Masters mine!
Your servant, much-honored Masters mine!
 Sa! Sa!
 Much-honored Masters mine!
Your servant, Masters mine!

How does the Herr Papa?
How does the Herr Papa?
How does the leathery Herr Papa?
 Sa! Sa!
 Herr Papa!
How does the Herr Papa?

He reads in Cicero!
He reads in Cicero!
He reads in leathery Cicero!
 Sa! Sa!
 Cicero!
He reads in Cicero!

How does the Frau Mamma?
How does the Frau Mamma?
How does the leathery Frau Mamma?
 Sa! Sa!
 Frau Mamma!
How does the Frau Mamma?

She makes the Papa tea!
She makes the Papa tea!
She makes the Papa leathery tea!
 Sa! Sa!
 Leathery tea!
She makes the Papa tea!

How does the Mamsell Sœur?
How does the Mamsell Sœur?
How does the leathery Mamsell Sœur?
 Sa! Sa!
 Mamsell Sœur!
How does the Mamsell Sœur?

She knits the Papa socks!
She knits the Papa socks!
She knits the Papa leathery socks!
 Sa! Sa!
 Leathery socks!
She knits the Papa socks!

How does the Herr Rector?
How does the Herr Rector?
How does the leathery Herr Rector?
 Sa! Sa!
 Herr Rector!
How does the Herr Rector?

He calls the scholar, Boy!
He calls the scholar, Boy!
He calls the scholar, leathery Boy!
 Sa! Sa!
 Leathery Boy!
He calls the scholar, Boy!

And smokes the Fox tobacco!
And smokes the Fox tobacco!
And smokes the leathery Fox tobacco!
 Sa! Sa!
 Fox tobacco!
And smokes the Fox tobacco!

A little, Masters mine!
A little, Masters mine!
A little, much-honored Masters mine!
 Sa! Sa!
 Much-honored Masters mine!
A little, masters mine!

Then let him fill a pipe!
Then let him fill a pipe!
Then let him fill a leathery pipe!
 Sa! Sa!
 Leathery pipe!
Then let him fill a pipe!

O Lord! it makes me sick!
O Lord! it makes me sick!
O Lord! it makes me leathery sick!
 Sa! Sa!
 Leathery sick!
O Lord! it makes me sick!

Then let him throw it off!
Then let him throw it off!
Then let him throw it leathery off!
 Sa! Sa!
 Leathery off!
Then let him throw it off!

Now I again am well!
Now I again am well!
Now I again am leathery well!
 Sa! Sa!
 Leathery well!
Now I again am well!

So grows the Fox a Bursch!
So grows the Fox a Bursch!
So grows the leathery Fox a Bursch!
 Sa! Sa!
 Fox a Bursch!
So grows the Fox a Bursch!

At length the song was finished. Meanwhile large tufts and strips of paper had been twisted into the hair of the Branders, as those are called who have been already one term at the University, and then at a given signal were set on fire, and the Branders rode round the table on chairs amid roars of laughter. When this ceremony was completed, the President rose and in a solemn voice pronounced a long discourse, in which old college jokes were mingled with much parental advice to young men on entering life, and the whole was

profusely garnished with select passages from the
Old Testament. Then they all seated themselves
at the table and the heavy beer-drinking set in, as
among the Gods and Heroes of the old Northern
mythology.

"Brander! Brander!" screamed a youth whose
face was hot and flushed with supper and with
beer; "Brander, I say! Thou art a Doctor! No,
— a Pope; — thou art a Pope, by — !"

These words were addressed to a pale, quiet-
looking person, who sat opposite, and was busy in
making a wretched shaved poodle sit on his hind
legs in a chair, by his master's side, and hold a
short clay pipe in his mouth, — a performance to
which the poodle seemed nowise inclined.

"Thou art challenged!" replied the pale stu-
dent, turning from his dog, who dropped the pipe
from his mouth, and leaped under the table.

Seconds were chosen on the spot, and the arms
ordered; namely, six mighty goblets, or Bass-
gläser, filled to the brim with foaming beer.
Three were placed before each duellist.

"Take your weapons!" cried one of the sec-
onds, and each of the combatants seized a goblet
in his hand.

"Strike!"

And the glasses rang, with a salutation like the
crossing of swords.

"Set to!"

Each set the goblet to his lips.

"Out!"

And each poured the contents down his throat,
as if he were pouring them through a tunnel into

a beer-barrel. The other two glasses followed in quick succession, hardly a long breath drawn between. The pale student was victorious. He was first to drain the third goblet. He held it for a moment inverted, to let the last drops fall out, and then, placing it quietly on the table, looked his antagonist in the face, and said : —

" Hit! "

Then, with the greatest coolness, looking under the table, he whistled for his dog. His antagonist stopped midway in his third glass. Every vein in his forehead seemed bursting; his eyes were wild and bloodshot, his hand gradually loosened its hold upon the table, and he sank and rolled together like a sheet of lead. He was drunk.

At this moment a majestic figure came stalking down the table, ghost-like, through the dim, smoky atmosphere. His coat was off, his neck bare, his hair wild, his eyes wide open, and looking straight before him, as if he saw some beckoning hand in the air, that others could not see. His left hand was upon his hip, and in his right he held a drawn sword extended and pointing downward. Regardless of every one, erect, and with a martial stride, he marched directly along the centre of the table, crushing glasses and overthrowing bottles at every step. The students shrank back at his approach ; till at length one more intoxicated, or more courageous, than the rest, dashed a glass full of beer into his face. A general tumult ensued, and the student with the sword leaped to the floor. It was Von Kleist. He was renowning it. In the midst of the uproar could be distinguished the offensive words : —

" Arrogant ! Absurd ! Impertinent ! Dummer Junge ! "

Von Kleist went home that night with no less than six duels on his hands. He fought them all out in as many days, and came off with only a gash through his upper lip and another through his right eyelid from a dexterous Suabian Schläger.

CHAPTER V.

THE WHITE LADY'S SLIPPER AND THE PASSION-FLOWER.

That night Emma of Ilmenau went to her chamber with a heavy heart, and her dusky eyes were troubled with tears. She was one of those gentle beings who seem created only to love and to be loved. A shade of melancholy softened her character. She shunned the glare of daylight and of society, and wished to be alone. Like the evening primrose, her heart opened only after sunset, but bloomed through the dark night with sweet fragrance. Her mother, on the contrary, flaunted in the garish light of society. There was no sympathy between them. Their souls never approached, never understood each other, and words were often spoken which wounded deeply. And therefore Emma of Ilmenau went to her chamber that night with tears in her eyes.

She was followed by her French chamber-maid, Madeleine, a native of Strasburg, who had grown old in the family. In her youth, she had been poor, — and virtuous, because she had never been

tempted; and now that she had grown old, and seen no immediate reward for her virtue, as is usual with weak minds, she despaired of Providence, and regretted she had never been tempted. Whilst this unfortunate personage was lighting the wax tapers on the toilet, and drawing the bed-curtains, and tattling about the room, Emma threw herself into an arm-chair, and, crossing her hands in her lap, and letting her head fall upon her bosom, seemed lost in a dream.

" Why have these gentle feelings been given me ? " said she in her heart. " Why have I been born with all these warm affections, these ardent longings after what is good, if they lead only to sorrow and disappointment? I would love some one, — love him once and for ever; — devote myself to him alone, — live for him, — die for him, — exist alone in him ! But, alas ! in all this wide world there is none to love me as I would be loved, — none whom I may love as I am capable of loving. How empty, how desolate, seems the world about me ! Why has Heaven given me these affections, only to fall and fade ? "

Alas ! poor child ! thou too must learn, like others, that the sublime mystery of Providence goes on in silence, and gives no explanation of itself, — no answer to our impatient questionings !

" Bless me, child, what ails you ? " exclaimed Madeleine, perceiving that Emma paid no attention to her idle gossip. " When I was of your age " —

" Do not talk to me now, good Madeleine. Leave me, I wish to be alone."

"Well, here is something," continued the maid, taking a billet from her bosom, "which I hope will enliven you. When I was of your age" —

"Hush! hush!" said Emma, taking the billet from the hard hand of Madeleine. "Once more I beg you, leave me. I wish to be alone."

Madeleine took the lamp and retired slowly, wishing her young mistress many good nights and rosy dreams. Emma broke the seal of the note. As she read, her face became deadly pale, and then, quick as thought, a crimson blush gleamed on her cheek, and her hands trembled. Tenderness, pity, love, offended pride, the weakness and dignity of woman, were all mingled in her look, changing and passing over her fine countenance like cloud-shadows. She sunk back in her chair, covering her face with her hands, as if she would hide it from herself and Heaven.

"He loves me!" said she to herself; "loves me; and is married to another, whom he loves not! and dares to tell me this! Oh, never, — never, — never! And yet he is so friendless and alone in this unsympathizing world, and an exile, and homeless! I can but pity him; yet I hate him, and will see him no more!"

This short reverie of love and hate was broken by the sound of a clear, mellow voice, which, in the universal stillness of the hour, seemed almost like the voice of a spirit. It was a voice, without the accompaniment of any instrument, singing those beautiful lines which Goethe wrote on the wall of a summer-house at Ilmenau: —

O'er all the hill-tops is quiet now !
In all the woodlands hearest thou
· Hardly a sound !
The little birds are asleep in the trees ;
Wait ! wait ! and soon, like these,
Sleepest thou !

Emma knew the voice, and started. She rushed to the window to close it. It was a beautiful night, and the stars were shining peacefully over the mountain of All-Saints. The sound of the Neckar was soft and low ; nightingales were singing among the brown shadows of the woods ; the large red moon shone like a ruby, in the horizon's ample ring ; and golden threads of light seemed braided together with the rippling current of the river. Tall and spectral stood the white statues on the bridge. The outlines of the hills, the castle, the arches of the bridge, and the spires and roofs of the town, were as strongly marked as if cut out of pasteboard. Amid this fairy scene, a little boat was floating silently down the stream. Emma closed the window hastily, and drew the curtains close.

" I hate him ; and yet I will pray for him," said she, as she laid her weary head upon that pillow, from which, but a few months before, she thought she should never raise it again. " Oh that I had died then ! I dare not love him, but I will pray for him ! "

Sweet child ! If the face of the deceiver comes so often between thee and Heaven, I tremble for thy fate ! The plant that sprang from Helen's tears destroyed serpents ; would that from thine might spring up heart's-ease, — some plant, at

least, to destroy the serpents in thy bosom! Believe me, upon the margin of celestial streams alone those simples grow which cure the heart-ache!

And this the silent stars beheld, looking down from heaven, and told it not again. This likewise the Frau Himmelauen beheld, looking from her chamber-window, and was not so discreet as the silent stars.

CHAPTER VI.

GLIMPSES INTO CLOUD-LAND.

"There are many things which, having no corporeal evidence, can be perceived and comprehended only by the discursive energies of reason. Hence the ambiguous nature of matter can be comprehended only by adulterated opinion. Matter is the principle of all bodies, and is stamped with the impression of forms. Fire, air, and water derive their origin and principle from the scalene triangle. But the earth was created from right-angled triangles, of which two of the sides are equal. The sphere and the pyramid contain in themselves the figure of fire; but the octahedron was destined to be the figure of air, and the icosahedron of water. The right-angled isosceles triangle produces from itself a square, and the square generates from itself the cube, which is the figure peculiar to earth. But the figure of a beautiful and perfect sphere was imparted to the most beautiful and perfect world, that it might be indigent of nothing, but contain all things, embracing

and comprehending them in itself, and thus might
be excellent and admirable, similar to and in con-
cord with itself, ever moving musically and melo-
diously. If I use a novel language, excuse me.
As Apuleius says, pardon must be granted to nov-
elty of words, when it serves to illustrate the ob-
scurity of things."

These words came from the lips of the lion-like
philosopher who has been noticed before in these
pages. He was sitting with Flemming, smoking a
long pipe. As the Baron said, he was indeed a
strange owl, for the owl is a grave bird ; a monk,
who chants midnight mass in the great temple
of Nature ; an anchorite, a pillar saint, the very
Simeon Stylites of his neighborhood. Such, like-
wise, was the philosophical Professor. Solitary,
but with a mighty current, flowed the river of his
life, like the Nile, without a tributary stream, and
making fertile only a single strip in the vast desert.
His temperament had been in youth a joyous one ;
and now, amid all his sorrows and privations, —
for he had many, — he looked upon the world as
a glad, bright, glorious world. On the many joys
of life he gazed still with the eyes of childhood,
from the far-gone Past upward, trusting, hoping ;
— and upon its sorrows with the eyes of age, from
the distant Future, downward, triumphant, not de-
spairing. He loved solitude, and silence, and can-
dle-light, and the deep midnight. " For," said he,
" if the morning hours are the wings of the day,
I only fold them about me to sleep more sweetly ;
knowing that, at its other extremity, the day, like
the fowls of the air, has an epicurean morsel, — a

parson's nose ; and on this oily midnight my spirit revels and is glad."

Such was the Professor, who had been talking in a half-intelligible strain for two hours or more. The Baron had fallen fast asleep in his chair ; but Flemming sat listening with excited imagination, and the Professor continued in the following words, which, to the best of his listener's memory, seemed gleaned here and there from Fichte's Destiny of Man, and Schubert's History of the Soul.

" Life is one and universal, its forms many and individual. Throughout this beautiful and wonderful creation there is never-ceasing motion, without rest by night or day, ever weaving to and fro. Swifter than a weaver's shuttle it flies from Birth to Death, from Death to Birth ; from the beginning seeks the end, and finds it not, for the seeming end is only a dim beginning of a new out-going and endeavor after the end. As the ice upon the mountain, when the warm breath of the summer sun breathes upon it, melts, and divides into drops, each of which reflects an image of the sun ; so life, in the smile of God's love, divides itself into separate forms, each bearing in it and reflecting an image of God's love. Of all these forms the highest and most perfect in its God-likeness is the human soul. The vast cathedral of Nature is full of holy scriptures, and shapes of deep, mysterious meaning, but all is solitary and silent there — no bending knee, no uplifted eye, no lip adoring, praying. Into this vast cathedral comes the human soul, seeking its Creator ; and the universal silence is changed to sound, and

the sound is harmonious, and has a meaning, and is comprehended and felt. It was an ancient saying of the Persians, that the waters rush from the mountains and hurry forth into all the lands to find the Lord of the Earth ; and the flame of the fire, when it awakes, gazes no more upon the ground, but mounts heavenward, to seek the Lord of Heaven ; and here and there the Earth has built the great watch-towers of the mountains, and they lift their heads far up into the sky, and gaze ever upward and around, to see if the Judge of the World comes not ! Thus in Nature herself, without man, there lies a waiting and hoping, a looking and yearning, after an unknown somewhat. Yes ; when, above there, where the mountain lifts its head over all others, that it may be alone with the clouds and storms of heaven, the lonely eagle looks forth into the gray dawn, to see if the day comes not ; when, by the mountain torrent, the brooding raven listens to hear if the chamois is returning from his nightly pasture in the valley ; and when the soon uprising sun calls out the spicy odors of the thousand flowers, the Alpine flowers, with heaven's deep blue and the blush of sunset on their leaves ; — then there awake in Nature, and the soul of man can see and comprehend them, an expectation and a longing for a future revelation of God's majesty. They awake, also, when, in the fulness of life, field and forest rest at noon, and through the stillness are heard only the song of the grasshopper and the hum of the bee ; and when at evening the singing lark up from the sweet-smelling vineyards rises, or in the later hours of

night Orion puts on his shining armor, to walk forth into the fields of heaven. But in the soul of man alone is this longing changed to certainty, and fulfilled. For, lo ! the light of the sun and the stars shines through the air, and is nowhere visible and seen ; the planets hasten with more than the speed of the storm through infinite space, and their footsteps are not heard ; but where the sunlight strikes the firm surface of the planets, where the storm-wind smites the wall of the mountain cliff, there is the one seen and the other heard. Thus is the glory of God made visible, and may be seen, where in the soul of man it meets its likeness changeless and steadfast. Thus, then, stands Man ; — a mountain on the boundary between two worlds ; — its foot in one, its summit far-rising into the other. From this summit the manifold landscape of life is visible, the way of the Past and Perishable, which we have left behind us ; and as we evermore ascend, bright glimpses of the daybreak of Eternity beyond us ! "

Flemming would fain have interrupted this discourse at times, to answer and inquire ; but the Professor went on, warming and glowing more and more. At length there was a short pause, and Flemming said : —

" All these indefinite longings, these yearnings after an unknown somewhat, I have felt and still feel within me, but not yet their fulfilment."

" That is because you have not faith," answered the Professor. " The Present is an age of doubt, and disbelief, and darkness ; out of which shall arise a clear and bright Hereafter. In the second

part of Goethe's Faust, there is a grand and strik-
ing scene, where in the classical Walpurgis Night,
on the Pharsalian Plains, the mocking Mephis-
topheles sits down between the solemn antique
Sphinxes, and boldly questions them, and reads
their riddles. The red light of innumerable watch-
fires glares round about, and shines upon the terri-
ble face of the arch-scoffer; while on either side,
severe, majestic, solemnly serene, we behold the
gigantic forms of the children of Chimæra, half
buried in the sand, their mild eyes gazing fixedly,
as if they heard through the midnight the swift-
rushing wings of the Stymphalides, striving to out-
strip the speed of Alcides' arrows! Angry Griffins
are near them, and not far are Sirens, singing
their wondrous songs from the rocking branches
of the willow-trees! Even thus does a scoffing and
unbelieving Present sit down between an unknown
Future and a too believing Past, and question and
challenge the gigantic forms of Faith, half buried
in the sands of Time, and gazing forward stead-
fastly into the night, whilst sounds of anger and
voices of delight alternate vex and soothe the ear
of man! — But the time will come when the soul
of man shall return again childlike and trustful to
its faith in God, and look God in the face and die;
for it is an old saying, full of deep, mysterious
meaning, that he must die who hath looked upon
a God. And this is the fate of the soul, that it
should die continually. No sooner here on earth
does it awake to its peculiar being, than it strug-
gles to behold and comprehend the Spirit of Life.
In the first dim twilight of its existence, it beholds

this spirit, is pervaded by its energies, — is quick and creative like the spirit itself, and yet slumbers away into death after having seen it. But the image it has seen remains; in the eternal procreation, as a homogeneal existence, is again renewed, and the seeming death, from moment to moment, becomes the source of kind after kind of existences in ever-ascending series. The soul aspires ever onward to love and to behold. It sees the image more perfect in the brightening twilight of the dawn, in the ever higher-rising sun. It sleeps again, dying in the clearer vision; but the image seen remains as a permanent kind; and the slumberer awakes anew and ever higher after its own image, till at length, in the full blaze of noonday, a being comes forth, which, like the eagle, can behold the sun and die not. Then both live on, even when this bodily element, the mist and vapor through which the young eagle gazed, dissolves and falls to earth."

"I am not sure that I understand you," said Flemming; "but if I do, you mean to say, that, as the body continually changes and takes unto itself new properties, and is not the same to-day as yesterday, so likewise the soul lays aside its idiosyncrasies, and is changed by acquiring new powers, and thus may be said to die. And hence, properly speaking, the soul lives always in the Present, and has, and can have, no Future; for the Future becomes the Present, and the soul that then lives in me is a higher and more perfect soul, and so onward for evermore."

"I mean what I say," continued the Professor;

" and can find no more appropriate language to express my. meaning than that which I have used. But, as I said before, pardon must be granted to the novelty of words, when it serves to illustrate the obscurity of things. And I think you will see clearly from what I have said, that this earthly life, when seen hereafter from heaven, will seem like an hour passed long ago, and dimly remembered ; — that long, laborious, full of joys and sorrows as it is, it will then have dwindled down to a mere point, hardly visible to the far-reaching ken of the disembodied spirit. But the spirit itself soars onward. And thus death is neither an end nor a beginning. It is a transition, not from one existence to another, but from one state of existence to another. No link is broken in the chain of being, any more than in passing from infancy to manhood, from manhood to old age. There are seasons of reverie and deep abstraction, which seem to me analogous to death. The soul gradually loses its consciousness of what is passing around it, and takes no longer cognizance of objects which are near. It seems for the moment to have dissolved its connection with the body. It has passed, as it were, into another state of being. It lives in another world. It has flown over lands and seas, and holds communion with those it loves, in distant regions of the earth, and the more distant heaven. It sees familiar faces and hears beloved voices, which to the bodily senses are no longer visible and audible. And this likewise is death ; save that, when we die, the soul returns no more to the dwelling it has left."

" You seem to take it for granted," interrupted Flemming, " that, in our reveries, the soul really goes out of the body into distant places, instead of summoning up their semblance within itself by the power of memory and imagination."

"Something I must take for granted," replied the Professor. " We will not discuss that point now. I speak not without forethought. Just observe what a glorious thing human life is, when seen in this light; and how glorious man's destiny. I am; thou art; he is! seems but a school-boy's conjugation. But therein lies a mysterious meaning. We behold all round about us one vast union, in which no man can labor for himself, without laboring at the same time for all others; a glimpse of truth, which, by the universal harmony of things, becomes an inward benediction, and lifts the soul mightily upward. Still more so, when a man regards himself as a necessary member of this union. The feeling of our dignity and our power grows strong, when we say to ourselves: My being is not objectless and in vain; I am a necessary link in the great chain, which, from the full development of consciousness in the first man, reaches forward into eternity. All the great and wise and good among mankind, all the benefactors of the human race, whose names I read in the world's history, and the still greater number of those whose good deeds have outlived their names, — all those have labored for me. I have entered into their harvest. I walk the green earth which they inhabited. I tread in their footsteps, from which blessings grow. I can undertake the sub-

lime task which they once undertook, the task of
making our common brotherhood wiser and hap-
pier. I can build forward, where they were forced
to leave off, and bring nearer to perfection the
great edifice which they left uncompleted. And at
length I, too, must leave it, and go hence. Oh,
this is the sublimest thought of all! I can never
finish the noble task; therefore, so sure as this
task is my destiny, I can never cease to work, and
consequently never cease to be. What men call
death cannot break off this task, which is never-
ending; consequently no period is set to my being,
and I am eternal. I lift my head boldly to the
threatening mountain-peaks, and to the roaring
cataract, and to the storm-clouds swimming in the
fire-sea overhead, and say, — I am eternal and
defy your power! Break, break over me! and
thou Earth, and thou Heaven, mingle in the wild
tumult! and ye Elements, foam and rage, and de-
stroy this atom of dust, — this body, which I call
mine! My will alone, with its fixed purpose, shall
hover brave and triumphant over the ruins of the
universe; for I have comprehended my destiny;
and it is more durable than ye! It is eternal; and
I, who recognize it, I likewise am eternal! Tell
me, my friend, have you no faith in this?"

"I have," answered Flemming, and there was
another pause. He then said : —

"I have listened to you patiently and without
interruption. Now listen to me. You complain
of the scepticism of the age. This is one form in
which the philosophic spirit of the age presents it-
self. Let me tell you that another form which it

assumes is that of poetic reverie. Plato of old had dreams like these, and the Mystics of the Middle Ages; and still their disciples walk in the cloud-land and dream-land of this poetic philosophy. Pleasant and cool upon their souls lie the shadows of the trees under which Plato taught. From their whispering leaves comes wafted across the noise of populous centuries a solemn and .mysterious sound, which to them is the voice of the Soul of the World. All nature has become spiritualized and transfigured; and, wrapped in beautiful, vague dreams of the real and the ideal, they live in this green world, like the little child in the German tale, who sits by the margin of a woodland lake, and hears the blue heaven and the branches overhead dispute with their reflection in the 'water, which is the reality and which the image. I willingly confess that such day-dreams as these appeal strongly to my imagination. Visitants and attendants are they of those lofty souls which, soaring ever higher and higher, build themselves nests under the very eaves of the stars, forgetful that they cannot live on air, but must descend to earth for food. Yet I recognize them as day-dreams only; as shadows, not substantial things. What I mainly dislike in the New Philosophy is the cool impertinence with which an old idea folded in a new garment looks you in the face and pretends not to know you, though you have been familiar friends from childhood. I remember an English author, who, in speaking of your German philosophies, says very wisely: 'Often a proposition of inscrutable and dread aspect, when resolutely grappled with,

and torn from its shady den and its bristling in-
trenchments of uncouth terminology, and dragged
forth into the open light of day, to be seen by the
natural eye and tried by merely human understand-
ing, proves to be a very harmless truth, familiar
to us from old, sometimes so familiar as to be a
truism. Too frequently the anxious novice is re-
minded of Dryden in the Battle of the Books ;
there is a helmet of rusty iron, dark, grim, gigan-
tic, and within it, at the farthest corner, is a head
no bigger than a walnut.' — Can you believe that
these words ever came from the pen of Thomas
Carlyle ? He has himself taken up the uncouth
terminology, of late, and many pure, simple minds
are much offended at it. They seem to take it as
a personal insult. They are angry, and deny the
just meed of praise. It is, however, hardly worth
while to lose our presence of mind. Let us rather
profit as we may, even from this spectacle, and
recognize the monarch in his masquerade. For,
hooded and wrapped about with that strange and
antique garb, there walks a kingly, a most royal
soul, even as the Emperor Charles walked amid
solemn cloisters under a monk's cowl, — a mon-
arch still in soul. Such things are not new in
the history of the world. Ever and anon they
sweep over the earth, and blow themselves out
soon ; and then there is quiet for a season,
and the atmosphere of Truth seems more serene.
Why would you preach to the wind ? Why rea-
son with thunder-storms ? Better sit quiet, and
see them pass over like a pageant, cloudy, superb,
and vast."

The Professor smiled self-complacently, but said not a word. Flemming continued : —

" I will add no more than this, — there are many speculations in literature, philosophy, and religion, which, though pleasant to walk in, and lying under the shadow of great names, yet lead to no important result. They resemble rather those roads in the Western forests of my native land, which, though broad and pleasant at first, and lying beneath the shadow of great branches, finally dwindle to a squirrel track, and run up a tree ! "

The Professor hardly knew whether he should laugh or be offended at this sally ; and, laying his hand upon Flemming's arm, he said seriously : —

" Believe me, my young friend, the time will come when you will think more wisely on these things. And with you, I trust, that time will soon come, since it moves more speedily with some than with others. For what is Time ? The shadow on the dial, the striking of the clock, the running of the sand, day and night, summer and winter, months, years, centuries — these are but arbitrary and outward signs, the measure of Time, not Time itself. Time is the Life of the soul. If not this, then tell me, what is Time ? "

The high and animated tone of voice in which the Professor uttered these words aroused the Baron from his sleep ; and, not distinctly comprehending what was said, but thinking the Professor asked what time it was, he innocently exclaimed : —

" I should think it must be near midnight ! "

This somewhat disconcerted the Professor, who took his leave soon afterward. When he was gone, the Baron said : —

" Excuse me for treating your guest so cavalierly. His philosophy annoyed me not a little; and I took refuge in sleep. One would think, to judge by the language of this sect, that they alone saw any beauty in Nature; and when I hear one of them discourse, I am instantly reminded of Goethe's Baccalaureus, when he exclaims : ' The world was not, before I created it ; I brought the sun up out of the sea ; with me began the changeful course of the moon; the day decked itself on my account; the earth grew green and blossomed to meet me ; at my nod, in that first night, the pomp of all the stars developed itself; who but I set you free from all the bonds of Philister-like, contracting thoughts ? I, however, emancipated as my mind assures me I am, gladly pursue my inward light, advance boldly in a transport peculiarly my own, the bright before me, and the dark behind !' — Do you not see a resemblance ? Oh, they might be modest enough to confess that one straggling ray of light may, by some accident, reach the blind eyes of even us poor, benighted heathen ! "

" Alas ! how little veneration we have ! " said Flemming. " I could not help closing the discussion with a jest. An ill-timed levity often takes me by surprise. On all such occasions, I think of a scene at the University, where, in the midst of a grave discussion on the possibility of Absolute Motion, a scholar said he had seen a rock split

open, from which sprang a toad, who could not be supposed to have any knowledge of the external world, and consequently his motion must have been absolute. The learned Professor who presided on that occasion was hardly more startled and astonished than was our learned Professor, five minutes ago. But come; wind up your watch, and let us go to bed."

" By the way," said the Baron, " did you mind what a curious head he has? There are two crowns upon it."

" That is a sign," replied Flemming, " that he will eat his bread in two kingdoms."

" I think the poor man would be very thankful," said the Baron, with a smile, " if he were always sure of eating it in one. He is what the Transcendentalists call a God-intoxicated man; and I advise him, as Santeul advised Bossuet, to go to Patmos and write a new Apocalypse."

CHAPTER VII.

MILL-WHEELS AND OTHER WHEELS.

A few days after this, the Baron received letters from his sister, telling him that her physicians had prescribed a few weeks at the Baths of Ems, and urging him to meet her there before the fashionable season.

" Come," said he to Flemming; "make this short journey with me. We will pass a few pleasant days at Ems, and visit the other watering-places of Nassau. It will drive away the melan-

choly day-dreams that haunt you. Perhaps some
future bride is even now waiting for you, with dim
presentiments and undefined longings, at the Ser-
pent's Bath."

"Or some widow of Ems, with a cork leg!"
said Flemming, smiling; and then added, in a tone
of voice half jest, half earnest, "Certainly; let us
go in pursuit of her: —

> "Whoe'er she be,
> That not impossible she,
> That shall command my heart and me:
> Where'er she lie,
> Hidden from mortal eye,
> In shady leaves of destiny."

They started in the afternoon for Frankfort, pur-
suing their way slowly along the lovely Bergstrasse,
famed throughout Germany for its beauty. They
passed the ruined house where Martin Luther lay
concealed after the Diet of Worms, and through
the village of Handschuhsheim, as old as the days
of King Pepin the Short, — a hamlet, lying under
the hills, half buried in blossoms and green leaves.
Close on the right rose the mountains of the mys-
terious Odenwald; and on the left lay the Neckar,
like a steel bow in the meadow. Farther westward,
a thin, smoky vapor betrayed the course of the
Rhine; beyond which, like a troubled sea, ran the
blue, billowy Alsatian hills. Song of birds and
sound of evening bells, and fragrance of sweet
blossoms, filled the air; and silent and slow sank
the broad red sun, half hidden amid folding clouds.

"We shall not pass the night at Weinheim,"
said the Baron to the postilion, who had dis-

mounted to walk up the hill leading to the town. "You may drive to the mill in the valley of Birkenau."

The postilion seized one of his fat horses by the tail, and swung himself up to his seat again. They rattled over the paved streets of Weinheim, and took no heed of the host of the Golden Eagle, who stood so invitingly at the door of his own inn ; and the ruins of Burg Windeck, above there, on its mountain throne, frowned at them for hurrying by, without staying to do him homage.

"The old ruin looks well from the valley," said the Baron; "but let us beware of climbing that steep hill. Most travellers are like children ; they must needs touch whatever they behold. They climb up to every old broken tooth of a castle which they find on their way; get a toilsome ascent and hot sunshine for their pains, and come down wearied and disappointed. I trust we are wiser."

They crossed the bridge, and turned up the stream, passing under an arch of stone which serves as a gateway to this enchanted valley of Birkenau. A cool and lovely valley, shut in by high hills ; shaded by alder-trees and tall poplars, under which rushes the Wechsnitz, a noisy mountain-brook, that ever and anon puts its broad shoulder to the wheel of a mill, and shows that it can labor as well as laugh. At one of these mills they stopped for the night.

A mill forms as characteristic a feature in the romantic German landscape as in the romantic German tale. It is not only a mill, but likewise

an alehouse and rural inn ; so that the associations
it suggests are not of labor only, but also of pleas-
ure. It stands in the narrow defile, with its pic-
turesque thatched roof ; thither throng the peas-
ants, of a holiday ; and there are rustic dances
under the trees.

In the twilight of the fast-approaching summer
night, the Baron and Flemming walked forth along
the borders of the stream. As they heard it rush-
ing and gushing among the stones and tangled
roots, and the great wheel turning in the current,
with its never-ceasing plash ! plash ! it brought to
their minds that exquisite, simple song of Goethe,
the Youth and the Mill-brook. It was for the
moment a nymph which sang to them in the voice
of the waters.

"I am persuaded," said Flemming, "that, in
order fully to understand and feel the popular
poetry of Germany, one must be familiar with the
German landscape. Many sweet little poems are
the outbreaks of momentary feelings ; — words to
which the song of birds, the rustling of leaves, and
the gurgle of cool waters form the appropriate
music. Or perhaps I should say they are words
which man has composed to the music of nature.
Can you not, even now, hear this brooklet telling
you how it is on its way to the mill, where at day-
break the miller's daughter opens her window, and
comes down to bathe her face in its stream, and her
bosom is so full and white that it kindles the glow
of love in the cool waters ? "

"A most delightful ballad, truly," said the
Baron. "But, like many others of our little

songs, it requires a poet to feel and understand
it. Sing them in the valley and woodland shad-
ows, and under the leafy roofs of garden walks,
and at night, and alone, as they were written. Sing
them not in the loud world, — for the loud world
laughs such things to scorn. It is Müller who
says, in that little song where the maiden bids the
moon good evening : —

> " This song was made to be sung at night,
> And he who reads it in broad daylight
> Will never read the mystery right ;
> And yet it is childlike easy !

He has written a great many pretty songs, in
which the momentary, indefinite longings and im-
pulses of the soul of man find an expression.
He calls them the Songs of a Wandering Horn-
player. There is one among them much to our
present purpose. He expresses in it the feeling
of unrest and desire of motion, which the sight
and sound of running waters often produce in us.
It is entitled ' Whither ? ' and is worth repeating
to you.

> " I heard a brooklet gushing
> From its rocky fountain near,
> Down into the valley rushing,
> So fresh and wondrous clear.
>
> " I know not what came o'er me,
> Nor who the counsel gave ;
> But I must hasten downward,
> All with my pilgrim-stave.
>
> " Downward, and ever farther,
> And ever the brook beside ;
> And ever fresher murmured,
> And ever clearer, the tide.

" Is this the way I was going ?
 Whither, O brooklet ? say !
 Thou hast, with thy soft murmur,
 Murmured my senses away.

" What do I say of a murmur ?
 That can no murmur be ;
 'T is the water-nymphs that are singing
 Their roundelays under me.

" Let them sing, my friend, let them murmur
 And wander merrily near ;
 The wheels of a mill are going
 In every brooklet clear."

"There you have the poetic reverie," said Flem-
ming, " and the dull prose commentary and expla-
nation in matter of fact. The song is pretty, and
was probably suggested by some such scene as this
which we are now beholding. Doubtless, all your
old national traditions sprang up in the popular
mind as this song in the poet's."

"Your opinion is certainly correct," answered
the Baron ; "and yet all this play of poetic fancy
does not prevent me from feeling the chill night-
air and the pangs of hunger. Let us go back to
the mill, and see what our landlady has for sup-
per. Did you observe what a loud, sharp voice
she has ? "

"People always have who live in mills and near
waterfalls."

On the following morning, they emerged unwil-
lingly from the green, dark valley, and journeyed
along the level highway to Frankfort, where in
the evening they heard the glorious Don Giovanni
of Mozart. Of all operas, this was Flemming's
favorite. What rapturous flights of sound ! what

thrilling, pathetic chimes! what wild, joyous rev-
elry of passion! what a delirium of sense! what
an expression of agony and woe! — all the feel-
ings of suffering and rejoicing humanity sympa-
thized with and finding a voice in those tones.
Flemming and the Baron listened with ever in-
creasing delight.

"How wonderful this is!" exclaimed Flemming,
transported by his feelings. "How the chorus
swells and dies, like the wind of summer! How
those passages of mysterious import seem to wave
to and fro, like the swaying branches of trees;
from which anon some solitary sweet voice darts
off like a bird, and floats away and revels in the
bright, warm sunshine! and then mark! how, amid
the chorus of a hundred voices and a hundred in-
struments, of flutes and drums and trumpets, this
universal shout and whirlwind of the vexed air,
you can so clearly distinguish the melancholy vi-
bration of a single string, touched by the finger, —
a mournful, sobbing sound! Ah, this is indeed
human life! where, in the rushing, noisy crowd,
and amid sounds of gladness, and a thousand min-
gling emotions, distinctly audible to the ear of
thought, are the pulsations of some melancholy
string of the heart, touched by an invisible hand."

Then came, in the midst of these excited feel-
ings, the ballet, drawing its magic net about the
soul. And soon, from the tangled yet harmonious
mazes of the dance, came forth a sylph-like form,
her scarf floating behind her, as if she were fan-
ning the air with gauze-like wings. Noiseless as a
feather or a snow-flake falls, did her feet touch the

earth. She seemed to float in the air, and the floor to bend and wave under her, as a branch when a bird alights upon it and takes wing again. Loud and rapturous applause followed each wonderful step, each voluptuous movement; and, with a flushed cheek and burning eye, and bosom panting to be free, stood the gracefully majestic figure for a moment still, and then the winged feet of the swift dancing-girls glanced round her, and she was lost again in the throng.

"How truly exquisite this is!" exclaimed the Baron, after joining loudly in the applause.

"What a noble figure! What grace! what attitudes! How much soul in every motion! how much expression in every gesture! I assure you, it produces upon me the same effect as a beautiful poem. It is a poem. Every step is a word; and the whole together a poem!"

The Baron and Flemming were delighted with the scene; and at the same time exceedingly amused with the countenance of an old prude in the next box, who seemed to look upon the whole magic show with such feelings as Michal, Saul's daughter, experienced, when she looked from her window and saw King David dancing and leaping with his scanty garments.

"After all," said Flemming, "the old French priest was not so far out of the way, when he said, in his coarse dialect, 'The dance is the Devil's procession, and paint and ornaments, the whetting of the Devil's sword; and the ring that is made in dancing, the Devil's grindstone, whereon he sharpens his sword; and finally, — a ballet is the pomp

and mass of the Devil, and whosoever entereth therein entereth into his pomp and mass; for the woman who singeth is the prioress of the Devil, and they that answer are clerks, and they that look on are parishioners, and the cymbals and flutes are the bells, and the musicians that play are the ministers of the Devil.' "

" No doubt, this good lady near us thinks so likewise," answered the Baron, laughing ; " but she likes it for all that."

When the play was over, the Baron begged Flemming to sit still till the crowd had gone.

" I have a strange fancy," said he, " whenever I come to the theatre, to see the end of all things. When the crowd is gone, and the curtain raised again to air the house, and the lamps are all out, save here and there one behind the scenes, the contrast with what has gone before is most impressive. Everything wears a dream-like aspect. The empty boxes and stalls, the silence, the smoky twilight, and the magic scene dismantled, produce in me a strange, mysterious feeling. It is like a dim reflection of a theatre in water or in a dusty mirror, and reminds me of some of Hoffmann's wild tales. It is a practical moral lesson, a commentary on the play, and makes the show complete."

It was truly as he said, only tenfold more desolate, solemn, and impressive ; and produced upon the mind the effect we experience when slumber is suddenly broken, and dreams and realities mingle, and we know not yet whether we sleep or wake. As they at length passed out through the dimly lighted passage, they heard a vulgar-looking fel-

low, with a sensual face and shaggy whiskers, say to some persons who were standing near him, and seemed to be hangers-on of the play-house : —

" I shall run her six nights at Munich, and then take her on to Vienna."

Flemming thought he was speaking of some favorite horse. He was speaking of his beautiful wife, the ballet-dancer.

CHAPTER VIII.

GOETHE.

What most interested our travellers in the ancient city of Frankfort was neither the opera, nor the Ariadne of Dannecker, but the house in which Goethe was born, and the scenes he frequented in his childhood and remembered in his old age. Such, for example, are the walks around the city, outside the moat ; the bridge over the Main, with the golden cock on the cross, which the poet beheld and marvelled at when a boy ; the cloister of the Barefooted Friars, through which he stole with mysterious awe to sit by the oilcloth-covered table of old Rector Albrecht ; and the garden in which his grandfather walked up and down among fruit-trees and rose-bushes, in long morning-gown, black velvet cap, and the antique leather gloves, which he annually received as Mayor on Pipers-Dooms-day representing a kind of middle personage between Alcinous and Laertes. Thus, O Genius ! are thy footprints hallowed, and the star shines forever over the place of thy nativity.

" Your English critics may rail as they list,"
said the Baron, while he and Flemming were re-
turning from a stroll in the leafy gardens out-
side the moat; " but, after all, Goethe was a mag-
nificent old fellow. Only think of his life; his
youth of passion, alternately aspiring and despond-
ing, stormy, impetuous, headlong ; — his romantic
manhood, in which passion assumes the form of
strength ; assiduous, careful, toiling, without haste,
without rest ; — and his sublime old age, — the
age of serene and classic repose, where he stands
like Atlas, as Claudian has painted him in the
Battle of the Giants, holding the world aloft upon
his head, the ocean-streams hard frozen in his
hoary locks."

" A good illustration of what the world calls his
indifferentism."

" And do you know I rather like this indifferent-
ism ? Did you never have the misfortune to live
in a community, where a difficulty in the parish
seemed to announce the end of the world ? or to
know one of the benefactors of the human race, in
the very storm and pressure period of his indis-
creet enthusiasm ? If you have, I think you will
see something beautiful in the calm and dignified
attitude which the old philosopher assumes."

" It is a pity that his admirers had not a little
of this philosophic coolness. It amuses me to
read the various epithets which they apply to
him : — The Dear, dear Man ! The Life-enjoying
Man ! The All-sided One ! The Representative
of Poetry upon Earth ! The Many-sided Master-
Mind of Germany ! His enemies rush into the

other extreme, and hurl at him the fierce names of
Old Humbug! and Old Heathen! which hit like
pistol-bullets."

" I confess he was no saint."

" No ; his philosophy is the old ethnic philoso-
phy. You will find it all in a convenient and
concentrated portable form in Horace's beautiful
Ode to Thaliarchus. What I most object to in the
old gentleman is his sensuality."

" Oh, nonsense ! Nothing can be purer than the
Iphigenia; it is as cold and passionless as a marble
statue."

" Very true, but you cannot say the same of
some of the Roman Elegies, and of that strange
book, the Elective Affinities."

" Ah, my friend, Goethe is an artist, and looks
upon all things as objects of art merely. Why
should he not be allowed to copy in words what
painters and sculptors copy in colors and in
marble ? "

" The artist shows his character in the choice of
his subject. Goethe never sculptured an Apollo,
nor painted a Madonna. He gives us only sinful
Magdalens and rampant Fauns. He does not so
much idealize as realize."

" He only copies nature."

" So did the artists who made the bronze lamps
of Pompeii. Would you hang one of those in your
hall? To say that a man is an artist and copies
nature is not enough. There are two great schools
of art, — the imitative and the imaginative. The
latter is the most noble, and the most enduring ;
and Goethe belonged rather to the former. Have
you read Menzel's attack upon him ? "

" It is truly ferocious. The Silesian hews into him lustily. I hope you do not take sides with him."

" By no means. He goes too far. He blames the poet for not being a politician. He might as well blame him for not being a missionary to the Sandwich Islands."

" And what do you think of Eckermann?"

" I think he is a kind of German Boswell. Goethe knew he was drawing his portrait, and sat for it accordingly. He works very hard to make a Saint Peter out of an old Jupiter, as the Catholics did at Rome."

" Well, call him Old Humbug, or Old Heathen, or what you please ; I maintain that, with all his errors and shortcomings, he was a glorious specimen of a man."

" He certainly was. Did it ever occur to you that he was in some points like Ben Franklin, — a kind of rhymed Ben Franklin? The practical tendency of his mind was the same; his love of science was the same; his benignant, philosophic spirit was the same; and a vast number of his little poetic maxims and soothsayings seem nothing more than the worldly wisdom of Poor Richard, versified."

" What most offends me is, that now every German jackass must have a kick at the dead lion."

" And every one who passes through Weimar must throw a book upon his grave, as travellers did of old a stone upon the grave of Manfredi, at Benevento. But, of all that has been said or sung, what most pleases me is Heine's Apologetic, if I

may so call it; in which he says, that 'the minor poets, who flourished under the imperial reign of Goethe, resemble a young forest, where the trees first show their own magnitude after the oak of a hundred years, whose branches had towered above and overshadowed them, has fallen. There was not wanting an opposition that strove against Goethe, this majestic tree. Men of the most warring opinions united themselves for the contest. The adherents of the old faith, the orthodox, were vexed that in the trunk of the vast tree no niche with its holy image was to be found; nay, that even the naked Dryads of paganism were permitted to play their witchery there; and gladly, with consecrated axe, would they have imitated the holy Boniface, and levelled the enchanted oak to the ground. The followers of the new faith, the apostles of Liberalism, were vexed, on the other hand, that the tree could not serve as a Liberty Tree, or, at any rate, as a barricade. In fact the tree was too high; no one could plant the red cap upon its summit, or dance the Carmagnole beneath its branches. The multitude, however, venerated this tree for the very reason that it reared itself with such independent grandeur, and so graciously filled the world with its odor, while its branches streaming magnificently toward heaven made it appear as if the stars were only the golden fruit of its wondrous limbs.' Do you not think that beautiful?"

"Yes, very beautiful. And I am glad to see that you can find something to admire in my favorite author, notwithstanding his frailties; or, to

use an old German saying, that you can drive the
hens out of the garden without trampling down
the beds."

" Here is the old gentleman himself! " exclaimed
Flemming.

" Where? " cried the Baron, as if for the mo-
ment he expected to see the living figure of the
poet walking before them.

" Here at the window, — that full-length cast.
Excellent, is it not? He is dressed, as usual, in
his long yellow nankeen surtout, with a white cra-
vat crossed in front. What a magnificent head!
and what a posture! He stands like a tower of
strength. And, by Heavens! he was nearly eighty
years old when that was made."

" How do you know? "

" You can see by the date on the pedestal."

" You are right. And yet how erect he stands.
with his square shoulders braced back, and his
hands behind him! He looks as if he were stand-
ing before the fire. I feel tempted to put a live
coal into his hand, it lies so invitingly half-open.
Gleim's description of him, soon after he went to
Weimar, is very different from this. Do you
recollect it? "

" No, I do not."

" It is a story which good old father Gleim used
to tell with great delight. He was one evening
reading the Göttingen Musen-Almanach in a select
society at Weimar, when a young man came in,
dressed in a short, green shooting-jacket, booted
and spurred, and having a pair of brilliant, black,
Italian eyes. He, in turn, offered to read; but

finding, probably, the poetry of the Musen-Alma-
nach of that year rather too insipid for him, he
soon began to improvise the wildest and most fan-
tastic poems imaginable, and in all possible forms
and measures, pretending all the while to read
from the book. 'That is either Goethe or the
Devil,' said good old father Gleim to Wieland,
who sat near him. To which the Great I of
Osmannstadt replied, 'It is both, for he has the
Devil in him to-night; and at such times he is like
a wanton colt, that flings out before and behind,
and you will do well not to go too near him!'"

"Very good!"

"And now that noble figure is but mould. Only
a few months ago, those majestic eyes looked for
the last time on the light of a pleasant spring
morning. Calm, like a god, the old man sat; and
with a smile seemed to bid farewell to the light of
day, on which he had gazed for more than eighty
years. Books were near him, and the pen which
had just dropped, as it were, from his dying
fingers. — Open the shutters, and let in more
light! were the last words that came from those
lips. Slowly stretching forth his hand, he seemed
to write in the air; and, as it sank down again
and was motionless, the spirit of the old man de-
parted."

"And yet the world goes on. It is strange
how soon, when a great man dies, his place is
filled; and so completely that he seems no longer
wanted. But let us step in here. I wish to buy
that cast."

CHAPTER IX.

THE DAYLIGHT OF THE DWARFS, AND THE FALL-ING STAR.

After lingering a day or two in Frankfort, the two friends struck across through Hochheim to the Rhine, and up among the hills of the Rheingau to Schlangenbad, where they tarried only to bathe and to dine, and then pursued their way to Langen-schwalbach. The town lies in a valley, with gently sloping hills around it, and long avenues of poplars leading forth into the fields. One interminable street cuts the town in twain, and there are old houses with curious faces carved upon their fronts, and dates of the olden time.

Our travellers soon sallied forth from their hotel, impatient to drink the strength-giving waters of the fountains. They continued their walk far up the valley under the poplars. The new grain was waving in the fields; the birds singing in the trees and in the air; and everything seemed glad, save a poor, old man, who came tottering out of the woods, with a heavy bundle of sticks on his shoulders.

Returning upon their steps, they passed down the valley and through the long street to the tumble-down old Lutheran church. A flight of stone steps leads from the street to the green ter-race or platform on which the church stands, and which in ancient times was the church-yard, or, as the Germans more devoutly say, God's-acre; where generations are scattered like seeds, and

that which is sown in corruption shall be raised
hereafter in incorruption. On the steps stood an
old man, — a very old man, — holding a little girl
by the hand. He took off his greasy cap as they
passed, and wished them good day. His teeth
were gone; he could hardly articulate a syllable.
The Baron asked him how old the church was.
He gave no answer; but when the question was
repeated, came close up to them, and, taking off
his cap again, turned his ear attentively, and
said : —

"I am hard of hearing."

"Poor old man," said Flemming; "he is as
much a ruin as the church we are entering. It
will not be long before he, too, shall be sown as
seed in this God's-acre! "

The little girl ran into a house close at hand,
and brought out the great key. The church-door
swung open, and, descending a few steps, they
passed through a low-roofed passage into the
church. All was in ruin. The gravestones in
the pavement were started from their places; the
vaults beneath yawned; the roof above was falling
piecemeal; there were rents in the old tower; and
mysterious passages, and side doors with crazy
flights of wooden steps, leading down into the
churchyard. Amid all this ruin, one thing only
stood erect; it was a statue of a knight in armor,
standing in a niche under the pulpit.

"Who is this?" said Flemming to the old sex-
ton; "who is this, that stands here so solemnly in
marble, and seems to be keeping guard over the
dead men below?"

" I do not know," replied the old man ; "but I have heard my grandfather say it was the statue of a great warrior ! "

" There is history for you ! " exclaimed the Baron. " There is fame ! To have a statue of marble, and yet have your name forgotten by the sexton of your parish, who can remember only that he once heard his grandfather say that you were a great warrior ! "

Flemming made no reply, for he was thinking of the days, when, from that old pulpit, some bold reformer thundered down the first tidings of a new doctrine, and the roof echoed with the grand old hymn of Martin Luther.

When he communicated his thoughts to the Baron, the only answer he received was : —

" After all, what is the use of so much preaching ? Do you think the fishes, that heard the sermon of St. Anthony, were any better than those who did not ? I commend to your favorable notice the fish-sermon of this saint, as recorded by Abraham à Sancta Clara. You will find it in your favorite Wonder-Horn."

Thus passed the day at Langenschwalbach, and the evening at the Allée-Saal was quite solitary, for as yet no company had arrived to fill its chambers, or sit under the trees before the door. The next morning even Flemming and the Baron were gone, for the German's heart was beating with strong desire to embrace his sister, and the heart of his friend cared little whither he went, sobeit he were not too much alone.

After a few hours' drive, they were looking down

from the summit of a hill directly upon the house-
tops of Ems. · There it lay, deep sunk in the
hollow beneath them, as if some inhabitant of
Sirius, like him spoken of in Voltaire's tale of
Micromegas, held it in the hollow of his hand.
High and peaked rise the hills that throw their
shadows into this romantic valley, and at their
base winds the river Lahn. Our travellers drove
through the one long street composed entirely of
hotels and lodging-houses. Sick people looked out
of the windows as they passed. Others were walk-
ing leisurely up and down, beneath the few decap-
itated trees, which represent a public promenade,
and a boy, with a blue frock and crimson cap, was
driving three donkeys down the street. In short,
they were in a fashionable watering-place ; as yet
sprinkled only by a few pattering drops of the
summer rain of strangers, which generally follows
the first hot days.

On alighting at the London Hotel, the Baron
found — not his sister, but only a letter from her,
saying she had changed her mind and gone to the
Baths of Franconia. This was a disappointment,
which the Baron pocketed with the letter, and said
not a word more about either. It was his way, —
his philosophy in small things and great. In the
evening, they went to an æsthetic tea, at the house
of the Frau Kranich, the wife of a rich banker of
Frankfort.

"I must tell you about this Frau Kranich," said
the Baron to Flemming, on the way. "She is a
woman of talent and beauty, and just in the prime
of life, but, unfortunately, very ambitious. Her

mania is to make a figure in the fashionable world;
and to this end she married a rich banker of Frank-
fort, old enough to be her father, not to say her
grandfather, hoping, doubtless, that he would soon
die; for, if ever a woman wished to be a widow,
she is that woman. But the old fellow is tough
and won't die. Moreover, he is deaf, and crabbed,
and penurious, and half the time bedridden. The
wife is a model of virtue, notwithstanding her
weakness. She nurses the old gentleman as if he
were a child. And, to crown all, he hates society,
and will not hear of his wife's receiving or going
into company."

"How, then, can she give æsthetic teas?" asked
Flemming.

"I was just going to tell you," continued the
Baron. "The gay lady has no taste for long even-
ings with the old gentleman in the back chamber,
— for being thus chained like a criminal under
Mezentius, face to face with a dead body. So she
puts him to bed first, and" —

"Gives him opium."

"Yes, I dare say; and then gives herself a tea-
party, without his knowing anything about it.
This course of deception is truly hateful in itself,-
and must be particularly so to her, for she is not a
low or an immoral woman, but one of those who,
not having strength enough to complete the sacri-
fice they have had strength enough to commence,
are betrayed into a life of duplicity and false-
hood."

They had now reached the house, and were
ushered into a room gayly lighted and filled with

guests. The hostess came forward to receive them, dressed in white, and sailing down the room like a swan. When the customary salutations had passed and Flemming had been duly presented, the Baron said, not without a certain degree of malice : —

"And, my dear Frau Kranich, how is your good husband to-night?"

This question was about as discreet as a cannon-ball. But the lady replied, in the simplicity of her heart, and not in the least disconcerted : —

"The same as ever, my dear Baron. It is astonishing how he holds out. But let us not talk of these things now. I must introduce your friend to his countryman, the Grand Duke of Mississippi; alike remarkable for his wealth, his modesty, and the extreme simplicity of his manners. He drives only six horses. Besides, he is known as a man of learning and piety, — has his private chapel, and private clergyman, who always preaches against the vanity of worldly riches. He has also a private secretary, whose sole duty is to smoke to him, that he may enjoy the aroma of Spanish cigars, without the trouble of smoking."

"Decidedly a man of genius!"

Here Flemming was introduced to his illustrious countryman — a person who seemed to consist chiefly of linen, such a display did he make of collar, bosom, and wristbands.

"Pray, Mr. Flemming, what do you think of that Rembrandt?" said he, pointing to a picture on the wall. "Exquisite picture! The grandeur of sentiment and splendor of chiaroscuro are of

the first order. Just observe the liquidity of the
water, and the silveriness of the clouds! Great
power! There is a bravura of handling in that
picture, Sir, which it requires the eye of a con-
noisseur to appreciate."

"Yes, a most undoubted — copy!"

And here their conversation ended; for at that
moment the little Moldavian Prince Jerkin made
his way through the crowd, with his snuff-box as
usual in his hand, and hurried up to Flemming,
whom he had known in .Heidelberg. He was
eager to let every one know that he spoke Eng-
lish, and in his haste began by making a mis-
take.

"Good-by! Good-by! Mr. Flemming!" said he,
instead of "good evening." "I am ravished to
see you in Ems. Nice place; — all that there is
of most nice. I drink my water and am good!
Do you not think the Frau Kranich has a very
beautiful leather?"

He meant skin. Flemming laughed outright;
but it was not perceived by the Prince, because at
that moment he was pushed aside, in the rush of
a gallopade, and Flemming beheld his face no
more. At the same moment the Baron introduced
a friend of his, who also spoke English, and said:

"You will sup with me to-night. I have some
Rhine-wine, which will be a seduction to you."

Soon after, the Baron stood, with an impassioned,
romantic lady leaning on his arm, examining a copy
of Raphael's Fornarina.

"Ach! I wish I had been the Fornarina,"
sighed the impassioned, romantic lady.

"Then, my dear madam," replied the Baron, "I
wish I had been Raphael."

And so likewise said to himself a very tall man
with fiery red hair and fancy whiskers, who was
waltzing round and round in one spot, and in a
most extraordinary waistcoat; thus representing a
fiery floating-light, to warn men of the hidden
rocks on which the breath of vanity drives them
shipwreck. At length his partner, tired of spin-
ning, sank upon a sofa, like a child's top, when it
reels and falls.

"You do not like the waltz?" said an elderly
French gentleman, remarking the expression of
Flemming's countenance.

"Oh, yes; among the figurantes of the opera.
But I confess it sometimes makes me shudder to
see a young rake clasp his arms round the waist of
a pure and innocent girl. What would you say,
were you to see him sitting on a sofa with his arms
round your wife?" -

"Mere prejudice of education," replied the
French gentleman. "I know that situation. I
have read all about it in the *Bibliothèque de Ro-
mans Choisis!*"

And merrily went the dance; and bright eyes
and flushed cheeks were not wanting among the
dancers;

> And they waxed red, and waxed warm,
> And rested, panting, arm in arm;

and the Strauss-waltzes sounded pleasantly in the
ears of Flemming, who, though he never danced,
yet, like Henry of Ofterdingen, in the romance of
Novalis, thought to music. The wheeling waltz

set the wheels of his fancy going. And thus the moments glided on, and the footsteps of Time were not heard amid the sound of music and voices.

But suddenly this scene of gayety was interrupted. The door opened wide; and the short figure of a gray-haired old man presented itself, with a flushed countenance and wild eyes. He was but half dressed, and in his hand held a silver candlestick without a light. A sheet was wound round his head, like a turban; and he tottered forward with a vacant, bewildered look, exclaiming: —

" I am Mahomet, the king of the Jews ! "

At the same moment he fell in a swoon, and was borne out of the room by the servants. Flemming looked at the lady of the festival, and she was deadly pale. For a moment, all was confusion; and the dance and the music stopped. The impression produced on the company was at once ludicrous and awful. They tried in vain to rally. The whole society was like a dead body, from which the spirit has departed. Erelong, the guests had all dispersed, and left the lady of the mansion to her mournful, expiring lamps, and still more mournful reflections.

" Truly," said Flemming to the Baron, as they wended their way homeward, " this seems not like reality; but like one of the sharp contrasts we find in novels. Who shall say, after this, that there is not more romance in real life than we find written in books ? "

" Not more romance," said the Baron, " but a different romance."

A still more tragic scene had been that evening

enacted in Heidelberg. Just as the sun set, two female figures walked along the romantic woodland pathway leading to the Angel's Meadow, a little green opening on the brow of one of the high hills which see themselves in the Neckar and hear the solemn bells of Kloster-Neuburg. The evening shadows were falling broad and long, and the cuckoo began to sing.

" Cuckoo ! cuckoo ! " said the eldest of the two figures, repeating an old German popular rhyme, —

> " Cuckoo ! cuckoo !
> Tell me true,
> Tell me fair and fine,
> How long must I unmarried pine ? "

It was the voice of an evil spirit that spoke in the person of Madeleine ; and the pale and shrinking figure that walked by her side, and listened to those words, was Emma of Ilmenau. A young man joined them, where the path turns into the thick woodlands ; and they disappeared among the shadowy branches. It was the Polish Count.

The forget-me-nots looked up to heaven with their meek blue eyes, from their home in Angel's Meadow. Calmly stood the mountain of All-Saints, in its majestic, holy stillness ; the river flowed so far below that the murmur of its waters was not heard ; there was not a sigh of the evening wind among the leaves, not a sound upon the earth nor in the air ; — and yet that night there fell a star from heaven !

CHAPTER X.

THE PARTING.

It was now that season of the year which an old English writer calls the amiable month of June, and at that hour of the day, when, face to face, the rising moon beholds the setting sun. As yet the stars were few in heaven. But, after the heat of the day, the coolness and the twilight descended like a benediction upon the earth, by all those gentle sounds attended which are the meek companions of the night.

Flemming and the Baron had passed the afternoon at the Castle. They had rambled once more together, and for the last time, over the magnificent ruin. On the morrow they were to part, perhaps for ever. The Baron was going to Berlin, to join his sister; and Flemming, driven forward by the restless spirit within him, longed once more for a change of scene, and was to start for the Tyrol and Switzerland. Alas! he never said to the passing hour, " Stay, for thou art fair ! " but reached forward into the dark future, with unsatisfied longings and aimless desires that were never still.

As the day was closing, they sat down on the terrace of Elizabeth's Garden. The sun had set beyond the blue Alsatian hills ; and on the valley of the Rhine fell the purple mist, like the mantle of the departing prophet from his fiery chariot. Over the castle walls and the trees of the garden rose the large moon, and between the contending daylight and moonlight there were as yet no shad-

ows. But at length the shadows came, — transparent and faint outlines, that deepened into form. In the valley below only the river gleamed, like steel, and here and there the lamps were lighted in the town. Solemnly stood the leafy linden-trees in the garden near them, their trunks in darkness and their summits bronzed with moonlight ; and in his niche in the great round tower, overhung with ivy, like a majestic phantom, stood the gray statue of Louis, with his venerable beard, and shirt of mail, and flowing mantle ; and the mild majestic countenance looked forth into the silent night, as the countenance of a seer who reads the stars. At intervals, the wind of the summer night passed through the ruined castle and the trees, and they sent forth a sound as if Nature were sighing in her dreams ; and for a moment, overhead, the broad leaves gently clashed together, like brazen cymbals, with a tinkling sound ; and then all was still, save the sweet, passionate song of nightingales, that nowhere sing more sweetly than in the gardens of Heidelberg Castle.

The hour, the scene, and the near-approaching separation of the two young friends had filled their hearts with a pleasant, though at the same time not painless excitement. They had been conversing about the magnificent old ruin, and the ages in which it had been built, and the vicissitudes of time and war, that had battered down its walls, and left it " tenantless, save to the crannying wind."

" How sorrowful and sublime is the face of that statue yonder ! " said Flemming. " It reminds

me of the old Danish hero Beowulf; for careful,
sorrowing, he seeth in his son's bower the wine-
hall deserted, the resort of the wind, noiseless;
the knight sleepeth; the warrior lieth in darkness;
there is no noise of the harp, no joy in the dwell-
ings, as there was before."

"Even as you say," replied the Baron; "but it
often astonishes me that, coming from that fresh
green world of yours beyond the sea, you should
feel so much interest in these old things; nay, at
times, seem so to have drunk in their spirit, as
really to live in the times of old. For my part, I
do not see what charm there is in the pale and
wrinkled countenance of the Past, so to entice the
soul of a young man. It seems to me like falling
in love with one's grandmother. Give me the
Present, — warm, glowing, palpitating with life.
She is my mistress; and the Future stands wait-
ing like my wife that is to be, — for whom, to tell
the truth, I care very little just now. Indeed, my
friend, I wish you would take more heed of this
philosophy of mine, and not waste the golden
hours of youth in vain regrets for the past, and in-
definite, dim longings for the future. Youth comes
but once in a lifetime."

"Therefore," said Flemming, "let us so enjoy
it as to be still young when we are old. For my
part, I grow happier as I grow older. When I
compare my sensations and enjoyments now with
what they were ten years ago, the comparison is
vastly in favor of the present. Much of the fever
and fretfulness of life is over. The world and I
look each other more calmly in the face. My mind

is more self-possessed. It has done me good to be somewhat parched by the heat and drenched by the rain of life."

"Now you speak like an old philosopher," answered the Baron, laughing. "But you deceive yourself. I never knew a more restless, feverish spirit than yours. Do not think you have gained the mastery yet. You are only riding at anchor here in an eddy of the stream; you will soon be swept away again in the mighty current and whirl of accident. Do not trust this momentary calm. I know you better than you know yourself. There is something Faust-like in you; you would fain grasp the highest and the deepest, and reel from desire to enjoyment, and in enjoyment languish for desire. When a momentary change of feeling comes over you, you think the change permanent, and thus live in constant self-deception."

"I confess," said Flemming, "there may be some truth in what you say. There are times when my soul is restless, and a voice sounds within me, like the trump of the archangel, and thoughts that were buried, long ago, come out of their graves. At such times my favorite occupations and pursuits no longer charm me. The quiet face of Nature seems to mock me."

"There certainly are seasons," replied the Baron, "when Nature seems not to sympathize with her beloved children. She sits there so eternally calm and self-possessed, so very motherly and serene, and cares so little whether the heart of her child breaks or not, that at times I almost lose my patience. About that, too, she cares so little that,

out of sheer obstinacy, I become good-humored again, and then she smiles."

" I think we must confess, however," continued Flemming, " that all this springs from our own imperfection, not from hers. How beautiful is this green world which we inhabit! See yonder, how the moonlight mingles with the mist! What a glorious night is this! Truly, every man has a Paradise around him, until he sins, and the angel of an accusing conscience drives him from his Eden. And even then there are holy hours, when this angel sleeps, and man comes back, and, with the innocent eyes of a child, looks into his lost Paradise again, — into the broad gates and rural solitudes of Nature. I feel this often. We have much to enjoy in the quiet and retirement of our own thoughts. Boisterous mirth and loud laughter are not my mood. I love that tranquillity of soul, in which we feel the blessing of existence, and which in itself is a prayer and a thanksgiving. I find, however, that, as I grow older, I love the country less, and the town more."

" Yes," interrupted the Baron ; " and presently you will love the town less and the country more. Say at once that you have an undefined longing for both, and prefer town or country, according to the mood you are in. I think a man must be of a very quiet and happy nature who can long endure the country ; and, moreover, very well contented with his own insignificant person, very self-complacent, to be continually occupied with himself and his own thoughts. To say the least, a town life makes one more tolerant and liberal in one's

judgment of others. One is not eternally wrapped up in self-contemplation; which, after all, is only a more holy kind of vanity."

In conversation like this, the hours glided away; till at length, from the Giant's Tower, the castle clock struck twelve, with a sound that seemed to come from the Middle Ages. Like watchmen from their belfries, the city clocks answered it, one by one. Then distant and muffled sounds were heard. Inarticulate words seemed to blot the foggy air, as if written on wet paper. These were the bells of Handschuhsheimer, and of other villages on the broad plain of the Rhine and among the hills of the Odenwald; mysterious sounds, that seemed not of this world.

Beneath them, in the shadow of the hills, lay the valley, — fathomless, black, impenetrable. Above were the cloistered stars, that, nun-like, walk the holy aisles of heaven. The city was asleep in the valley below; all asleep and silent, save the clocks, that had just struck twelve, and the veering, golden weathercocks, that were swimming in the moonlight, like golden fishes in a glass vase. And again the wind of the summer night passed through the old castle and the trees, and the nightingales recorded under the dark, shadowy leaves, and the heart of Flemming was full.

When he had retired to his chamber, a feeling of utter loneliness came over him. The night before one begins a journey is always a dismal night; for, as Byron says,

> In leaving even the most unpleasant people
> And places, one keeps looking at the steeple!

and how much more so when the place and peo-
ple are pleasant! as was the case with those that
Flemming was now leaving. No wonder he was
sad and sleepless. Thoughts came and went, and
bright and gloomy fancies, and dreams and vis-
ions, and sweet faces looked under his closed eye-
lids, and vanished away, and came again, and
again departed. He heard the clock strike from
hour to hour, and said, " Another hour is gone."
At length the birds began to sing, and ever and
anon the cock crew. He arose, and looked forth
into the gray dawn; and before him lay the city
he was so soon to leave, all white and ghastly, like
a city that had arisen from its grave.

" All things must change," said he to the Baron,
as he embraced him, and held him by the hand.
" Friends must be torn asunder, and swept along
in the current of events, to see each other seldom,
and perchance no more. For ever and ever in the
eddies of time and accident we whirl away. Be-
sides which, some of us have a perpetual motion
in our wooden heads, as Wodenblock had in his
wooden leg; and like him we travel on, without
rest or sleep, and have hardly time to take a
friend by the hand in passing; and at length are
seen hurrying through some distant land, worn to
a skeleton, and all unknown."

BOOK THE THIRD

Take away the lights, too;
The moon lends me too much to find my fears,
And those devotions I am now to pay
Are written in my heart, not in thy book;
And I shall read them there without a taper.

<div align="right">BEAUMONT AND FLETCHER.</div>

CHAPTER I.

SUMMER-TIME.

THEY were right — those old German Min-
nesingers — to sing the pleasant summer-time!
What a time it is! How June stands illuminated
in the calendar! The windows are all wide open;
only the Venetian blinds-closed. Here and there
a long streak of sunshine streams in through a
crevice. We hear the low sound of the wind
among the trees; and, as it swells and freshens,
the distant doors clap to, with a sudden sound.
The trees are heavy with leaves, and the gardens
full of blossoms, red and white. The whole at-
mosphere is laden with perfume and sunshine.
The birds sing. The cock struts about, and crows
loftily. Insects chirp in the grass. Yellow but-
tercups stud the green carpet like golden buttons,
and the red blossoms of the clover like rubies.
The elm-trees reach their long, pendulous branches
almost to the ground. White clouds sail aloft,

and vapors fret the blue sky with silver threads. The white village gleams afar against the dark hills. Through the meadow winds the river, — careless, indolent. It seems to love the country, and is in no haste to reach the sea. The bee only is at work, — the hot and angry bee. All things else are at play ; he never plays, and is vexed that any one should.

People drive out from town to breathe, and to be happy. Most of them have flowers in their hands ; bunches of apple-blossoms, and still oftener lilacs. Ye denizens of the crowded city, how pleasant to you is the change from the sultry streets to the open field, fragrant with clover-blossoms ! how pleasant the fresh, breezy country air, dashed with brine from the meadows ! how pleasant, above all, the flowers, — the manifold, beautiful flowers !

It is no longer day. Through the trees rises the red moon, and the stars are scarcely seen. In the vast shadow of night, the coolness and the dews descend. I sit at the open window to enjoy them ; and hear only the voice of the summer wind. Like black hulks, the shadows of the great trees ride at anchor on the billowy sea of grass. I cannot see the red and blue flowers, but I know that they are there. Far away in the meadow gleams the silver Charles. The tramp of horses' hoofs sounds from the wooden bridge. Then all is still, save the continuous wind of the summer night. Sometimes I know not if it be the wind, or the sound of the neighboring sea. The village clock strikes ; and I feel that I am not alone.

How different is it in the city! It is late, and the crowd is gone. You step out upon the balcony, and lie in the very bosom of the cool, dewy Night, as if you folded her garments about you. Beneath lies the public walk with trees, like a fathomless, black gulf, into whose silent darkness the spirit plunges and floats away, with some beloved spirit clasped in its embrace. The lamps are still burning up and down the long street. People go by, with grotesque shadows, now foreshortened, and now lengthening away into the darkness and vanishing, while a new one springs up behind the walker, and seems to pass him, revolving like the sail of a windmill. The iron gates of the park shut with a jangling clang. There are footsteps and loud voices; — a tumult, — a drunken brawl, — an alarm of fire; — then silence again. And now at length the city is asleep, and we can see the night. The belated moon looks over the roofs, and finds no one to welcome her. The moonlight is broken. It lies here and there in the squares, and the openings of streets, — angular, like blocks of white marble.

Under such a green, triumphal arch, O Reader, with the odor of flowers about thee, and the song of birds, shalt thou pass onward into the enchanted land, as through the Ivory Gate of dreams! And as a prelude and majestic march, one sweet human voice, coming from the bosom of the Alps, sings this sublime ode, which the Alpine echoes repeat afar.

Come, golden Evening! in the west
 Enthrone the storm-dispelling sun,
And let the triple rainbow rest
 O'er all the mountain-tops. 'T is done; —
The tempest ceases; bold and bright,
 The rainbow shoots from hill to hill;
Down sinks the sun; on presses night; —
 Mont Blanc is lovely still!

There take thy stand, my spirit; — spread
 The world of shadows at thy feet;
And mark how calmly, overhead,
 The stars, like saints in glory, meet.
While hid in solitude sublime,
 Methinks I muse on Nature's tomb,
And hear the passing foot of Time
 Step through the silent gloom.

All in a moment, crash on crash,
 From precipice to precipice,
An avalanche's ruins dash
 Down to the nethermost abyss,
Invisible; the ear alone
 Pursues the uproar till it dies;
Echo to echo, groan for groan,
 From deep to deep, replies.

Silence again the darkness seals,
 Darkness that may be felt; — but soon
The silver-clouded east reveals
 The midnight spectre of the moon;
In half-eclipse she lifts her horn,
 Yet o'er the host of heaven supreme
Brings the faint semblance of a morn,
 With her awakening beam.

Ah! at her touch, these Alpine heights
 Unreal mockeries appear;
With blacker shadows, ghastlier lights,
 Emerging as she climbs the sphere;
A crowd of apparitions pale!
 I hold my breath in chill suspense,
They seem so exquisitely frail,
 Lest they should vanish hence.

I breathe again, I freely breathe ;
 Thee, Leman's Lake, once more I trace,
Like Dian's crescent far beneath,
 As beautiful as Dian's face :
Pride of the land that gave me birth !
 All that thy waves reflect I love,
Where heaven itself, brought down to earth,
 Looks fairer than above.

Safe on thy banks again I stray ;
 The trance of poesy is o'er,
And I am here at dawn of day,
 Gazing on mountains as before,
Where all the strange mutations wrought
 Were magic feats of my own mind ;
For, in that fairy land of thought,
 Whate'er I seek, I find.*

CHAPTER II.

FOOT-TRAVELLING.

Tell me, my soul, why art thou restless ? Why
dost thou look forward to the future with such
strong desire ? The present is thine, — and the
past ; — and the future shall be ! Oh that thou
didst look forward to the great hereafter with
half the longing wherewith thou longest for an
earthly future, — which a few days, at most, will
bring thee ! to the meeting of the dead, as to the
meeting of the absent ! Thou glorious spirit-
land ! Oh that I could behold thee as thou art,
— the region of life and light and love, and the
dwelling-place of those beloved ones whose being
has flowed onward, like a silver-clear stream into

* James Montgomery.

the solemn-sounding main, into the ocean of Eternity !

Such were the thoughts that passed through the soul of Flemming, as he lay in utter solitude and silence on the rounded summit of one of the mountains of the Furca Pass, and gazed, with tears in his eyes, and ardent longing in his heart, into the blue, swimming heaven overhead, and at the glaciers and snowy mountain-peaks around him. Highest and whitest of all stood the peak of the Jungfrau, which seemed near him, though it rose afar off from the bosom of the Lauterbrunner Thal. There it stood, holy and high and pure, the bride of heaven, veiled and clothed in white, and lifting the thoughts of the beholder heavenward. Oh, he little thought then, as he gazed at it with longing and delight, how soon a form was to arise in his own soul, as holy and high and pure as this, and like this point heavenward !

Thus lay the traveller on the mountain summit, reposing his weary limbs on the short, brown grass, which more resembled moss than grass. He had sent his guide forward, that he might be alone. His soul within him was wild with a fierce and painful delight. The mountain air excited him; the mountain solitudes enticed yet maddened him. Every peak, every sharp, jagged iceberg, seemed to pierce him. The silence was awful and sublime. It was like that in the soul of a dying man, when he hears no more the sounds of earth. He seemed to be laying aside his earthly garments. The heavens were near unto him; but between him and heaven every evil deed he had done arose gigantic,

like those mountain-peaks, and breathed an icy
breath upon him. Oh, let not the soul that suffers
dare to look Nature in the face, where she sits ma-
jestically aloft in the solitude of the mountains!
for her face is hard and stern, and turns not in
compassion upon her weak and erring child. It
is the countenance of an accusing archangel, who
summons us to judgment. In the valley she
wears the countenance of a Virgin Mother, look-
ing at us with tearful eyes, and a face of pity and
love!

But yesterday Flemming had come up the val-
ley of the Saint Gothard Pass, through Amsteg,
where the Kerstelenbach comes dashing down the
Maderaner Thal, from its snowy cradle overhead.
The road is steep, and runs on zigzag terraces.
The sides of the mountains are barren cliffs ; and
from their cloud-capt summits, unheard amid the
roar of the great torrent below, come streams of
snow-white foam, leaping from rock to rock, like
the mountain chamois. As you advance, the scene
grows wilder and more desolate. There is not a
tree in sight, — not a human habitation. Clouds,
black as midnight, lower upon you from the ra-
vines above ; and the mountain torrent beneath is
but a sheet of foam, and sends up an incessant roar.
A sudden turn in the road brings you in sight of
a lofty bridge, stepping from cliff to cliff with a
single stride. A mighty cataract howls beneath it,
like an evil spirit, and fills the air with mist ; and
the mountain wind claps its hands and shrieks
through the narrow pass, Ha! ha! This is the
Devil's Bridge. It leads the traveller across the

fearful chasm, and through a mountain gallery into the broad, green, silent meadow of Andermath.

Even the sunny morning which followed this gloomy day had not chased the desolate impression from the soul of Flemming. His excitement increased as he lost himself more and more among the mountains; and now, as he lay alone on the summit of the sunny hill, with only glaciers and snowy peaks about him, his soul, as I have said, was wild with a fierce and painful delight.

A human voice broke his reverie. He looked, and beheld, at a short distance from him, the athletic form of a mountain herdsman, who was approaching the spot where he lay. He was a young man, clothed in a rustic garb, and holding a long staff in his hand. When Flemming rose, he stood still, and gazed at him, as if he loved the face of man, even of a stranger, and longed to hear a human voice, though it might speak in an unknown tongue. He answered Flemming's salutation in a rude mountain dialect, and in reply to his questions said: —

"I, with two others, have charge of two hundred head of cattle on these mountains. Through the two summer months, we remain here night and day, for which we receive each a napoleon."

Flemming gave him half his summer wages. He was glad to do a good deed in secret, and yet so near heaven. The man received it as his due, like a toll-keeper, and soon after departed, leaving the traveller alone. And the traveller went his

way down the mountain, as one distraught. He stopped only to pluck one bright blue flower, which bloomed alone in the vast desert, and looked up at him, as if to say, " Oh, take me with you! leave me not here companionless ! "

Erelong he reached the magnificent glacier of the Rhone — a frozen cataract, more than two thousand feet in height, and many miles broad at its base. It fills the whole valley between two mountains, running back to their summits. At the base it is arched, like a dome; and above, jagged and rough, and resembles a mass of gigantic crystals, of a pale emerald tint, mingled with white. A snowy crust covers its surface, but at every rent and crevice the pale green ice shines clear in the sun. Its shape is that of a glove, lying with the palm downwards, and the fingers crooked and close together. It is a gauntlet of ice, which, centuries ago, Winter, the king of these mountains, threw down in defiance to the Sun; and year by year the Sun strives in vain to lift it from the ground on the point of his glittering spear. A feeling of wonder and delight came over the soul of Flemming when he beheld it, and he shouted and cried aloud : —

" How wonderful ! how glorious ! "

After lingering a few hours in the cold, desolate valley, he climbed in the afternoon the steep Mayen-Wand, on the Grimsel; passed the Lake of the Dead, with its ink-black waters; and through the melting snow, and over slippery stepping-stones in the beds of numberless shallow brooks, descended to the Grimsel Hospital, where

he passed the night, and thought it the most lone and desolate spot that man ever slept in.

On the morrow he rose with the day; and the rising sun found him already standing on the rustic bridge which hangs over the verge of the Falls of the Aar at Handeck, where the river pitches down a precipice into a narrow and fearful abyss shut in by perpendicular cliffs. At right angles with it comes the beautiful Aerlenbach; and half-way down, the double cascade mingles into one. Thus he pursued his way down the Hasli Thal into the Bernese Oberland, — restless, impatient, he knew not why, — stopping seldom, and never long, — and then rushing forward again, like the rushing river whose steps he followed, and in whose ice-cold waters ever and anon he bathed his wrists, to cool the fever in his blood; for the noonday sun was hot.

His heart dilated in the dilating valley, that grew broader and greener at every step. The sight of human faces and human dwellings soothed him; and through the fields of summer grain, in the broad meadows of Imgrund, he walked with a heart that ached no more, but trembled only, as our eyelids when we have done weeping. As he climbed the opposite hill, which hems in this romantic valley, and, like a heavy yoke, chafes the neck of the Aar, he believed the ancient tradition, which says that once the valley was a lake. From the summit of the hill he looked southward upon a beautiful landscape of gardens, and fields of grain, and woodlands, and meadows, and the ancient castle of Resti, looking down upon Meyringen.

And now all around him were the singing of birds, and grateful shadows of the leafy trees, and sheeted waterfalls dropping from the woodland cliffs, seen only, but unheard, — the fluted columns breaking into mist, and fretted with frequent spires and ornaments of foam, and not unlike the towers of a Gothic church inverted. There, in one white sheet of foam, the Reichenbach pours down into its deep beaker, into which the sun never shines. Face to face it beholds the Alpbach falling from the opposite hill, "like a downward smoke." When Flemming saw the innumerable runnels, sliding down the mountain-side, and leaping, all life and gladness, he would fain have clasped them in his arms and been their playmate, and revelled with them in their freedom and delight. Yet he was weary with the day's journey, and entered the village of Meyringen, embowered in cherry-trees, which were then laden with fruit, more like a way-worn traveller than an enthusiastic poet. As he went up the tavern-steps, he said in his heart, with the Italian Aretino: " He who has not been at a tavern knows not what a paradise it is. O holy tavern! O miraculous tavern! — holy, because no carking cares are there, nor weariness, nor pain ; and miraculous, because of the spits, which of themselves turn round and round! Of a truth, all courtesy and good manners come from taverns, so full of bows, and *Signor, sì!* and *Signor, no!* "

But even in the tavern he could not rest long. The same evening at sunset he was floating on the lake of Brienz, in an open boat, close under the

cascade of the Giessbach, hearing the peasants sing the Ranz des Vaches. He slept that night at the other extremity of the lake, in a large house, which, like Saint Peter's at Joppa, stood by the water's side. The next day he wasted in writing letters, musing in this green nest, and paddling about the lake again; and in the evening went across the beautiful meadows to Interlachen, where many things happened to him, and detained him long.

CHAPTER III.

INTERLACHEN.

Interlachen ! How peacefully, by the margin of the swift-rushing Aar, thou liest on the broad lap of those romantic meadows, all overshadowed by the wide arms of giant trees ! Only the quaint towers of thine ancient cloister rise above their summits ; the quaint towers themselves but a child's playthings under the great church-towers of the mountains. Close beside thee are lakes, which the flowing band of the river ties together. Before thee opens the magnificent valley of Lauterbrunnen, where the cloud-hooded Monk and the pale Virgin stand like Saint Francis and his Bride of Snow ; and around thee are fields, and orchards, and hamlets green, from which the church-bells answer each other at evening. The evening sun was setting when I first beheld thee. The sun of life will set ere I forget thee ! Surely it was a scene like this that inspired the soul of the Swiss poet, in his Song of the Bell !

Bell ! thou soundest merrily,
When the bridal party
 .To the church doth hie !
Bell ! thou soundest solemnly,
When, on Sabbath morning,
 Fields deserted lie !

Bell ! thou soundest merrily;
Tellest thou at evening,
 Bedtime draweth nigh !
Bell ! thou soundest mournfully,
Tellest thou the bitter
 Parting hath gone by !

Say ! how canst thou mourn ?
How canst thou rejoice ?
 Art but metal dull !
And yet all our sorrowings,
And all our rejoicings,
 Thou dost feel them all !

God hath wonders many,
Which we cannot fathom,
 Placed within thy form !
When the heart is sinking,
Thou alone canst raise it,
 Trembling in the storm !

Paul Flemming alighted at one of the principal
hotels. The landlord came out to meet him. He
had great eyes and a green coat, and reminded
Flemming of the innkeeper mentioned in the
Golden Ass, who had been changed by magic into
a frog, and croaked to his customers from the lees
of a wine-cask. His house, he said, was full, and
so was every house in Interlachen ; but, if the gen-
tleman would walk in, he would find a chamber
for him in the neighborhood.

On the sofa sat a gentleman, reading ; a stout
gentleman of perhaps forty-five, round, ruddy, and

with a head which, being a little bald on the top, looked not unlike a crow's nest with one egg in it. A good-humored face turned from the book as Flemming entered, and a good-humored voice exclaimed : —

" Ha ! Mr. Flemming ! Is it you, or your apparition ? I told you we should meet again ! though you were for taking an eternal farewell of your fellow-traveller."

Saying these words the stout gentleman rose and shook Flemming heartily by the hand. And Flemming returned the shake as heartily, recognizing in this ruddy personage a former travelling-companion, Mr. Berkley, whom he had left, a week or two previous, toiling up the Righi. Mr. Berkley was an Englishman of fortune ; a good-humored, humane old bachelor, remarkable alike for his common sense and his eccentricity. That is to say, the basis of his character was good, sound common sense, trodden down and smoothed by education ; but this level groundwork his strange and whimsical fancy used as a dancing-floor whereon to exhibit her eccentric tricks. His ruling passion was cold-bathing, and he usually ate his breakfast sitting in a tub of cold water, and reading a newspaper. He kissed every child he met ; and to every old man said, in passing, " God bless you ! " with such an expression of voice and countenance that no one could doubt his sincerity. He reminded one of Roger Bontemps, or the Little Man in Gray, though with a difference.

" The last time I had the pleasure of seeing you, Mr. Berkley," said Flemming, " was at Goldau,

just as you were going up the Righi. I hope you were gratified with a fine sunrise on the mountain-top."

"No, I was not!" replied Mr. Berkley. "It is all a humbug! a confounded humbug! They made such a noise about their sunrise, that I determined I would not see it. So I lay snug in bed, and only peeped through the window-curtain. That was enough. Just above the house, on the top of the hill, stood some fifty half-dressed, romantic individuals, shivering in the wet grass; and, a short distance from them, a miserable wretch, blowing a long, wooden horn. That's your sunrise on the Righi, is it? said I; and went to sleep again. The best thing I saw at the Culm was the advertisement on the bed-room doors, saying that, if the women would wear the quilts and blankets for shawls when they went out to see the sunrise, they must pay for the washing. Take my word for it, the Righi is a great humbug!"

"Where have you been since?"

"At Zürich and Schaffhausen. If you go to Zürich, beware how you stop at the Raven. They will cheat you. They cheated me, but I had my revenge; for, when we reached Schaffhausen, I wrote in the Traveller's Book, —

> "Beware of the Raven of Zurich!
> 'T is a bird of omen ill;
> With a noisy and an unclean nest,
> And a very, very long bill.

If you go to the Golden Falken, you will find it there. I am the author of those lines!"

"Bitter as Juvenal!" exclaimed Flemming.

"Not in the least bitter," said Mr. Berkley. "It is all true. Go to the Raven and see. But this Interlachen! this Interlachen! It is the loveliest spot on the face of the earth," he continued, stretching out both arms, as if to embrace the object of his affection. "There, — only look out there!"

Here he pointed to the window. Flemming looked, and beheld a scene of transcendent beauty. The plain was covered already by the brown shade of the summer twilight. From the cottage roofs in Unterseen rose here and there a thin column of smoke over the tops of the trees, and mingled with the evening shadows. The valley of Lauterbrunnen was filled with a blue haze. Far above, in the clear, cloudless heaven, the white forehead of the Jungfrau blushed at the last kiss of the departing sun. It was a glorious transfiguration of Nature! And when the village bells began to ring, and a single voice at a great distance was heard *yodling* forth a ballad, it rather broke than increased the enchantment of a scene, where silence was more musical than sound.

For a long time they gazed at the gloaming landscape, and spake not. At length people came in, and laid aside their shawls and hats, and exchanged a word or two with Berkley. To Flemming they were all unknown. The conversation turned upon the various excursions of the day. Some had been at the Staubbach, others at the Grindelwald, others at the lake of Thun; and nobody before had ever experienced half the rapture which they had experienced that day. And thus they sat in the twi-

light, as people love to do, at the close of a summer
day. As yet the lamps had not been lighted, and
one could not distinguish faces; but voices only,
and forms like shadows.

Presently a female figure, clothed in black, en-
tered the room and sat down by the window. She
rather listened to the conversation than joined in
it; but the few words she said were spoken in a
voice so musical and full of soul, that it moved the
soul of Flemming, like a whisper from heaven.

Oh, how wonderful is the human voice ! It is in-
deed the organ of the soul ! The intellect of man
sits enthroned visibly upon his forehead and in his
eye, and the heart of man is written upon his
countenance. But the soul reveals itself in the
voice only; as God revealed himself to the prophet
of old in the still, small voice, and in the voice
from the burning bush. The soul of man is audi-
ble, not visible. A sound alone betrays the flow-
ing of the eternal fountain, invisible to man !

Flemming would fain have sat and listened for
hours to the sound of that unknown voice. He
felt sure, in his secret heart, that the being from
whom it came was beautiful. His imagination
filled up the faint outline which the eye beheld in
the fading twilight, and the figure stood already in
his mind like Raphael's beautiful Madonna, in the
Dresden gallery. He was never more mistaken in
his life. The voice belonged to a beautiful being,
it is true, but her beauty was different from that
of any Madonna which Raphael ever painted; as
he would have seen, had he waited till the lamps
were lighted. But in the midst of his reverie and

saint-painting, the landlord came in, and told him he had found a room, which he begged him to go and look at.

Flemming took his leave and departed. Berkley went with him, to see, he said, what kind of a nest his young friend was to sleep in.

"The room is not what I could wish," said the landlord, as he led them across the street. "It is in the old cloister. But to-morrow or next day, you can, no doubt, have a room at the house."

The name of the cloister struck Flemming's imagination pleasantly. He was owl enough to like ruins and old chambers, where nuns or friars had slept. And he said to Berkley : —

"So, you perceive, my nest is to be in a cloister. It already makes me think of a bird's nest I once saw on an old tower of Heidelberg Castle, built in the jaws of a lion, which formerly served as a spout. But pray tell me, who was that young lady with the soft voice ? "

"What young lady with the soft voice ? "

"The young lady in black who sat by the window."

"Oh, she is the daughter of an English officer, who died not long ago at Naples. She is passing the summer here with her mother."

"What is her name ? "

"Ashburton."

"Is she beautiful ? "

"Not beautiful, but very intellectual. A woman of genius, I should say."

And now they had reached the walls of the cloister, and passed under an arched gateway, and

close beneath the quaint towers, which Flemming had already seen, rising with their cone-shaped roofs above the trees, like tall tapers, with extinguishers upon them.

"It is not so bad as it looks," said the landlord, knocking at a small door, in the main building. "The bailiff lives in one part of it."

A servant girl, with a candle in her hand, opened the door, and conducted Flemming and Berkley to the chamber which had been engaged. It was a large room on the lower floor, wainscoted with pine, and unpainted. Three lofty and narrow windows, with leaden lattices and small panes, looked southward towards the valley of Lauterbrunnen and the mountains. In one corner was a large square bed, with a tester and checked curtains. In another, a huge stove of painted tiles, reaching almost to the ceiling. An old sofa, a few high-backed, antique chairs, and a table, completed the furniture of the room.

Thus Flemming took possession of his monkish cell and dormitory. He ordered tea, and began to feel at home. Berkley passed the evening with him. On going away, he said : —

"Good-night! I leave you to the care of the Virgin and all the Saints. If the ghost of any old monk comes back after his prayer-book, my compliments to him. If I were a younger man, you certainly should see a ghost. Good-night!"

When he had departed, Flemming opened the lattice of one of the windows. The moon had risen, and silvered the dark outline of the nearest hills; while, afar off, the snowy summits of the

Jungfrau and the Silver-Horn shone like a white cloud in the sky. Close beneath the windows was a flower-garden; and the breath of the summer night came to him with dewy fragrance. There was a grateful seclusion about the place. He blessed the happy accident which gave him such a lodging, and fell asleep that night thinking of the nuns who once had slept in the same quiet cells; but neither wimpled nun nor cowled monk appeared to him in his dreams; — not even the face of Mary Ashburton, nor did he hear her voice.

CHAPTER IV.

THE EVENING AND THE MORNING STAR.

Old Froissart tells us, in his Chronicles, that, when King Edward beheld the Countess of Salisbury at her castle-gate, he thought he had never seen before so noble nor so fair a lady; he was stricken thereupon to the heart with a sparkle of fine love, that endured long after; he thought no lady in the world so worthy to be beloved as she. And so likewise thought Paul Flemming, when he beheld the English lady in the fair light of a summer morning. I will not disguise the truth. She is my heroine, and I mean to describe her with great truth and beauty, so that all shall be in love with her, and I most of all.

Mary Ashburton was in her twentieth summer. Like the fair maiden Amoret, she was sitting in the lap of womanhood. They did her wrong who said she was not beautiful; and yet

She was not fair,
Nor beautiful ; — those words express her not.
But, oh, her looks had something excellent,
That wants a name!

Her face had a wonderful fascination in it. It
was such a calm, quiet face, with the light of the
rising soul shining so peacefully through it. At
times it wore an expression of seriousness, — of
sorrow even ; and then seemed to make the very
air bright with what the Italian poets so beauti-
fully call the *lampeggiar dell' angelico riso*, — the
lightning of the angelic smile.

And, oh, those eyes, — those deep unutterable
eyes, with " down-falling eyelids full of dreams and
slumber," and within them a cold, living light, as
in mountain lakes at evening, or in the river of
Paradise, forever gliding,

With a brown, brown current,
Under the shade perpetual, that never
Ray of the sun lets in, nor of the moon.

I dislike an eye that twinkles like a star. Those
only are beautiful which, like the planets, have
a steady light, — are luminous, but not sparkling.
Such eyes the Greek poets give to the Immor-
tals.

The lady's figure was striking. Every step,
every attitude, was graceful, and yet lofty, as if
inspired by the soul within. Angels in the old
poetic philosophy have such forms ; it was the soul
itself imprinted on the air. And what a soul was
hers! A temple dedicated to Heaven, and, like
the Pantheon at Rome, lighted only from above.
And earthly passions in the form of gods were no

longer there, but the sweet and thoughtful faces
of Christ, and the Virgin Mary, and the Saints.
Thus there was not one discordant thing in her;
but a perfect harmony of figure, and face, and
soul, — in a word, of the whole being. And he
who had a soul to comprehend hers must of neces-
sity love her, and, having once loved her, could
love no other woman forevermore.

No wonder, then, that Flemming felt his heart
drawn towards her, as, in her morning walk, she
passed him, sitting alone under the great walnut-
trees near the cloister, and thinking of heaven, not
of her. She, too, was alone. Her cheek was no
longer pale; but glowing and bright, with the in-
spiration of the summer air. Flemming gazed
after her, till she disappeared, even as a vision of
his dreams, he knew not whither. He was not yet
in love, but very near it, for he thanked God
that he had made such beautiful beings to walk
the earth.

Last night he had heard a voice to which his
soul responded; and he might have gone on his
way and taken no further heed. But he would
have heard that voice afterwards, whenever at
evening he thought of this evening at Interlachen.
To-day he had seen more clearly the vision, and
his restless soul grew calm. The place seemed
pleasant to him, and he could not go. He did
not ask himself whence came this calm. He felt
it, and was happy in the feeling; and blessed the
landscape and the summer morning, as if they pos-
sessed the wonder-working power.

"A pleasant morning-dream to you," said a

friendly voice; and at the same moment some one laid his hand upon Flemming's shoulder. It was Berkley. He had approached unseen and unheard.

"I see by the smile on your countenance," he continued, "that it is no day-incubus."

"You are right," replied Flemming. "It was a pleasant dream, which you have put to flight."

"And I am glad to see that you have also put to flight the gloomy thoughts which used to haunt you. I like to see people cheerful and happy. Why give way to sadness in this beautiful world?"

"Ah! this beautiful world!" said Flemming, with a smile. "Indeed, I know not what to think of it. Sometimes it is all gladness and sunshine, and heaven itself lies not far off. And then it changes suddenly, and is dark and sorrowful, and clouds shut out the sky. In the lives of the saddest of us, there are bright days like this, when we feel as if we could take the great world in our arms. Then come the gloomy hours, when the fire will neither burn on our hearths nor in our hearts, and all without and within is dismal, cold, and dark. Believe me, every heart has its secret sorrows which the world knows not, and oftentimes we call a man cold, when he is only sad."

"And who says we do not?" interrupted Berkley. "Come, come! Let us go to breakfast. The morning air has given me a rude appetite. I long to say grace over a fresh egg, and eat salt with my worst enemies; namely, the Cockneys at the hotel. After breakfast you must give yourself up wholly to me. I shall take you to the Grindelwald!"

"To-day, then, you do not breakfast like Di-
ogenes, but consent to leave your tub."

"Yes, for the pleasure of your company. I shall
also blow out the light in my lantern, having found
you."

"Thank you."

The breakfast passed without any unusual occur-
rence. Flemming watched the entrance of every
guest; but she came not, — the guest he most de-
sired to see.

"And now for the Grindelwald!" said Berkley.

"Why such haste? We have the whole day
before us. There is time enough."

"Not a moment to lose, I assure you. The car-
riage is at the door."

They drove up the valley of Lauterbrunnen, and
turned eastward among the mountains of Grindel-
wald. There they passed the day; half-frozen by
the icy breath of the Great Glacier, upon whose
surface stand pyramids and blocks of ice, like the
tombstones of a cemetery. It was a weary day to
Flemming. He wished himself at Interlachen;
and was glad, when, towards evening, he saw once
more the cone-roofed towers of the cloister rising
above the walnut-trees.

That evening is written in red letters in his his-
tory. It gave him another revelation of the beauty
and excellence of woman's character and intellect;
not wholly new to him, yet now renewed and forti-
fied. It was from the lips of Mary Ashburton that
the revelation came. Her form arose, like a trem-
ulous evening-star, in the firmament of his soul.
He conversed with her, and with her alone; and

knew not when to go. All others were to him as if they were not there. He saw their forms, but saw them as the forms of inanimate things. At length her mother came, and Flemming beheld in her but another Mary Ashburton, with beauty more mature ; — the same forehead and eyes, the same majestic figure ; and, as yet, no trace of age. He gazed upon her with a feeling of delight, not unmingled with holy awe. She was to him the rich and glowing Evening, from whose bosom the tremulous star was born.

Berkley took no active part in the conversation, but did what was much more to the purpose, — that is to say, arranged a drive for the next day with the Ashburtons, and of course invited Flemming, who went home that night with a halo round his head, and wondering much at a dandy, who stood at the door of the hotel, and said to his companion, as Flemming passed : —

"What do you call this place ? I have been here two hours already, and find it devilish dull ! "

CHAPTER V.

A RAINY DAY.

When Flemming awoke the next morning, he saw the sky dark and lowering. From the mountain-tops hung a curtain of mist, whose heavy folds waved to and fro in the valley below. Over all the landscape the soft summer rain was falling. No admiring eyes would look up that day at the Staubbach.

A rainy day in Switzerland puts a sudden stop to many diversions. The coachman may drive to the inn, and then back to the stable; but no farther. The sun-burnt guide may sit at the alehouse door, and welcome, and the boatman whistle and curse the clouds, at his own sweet will; — but no foot stirs abroad for all that; no traveller moves, if he has time to stay. The rainy day gives him time for reflection. He has leisure now to take cognizance of his impressions, and make up his account with the mountains. He remembers, too, that he has friends at home, and writes up the journal, neglected for a week or more, and letters neglected longer; or finishes the rough pencil-sketch begun yesterday in the open air. On the whole, he is not sorry it rains, — though disappointed.

Flemming was both sorry and disappointed; but he did not on that account fail to go over to the Ashburtons at the appointed hour. He found them sitting in the parlor. The mother was reading, and the daughter retouching a sketch of the Lake of Thun. After the usual salutations, Flemming seated himself near the daughter, and said : —

"We shall have no Staubbach to-day, I presume; only this Giessbach from the clouds."

"Nothing more, I suppose. So we must be content to stay in-doors, and listen to the sound of the eaves-dropping rain. It gives me time to finish some of these rough sketches."

"It is a pleasant pastime," said Flemming; "and I perceive you are very skilful. I am delighted to see that you can draw a straight line.

I never before saw a lady's sketch-book in which all the towers did not resemble the Leaning Tower of Pisa. I always tremble for the little men under them."

" How absurd ! " exclaimed Mary Ashburton, with a smile that passed through the misty air of Flemming's thoughts like a sunbeam. " For one, I succeed much better in straight lines than in any others. Here I have been trying a half-hour to make this water-wheel round, and round it never will be."

" Then let it remain as it is. It looks uncommonly picturesque, and may pass for a new invention."

The lady continued to sketch, and Flemming to gaze at her beautiful face; often repeating to himself those lines in Marlow's Faust : —

> Oh, thou art fairer than the evening air,
> Clad in the beauty of a thousand stars !

He certainly would have betrayed himself to the maternal eye of Mrs. Ashburton, had she not been wholly absorbed in the folliés of a fashionable novel. Erelong, the fair sketcher had paused for a moment; and Flemming had taken her sketch-book in his hands and was looking it through from the beginning with ever-increasing delight, half of which he dared not express, though he favored her with some comments and bursts of admiration.

" This is truly a very beautiful sketch of Murten and the battle-field ! How quietly the landscape sleeps there by the lake, after the battle ! Did you ever read the ballad of Veit Weber, the shoe-

maker, on this subject? He says, the routed Bur-
gundians jumped into the lake, and the Swiss
Leaguers shot them down like wild ducks among
the reeds. He fought in the battle, and wrote the
ballad afterwards ; —

"He had himself laid hand on sword,
He who this rhyme did write;
Till evening mowed he with the sword,
And sang the song at night."

" You must give me the whole ballad," said
Miss Ashburton; " it will serve to illustrate the
sketch."

" And the sketch to illustrate the ballad. And
now we suddenly slide down the Alps into Italy,
and are even in Rome, if I mistake not. This is
surely a head of Homer?"

" Yes," replied the lady, with a little enthusiasm.
" Do you not remember the marble bust at Rome?
When I first beheld that bust, it absolutely in-
spired me with awe. It is not the face of a man,
but of a god!'"

" And you have done it no injustice in your
copy," said Flemming, catching a new enthusiasm
from hers. " With what a classic grace the fillet,
passing round the majestic forehead, confines his
flowing locks, which mingle with his beard!
The countenance, too, is calm, majestic, godlike!
Even the fixed and sightless eyeballs do not mar
the image of the seer! Such were the sightless
eyes of the blind old man of Chios. They seem
to look with mournful solemnity into the myste-
rious future, and the marble lips to repeat that
prophetic passage in the Hymn to Apollo: 'Let

me also hope to be remembered in ages to come.
And when any one, born of the tribes of men,
comes hither, a weary traveller, and inquires, who
is the sweetest of the singing-men that resort to
your feasts, and whom you most delight to hear,
do you make answer for me : It is the Blind Man
who dwells in Chios; his songs excel all that can
ever be sung!' But do you really believe that
this is a portrait of Homer?"

"Certainly not! It is only an artist's dream.
It was thus that Homer appeared to him in his
visions of the antique world. Every one, you
know, forms an image in his fancy of persons and
things he has never seen, and the artist repro-
duces them in marble or on canvas."

"And what is the image in your fancy? Is it
like this?"

"No, not entirely. I have drawn my impres-
sions from another source. Whenever I think of
Homer, which is not often, he walks before me,
solemn and serene, as in the vision of the great
Italian ; in countenance neither sorrowful nor glad,
followed by other bards, and holding in his right
hand a sword!"

"That is a finer conception than this," said
Flemming. "And I perceive from your words, as
well as from this book, that you have a true feel-
ing for Art, and understand what it is. You have
had bright glimpses into the enchanted land."

"I trust," replied the lady, modestly, "that I
am not wholly without this feeling. Certainly I
have as strong and passionate a love of Art as of
Nature."

" But does it not often offend you to hear people speaking of Art and Nature as opposite and discordant things ? Surely nothing can be more false. Nature is a revelation of God ; Art a revelation of man. Indeed, Art signifies no more than this. Art is Power. That is the original meaning of the word. It is the creative power by which the soul of man makes itself known, through some external manifestation or outward sign. As we can always hear the voice of God, walking in the garden, in the cool of the day, or under the starlight, where, to quote one of this poet's verses, ' high prospects and the brows of all steep hills and pinnacles thrust up themselves for shows,' — so under the twilight and the starlight of past ages do we hear the voice of man, walking amid the works of his hands, and city walls and towers, and the spires of churches, thrust up themselves for shows."

The lady smiled at his warmth ; and he continued : —

" This, however, is but a similitude ; and Art and Nature are more nearly allied than by similitudes only. Art is the revelation of man ; and not merely that, but likewise the revelation of Nature, speaking through man. Art preëxists in Nature, and Nature is reproduced in Art. As vapors from the ocean, floating landward and dissolved in rain, are carried back in rivers to the ocean, so thoughts and the semblances of things that fall upon the soul of man in showers flow out again in living streams of Art, and lose themselves in the great ocean, which is Nature. Art and Nature are not, then, discordant, but ever harmoniously working in each other."

Enthusiasm begets enthusiasm. Flemming spake with such evident interest in the subject that Miss Ashburton did not fail to manifest some interest in what he said ; and encouraged by this, he proceeded : —

" Thus in this wondrous world wherein we live, which is the World of Nature, man has made unto himself another world hardly less wondrous, which is the World of Art. And it lies infolded and compassed about by the other,

> " And the clear region where 't was born
> Round in itself encloses.

Taking this view of Art, I think we understand more easily the skill of the artist, and the difference between him and the mere amateur. What we call miracles and wonders of Art are not so to him who created them, for they were created by the natural movements of his own great soul. Statues, paintings, churches, poems, are but shadows of himself ; shadows in marble, colors, stone, words. He feels and recognizes their beauty ; but he thought these thoughts and produced these things as easily as inferior minds do thoughts and things inferior ; perhaps more easily. Vague images and shapes of beauty floating through the soul, the semblances of things as yet indefinite or ill-defined, and perfect only when put in Art, — this Possible Intellect, as the Scholastic Philosophers have termed it, — the artist shares in common with us all. The lovers of Art are many. But the Active Intellect, the creative power, — the power to put these shapes and images in Art, to embody the indefinite, and render perfect, — is his

alone. He shares the gift with few. He knows not even whence nor how this is. He knows only that it is; that God has given him the power, which has been denied to others."

" I should have known you were just from Germany," said the lady, with a smile, " even if you had not told me so. You are an enthusiast for the Germans. For my part, I cannot endure their harsh language."

" You would like it better, if you knew it better," answered Flemming. " It is not harsh to me, but homelike, hearty, and full of feeling, — like the sound of happy voices at a fireside, of a winter's night, when the wind blows, and the fire crackles, and hisses, and snaps. I do indeed love the Germans ; the men are so hale and hearty, and the Fräuleins so tender and true ! "

" I always think of men with pipes and beer, and women with knitting-work."

" Oh, those are English prejudices !." exclaimed Flemming. " Nothing can be more " —

" And their very literature presents itself to my imagination under the same forms."

" I see you have read only English criticisms ; and have an idea, that all German books smell, as one of your English critics says, ' of groceries, of brown papers filled with greasy cakes and slices of bacon, and of fryings in frouzy back-parlors ; ' and this shuts you out from a glorious world of poetry, romance, and dreams ! "

Mary Ashburton smiled, and Flemming continued to turn over the leaves of the sketch-book, with an occasional criticism and witticism. At

length he came to a leaf which was written in pencil. People of a lively imagination are generally curious, and always so when a little in love.

" Here is a pencil-sketch," said he, with an entreating look, "which I would fain examine with the rest."

" You may do so, if you wish, but you will find it the poorest sketch in the book. I was trying one day to draw the picture of an artist's life in Rome, as it presented itself to my imagination ; and this is the result. Perhaps it may awaken some pleasant recollection in your mind."

Flemming waited no longer, but read with the eyes of a lover, not of a critic, the following description, which inspired him with a new enthusiasm for Art, and for Mary Ashburton.

" I often reflect with delight upon the young artist's life in Rome. A stranger from the cold and gloomy North, he has crossed the Alps, and with the devotion of a pilgrim journeyed to the Eternal City. He dwells, perhaps, upon the Pincian Hill, and hardly a house there, which is not inhabited by artists from foreign lands. The very room he lives in has been their abode time out of mind. Their names are written all over the walls; perhaps some further record of them is left in a rough sketch upon the window-shutter, with an inscription and a date. These things consecrate the place, in his imagination. Even these names, though unknown to him, are not without associations in his mind.

" In that warm latitude he rises with the day. The night-vapors are already rolling away over the

Campagna seaward. As he looks from his window,
above and beyond their white folds he recognizes
the tremulous blue sea at Ostia. The rising sun
salutes Soracte, — his own beloved mountain ;
though no longer worshipped there, as of old. Be-
fore him, the antique house of Claude Lorraine
casts its long brown shadow down into the heart of
modern Rome. The city lies still asleep and silent.
But above its dark roofs, more than two hundred
steeples catch the sunshine on their gilded weather-
cocks. Presently the bells begin to ring, and, as
the artist listens to their pleasant chimes, he knows
that in each of those churches, over the high altar,
hangs a painting by some great master's hand,
whose beauty comes between him and heaven, so
that he cannot pray, but wonder only.

" Among these works of art he passes the day ;
but oftenest in St. Peter's and the Vatican. Up
the vast marble staircase, through the Corridor
Chiaramonti, through vestibules, galleries, cham-
bers, he passes as in a dream. All are filled with
busts and statues, or painted in daring frescos.
What forms of strength and beauty ! what glorious
creations of the human mind ! and in that last
chamber of all, standing alone upon his pedestal,
the Apollo found at Antium, in such a majestic
attitude, with such a noble countenance, life-like,
god-like !

" Or perhaps he passes into the chambers of the
painters, but goes no farther than the second.
For in the middle of that chamber a large painting
stands upon the heavy easel, as if unfinished,
though more than three hundred years ago the

great artist completed it, and then laid his pencil away forever, leaving this last benediction to the world. It is the Transfiguration of Christ, by Raphael. A child looks not at the stars with greater wonder than the artist at this painting. He knows how many studious years are in that picture. He knows the difficult path that leads to perfection, having himself taken some of the first steps. Thus he recalls the hour when that broad canvas was first stretched upon its frame, and Raphael stood before it, and laid the first colors upon it, and beheld the figures one by one born into life, and looked upon the work of his own hands with a smile, that it should have succeeded so well. He recalls, too, the hour when, the task accomplished, the pencil dropped from the master's dying hand, and his eyes closed to open on a more glorious transfiguration, and at length the dead Raphael lay in his own studio, before this wonderful painting, more glorious than any conqueror under the banners and armorial hatchments of his funeral!

" Think you that such sights and thoughts as these do not move the heart of a young man and an artist? And when he goes forth into the open air, the sun is going down, and the gray ruins of an antique world receive him. From the Palace of the Cæsars he looks down into the Forum, or towards the Coliseum; or westward sees the last sunshine strike the Bronze Archangel which stands upon the Tomb of Adrian. He walks amid a world of Art in ruins. The very street-lamps, that light him homeward, burn before some painted or

sculptured image of the Madonna! What wonder
is it if dreams visit him in his sleep, — nay, if his
whole life seem to him a dream? What wonder,
if, with a feverish heart and quick hand, he strive
to reproduce those dreams in marble or on can-
vas?"

Foolish Paul Flemming! who both admired and
praised this little sketch, and yet was too blind to
see that it was written from the heart, and not
from the imagination! Foolish Paul Flemming!
who thought that a girl of twenty could write thus
without a reason! Close upon this followed
another pencil sketch, which he likewise read, with
her permission. It was this.

" The whole period of the Middle Ages seems
very strange to me. At times I cannot persuade
myself that such things could have been as history
tells us; that such a strange world was a part of
our world, — that such a strange life was a part of
the life which seems to us, who are living it now,
so passionless and commonplace. It is only when
I stand amid ruined castles, that look at me so
mournfully, and behold the heavy armor of old
knights, hanging upon the wainscot of Gothic
chambers; or when I walk amid the aisles of some
dusky minster, whose walls are narrative of hoar
antiquity, and whose very bells have been baptized,
and see the carved oaken stalls in the choir, where
so many generations of monks have sat and sung,
and the tombs, where now they sleep in silence, to
awake no more to their midnight psalms; — it is
only at such times that the history of the Middle
Ages is a reality to me, and not a passage in
romance.

" Likewise the illuminated manuscripts of those ages have something of this power of making the dead Past a living Present in my mind. What curious figures are emblazoned on the creaking parchment, making its yellow leaves laugh with gay colors! You seem to come upon them unawares. Their faces have an expression of wonder. They seem all to be just startled from their sleep by the sound you made when you unloosed the brazen clasps, and opened the curiously carved oaken covers, that turn on hinges, like the great gates of a city. To the building of that city some diligent monk gave the whole of a long life. With what strange denizens he peopled it! Adam and Eve standing under a tree, with apples in their hands ; — the patriarch Abraham, with a tree growing out of his body, and his descendants sitting like owls upon its branches ; — ladies with flowing locks of gold ; knights in armor, with most fantastic, long-toed shoes ; jousts and tournaments ; and Minnesingers, and lovers whose heads reach to the towers where their ladies sit ; and all so angular, so naïve, so childlike, all in such simple attitudes, with such great eyes, and holding up such long, lank fingers ! — These things are characteristic of the Middle Ages, and persuade me of the truth of history."

At this moment Berkley entered, with a Swiss cottage, which he had bought as a present for somebody's child in England ; and a cane with a chamois-horn on the end of it, which he had bought as a present for himself. This was the first time that Flemming had been sorry to see the good·

natured man, whose presence now interrupted the delightful conversation he was carrying on under four eyes with Mary Ashburton. He really thought him tedious, and wondered it had never occurred to him before. Mrs. Ashburton, too, must needs lay down her book, and the conversation became general. Strange to say, the Swiss dinner-hour of one o'clock did not come a moment too soon for Flemming. It did not even occur to him that it was early, for he was seated beside Mary Ashburton ; and at dinner one can say so much, without being overheard.

CHAPTER VI.

AFTER DINNER, AND AFTER THE MANNER OF THE BEST CRITICS.

When the learned Thomas Diafoirus wooed the fair Angélique, he drew from his pocket a medical thesis, and presented it to her, as the first-fruits of his genius, and at the same time invited her, with her father's permission, to attend the dissection of a woman, upon whom he was to lecture. Paul Flemming did nearly the same thing; and so often, that it had become a habit. He was continually drawing from his pocket or his memory some scrap of song or story ; and inviting some fair Angélique, either with her father's permission or without, to attend the dissection of an author upon whom he was to lecture. He soon gave proofs of this to Mary Ashburton.

" What books have we here for afternoon read-

ing?" said Flemming, taking a volume from the table, when they had returned from the dining-room. "Oh, it is Uhland's Poems. Have you read anything of his? He and Tieck are generally considered the best living poets of Germany. They dispute the palm of superiority. Let me give you a lesson in German this afternoon, Miss Ashburton; so that no one may accuse you of 'omitting the sweet benefit of time, to clothe your age with angel-like perfection.' I have opened at random upon the ballad of the Black Knight. Do you repeat the German after me, and I will translate to you. *Pfingsten war, das Fest der Freude!*"

"I should never persuade my unwilling lips to pronounce such sounds. So I beg you not to perplex me with your German, but read me the ballad in English."

"Well, then, listen. I will improvise a translation for your own particular benefit.

> "'T was Pentecost, the Feast of Gladness,
> When woods and fields put off all sadness.
> Thus began the king, and spake:
> 'So from the halls
> Of ancient Hofburg's walls
> A luxuriant spring shall break.'
>
> "Drums and trumpets echo loudly,
> Wave the crimson banners proudly.
> From balcony the king looked on;
> In the play of spears,
> Fell all the cavaliers
> Before the monarch's stalwart son.
>
> "To the barrier of the fight
> Rode at last a sable knight.

'Sir Knight! your name and scutcheon? say.'
'Should I speak it here,
Ye would stand aghast with fear;
I am a prince of mighty sway!'

"When he rode into the lists,
The arch of heaven grew black with mists,
And the castle 'gan to rock.
At the first blow,
Fell the youth from saddle-bow, —
Hardly rises from the shock.

"Pipe and viol call the dances,
Torchlight through the high halls glances,
Waves a mighty shadow in;
With manner bland
Doth ask the maiden's hand,
Doth with her the dance begin:

"Danced in sable iron sark,
Danced a measure weird and dark,
Coldly clasped her limbs around.
From breast and hair
Down fell from her the fair
Flowerets, faded, to the ground.

"To the sumptuous banquet came
Every knight and every dame.
'Twixt son and daughter all distraught,
With mournful mind
The ancient king reclined,
Gazed at them in silent thought.

"Pale the children both did look,
But the guest a beaker took:
'Golden wine will make you whole!'
The children drank,
Gave many a courteous thank:
'Oh, that draught was very cool!'

"Each the father's breast embraces,
Son and daughter; and their faces
Colorless grow utterly.

> Whichever way
> Looks the fear-struck father gray,
> He beholds his children die.

> " 'Woe! the blessed children both
> Takest thou in the joy of youth:
> Take me, too, the joyless father!'
> Spake the grim guest,
> From his hollow, cavernous breast:
> 'Roses in the spring I gather!' ' "

"That is indeed a striking ballad!" said Miss Ashburton, "but rather too grim and ghostly for this dull afternoon."

"It begins joyously enough with the feast of Pentecost, and the crimson banners at the old castle. Then the contrast is well managed. The knight in black mail, and the waving in of the mighty shadow in the dance, and the dropping of the faded flowers, are all strikingly presented to the imagination. However, it tells its own story, and needs no explanation. Here is something in a different vein, though still melancholy. The Castle by the Sea. Shall I read it?"

"Yes, if you like."

Flemming read:—

> " 'Hast thou seen that lordly castle,
> That castle by the sea?
> Golden and red above it
> The clouds float gorgeously.

> " 'And fain it would stoop downward
> To the mirrored wave below;
> And fain it would soar upward
> In the evening's crimson glow.'

> " 'Well have I seen that castle,
> That castle by the sea,

And the moon above it standing,
And the mist rise solemnly.'

" 'The winds and the waves of ocean,
Had they a merry chime ?
Didst thou hear, from those lofty chambers,
The harp and the minstrel's rhyme ? '

" 'The winds and the waves of ocean,
They rested quietly ;
But I heard on the gale a sound of wail,
And tears came to mine eye.'

" ' And sawest thou on the turrets
The king and his royal bride,
And the wave of their crimson mantles,
And the golden crown of pride ?

" ' Led they not forth, in rapture,
A beauteous maiden there,
Resplendent as the morning sun,
Beaming with golden hair ? '

" ' Well saw I the ancient parents,
Without the crown of pride ;
They were moving slow, in weeds of woe;
No maiden was by their side ! ' "

" How do you like that ? "

" It is very graceful, and pretty. But Uhland
seems to leave a great deal to his reader's imagina-
tion. All his readers should be poets themselves,
or they will hardly comprehend him. I confess, I
hardly understand the passage where he speaks of
the castle's stooping downward to the mirrored
wave below, and then soaring upward into the
gleaming sky. I suppose, however, he wishes to
express the momentary illusion we experience
when beholding a perfect reflection of an old tower
in the sea. We look at it as if it were not a mere

shadow in the water; and yet the real tower rises far above, and seems to float in the crimson evening clouds. Is that the meaning?"

"I should think it was. To me it is all a beautiful cloud landscape, which I comprehend and feel, and yet should find some difficulty perhaps in explaining."

"And why need one always explain? Some feelings are quite untranslatable. No language has yet been found for them. They gleam upon us beautifully through the dim twilight of fancy, and yet, when we bring them close to us, and hold them up to the light of reason, lose their beauty, all at once; as glowworms, which glimmer with such a spiritual light in the shadows of evening, when brought in where the candles are lighted, are found to be only worms, like so many others."

"Very true. We ought sometimes to be content with feeling. Here, now, is an exquisite piece, which soothes one like the fall of evening shadows, — like the dewy coolness of twilight after a sultry day. I shall not give you a bald translation of my own, because I have laid up in my memory another, which, though not very literal, equals the original in beauty. Observe how finely it commences.

> "Many a year is in its grave
> Since I crossed this restless wave,
> And the evening, fair as ever,
> Shines on ruin, rock, and river.
>
> "Then, in this same boat, beside,
> Sat two comrades old and tried;
> One with all a father's truth,
> One with all the fire of youth.

" One on earth in silence wrought,
And his grave in silence sought ;
But the younger, brighter form
Passed in battle and in storm.

" So, whene'er I turn my eye
Back upon the 'days gone by,
Saddening thoughts of friends come o'er me,
Friends who closed their course before me.

" Yet what binds us, friend to friend,
But that soul with soul can blend ?
Soul-like were those hours of yore ;
Let us walk in soul once more !

" Take, O boatman, thrice thy fee ;
Take, — I give it willingly ;
For, invisible to thee,
Spirits twain have crossed with me ! "

" Oh, that is beautiful, — beautiful exceedingly !
Who translated it ? "

" I do not know. I wish I could find out. It
is certainly admirably well done ; though in the
measure of the original there is something like the
rocking motion of a boat, which is not preserved
in the translation."

" And is Uhland always so soothing and spir-
itual ? "

" Yes, he generally looks into the spirit-world.
I am now trying to find here a little poem on the
Death of a Country Clergyman, in which he intro-
duces a striking picture. But I cannot turn to it.
No matter. He describes the spirit of the good
old man, returning to earth on a bright summer
morning, and standing amid the golden corn and
the red and blue flowers, and mildly greeting the
reapers as of old. But there is nothing morbid

in Uhland's mind. He is always fresh and in-
vigorating, like a breezy morning. In this he
differs entirely from such writers as Salis and Mat-
thisson."

"And who are they?"

"Two melancholy gentlemen to whom life was
only a Dismal Swamp, upon whose margin they
walked with cambric handkerchiefs in their hands,
sobbing and sighing, and making signals to Death
to come and ferry them over the lake. And now
their spirits stand in the green fields of German
song like two weeping-willows bending over a
grave. To read their poems is like wandering
through a village churchyard on a summer even-
ing, reading the inscriptions upon the grave-stones,
and recalling sweet images of the departed; while
above you,

> "Hark! in the holy grove of palms
> Where the stream of life runs free,
> Echoes, in the angels' psalms,
> Sister spirit! hail to thee!"

"How musically those lines flow! Are they
Matthisson's?"

"Yes; and they do indeed flow musically. I
wish I had his poems here. I should like to read
to you his Elegy on the Ruins of an Ancient
Castle. It is an imitation of Gray's Elegy. You
have been at Baden-Baden?"

"Yes; last summer."

"And have not forgotten" —

"The old castle? Of course not. What a mag-
nificent ruin it is?"

"That is the scene of Matthisson's poem, and

seems to have filled the melancholy bard with more than wonted inspiration."

"I should very much like to see the poem, — I remember that old ruin with so much delight."

"I am sorry I have not a translation of it for you. Instead of it, I will give you a sweet and mournful poem from Salis. It is called The Song of the Silent Land.

> "Into the Silent Land!
> Ah ! who shall lead us thither ?
> Clouds in the evening sky more darkly gather,
> And shattered wrecks lie thicker on the strand.
> Who leads us with a gentle hand
> Thither, oh, thither,
> Into the Silent Land ?
>
> "Into the Silent Land!
> To you, ye boundless regions
> Of all perfection ! Tender morning-visions
> Of beauteous souls ! The Future's pledge and band !
> Who in Life's battle firm doth stand
> Shall bear Hope's tender blossoms
> Into the Silent Land!
>
> "O Land ! O Land !
> For all the broken-hearted
> The mildest herald by our fate allotted
> Beckons, and with inverted torch doth stand
> To lead us with a gentle hand
> Into the land of the great departed,
> Into the Silent Land!

Is not that a beautiful poem ? "

Mary Ashburton made no answer. She had turned away to hide her tears. Flemming wondered that Berkley could say she was not beautiful. Still he was rather pleased than offended at it. He felt at that moment how sweet a thing it would be to possess one who should seem beautiful

to him alone, and yet to him be more beautiful
than all the world beside ! How bright the world
became to him at that thought ! It was like one
of those paintings in which all the light streams
from the face of the Virgin. Oh, there is nothing
holier, in this life of ours, than the first conscious-
ness of love, — the first fluttering of its silken
wings ; the first rising sound and breath of wind
which is so soon to sweep through the soul, to
purify or to destroy !

Old histories tell us that the great Emperor
Charlemagne stamped his edicts with the hilt of
his sword. The greater Emperor, Death, stamps
with the blade, and they are signed and executed
with the same stroke. Flemming received that
night a letter from Heidelberg, which told him
that Emma of Ilmenau was dead. The fate of
this poor girl affected him deeply ; and he said in
his heart : —

"Father in heaven ! Why was the lot of this
weak and erring child so hard ? What had she
done, to be so tempted in her weakness, and perish ?
Why didst thou suffer her gentle affections to lead
her thus astray ? "

And, through the silence of the awful midnight,
the voice of an avalanche answered from the dis-
tant mountains, and seemed to say : —

"Peace ! peace ! Why dost thou question God's
providence ? "

CHAPTER VII.

TAKE CARE!

Fair is the valley of Lauterbrunnen, with its green meadows and overhanging cliffs. The ruined castle of Unspunnen stands like an armed warder at the gate of the enchanted land. In calm serenity the snowy mountains rise beyond. Fairer than the Rock of Balmarusa, yon frowning precipice looks down upon us; and, from the topmost cliff, the white pennon of the Brook of Dust shimmers and waves in the sunny air!

It was a bright, beautiful morning after nightrain. Every dew-drop and rain-drop had a whole heaven within it; and so had the heart of Paul Flemming, as, with Mrs. Ashburton and her dark-eyed daughter, he drove up the Valley of Lauterbrunnen, — the Valley of Fountains-Only.

"How beautiful the Jungfrau looks this morning!" exclaimed he, looking at Mary Ashburton.

She thought he meant the mountain, and assented. But he meant her likewise.

"And the mountains beyond," he continued, "the Monk and the Silver-horn, the Wetter-horn, the Schreck-horn, and the Schwarz-horn, — all those sublime apostles of Nature, whose sermons are avalanches! Did you ever behold anything more grand?"

"Oh yes! Mont Blanc is more grand, when you behold it from the hills opposite. It was there that I was most moved by the magnificence of Swiss scenery. It was a morning like this; and

the clouds, that were hovering about on their huge, shadowy wings, made the scene only the more magnificent. Before me lay the whole panorama of the Alps; pine forests standing dark and solemn at the base of the mountains; and half-way up a veil of mist, above which rose the snowy summits and sharp needles of rock, which seemed to float in the air, like a fairy world. Then the glaciers stood on either side, winding down through the mountain ravines, and high above all rose the white, dome-like summit of Mont Blanc. And ever and anon from the shroud of mist came the awful sound of an avalanche, and a continual roar, as of the wind through a forest of pines, filled the air. It was the roar of the Arve and Aveiron, breaking from their icy fountains. Then the mists began to pass away; and it seemed as if the whole firmament were rolling together. It recalled to my mind that sublime passage in the Apocalypse : ' I saw a great white throne, and him that sat thereon, before whose face the heavens and the earth fled away, and found no place ! ' — I cannot believe that upon this earth there is. a more magnificent scene ! "

"It must be grand indeed," replied Flemming. " And those mighty glaciers, — huge monsters with bristling crests, creeping down into the valley ! for it is said they really move."

" Yes ; it filled me with a strange sensation of awe to think of this. They seemed to me like the dragons of Northern Romance, which come down from the mountains and devour whole villages. A little hamlet in Chamouni was once abandoned

by its inhabitants, terrified at the approach of the
icy dragon. But is it possible you have never
been at Chamouni?"

"Never. The great marvel still remains unseen
by me."

"Then how can you linger here so long? Were
I in your place, I would not lose an hour."

These words passed over the opening blossoms
of hope in the soul of Flemming like a cold wind
over the flowers in spring-time. He bore it as
best he could, and changed the subject.

I do not mean to describe the valley of Lauter-
brunnen, nor the bright day passed there. I know
that my gentle reader is blessed with the divine
gift of a poetic fancy; and can see already how
the mountains rise, and the torrents fall, and the
beautiful valley lies between; and how, along the
dusty road, the herdsman blows his horn, and
travellers come and go in *charabancs*, like Punch
and Judy in a show-box. He knows already how
romantic ladies sketch romantic scenes; and how
cold meat tastes under the shadow of trees; and
how time flies, when we are in love, and the be-
loved one near. One little incident I must, how-
ever, mention, lest his fancy should not suggest it.

Flemming was still sitting with the ladies on
the green slope near the Staubbach, or Brook of
Dust, when a young man clad in green came down
the valley. It was a German mechanic, with
flaxen ringlets hanging over his shoulders, and a
guitar in his hand. His step was free and elastic,
and his countenance wore the joyous expression of
youth and health. He approached the company

with a courteous salutation ; and, after the manner
of travelling apprentices, asked charity with the
confident air of one unaccustomed to refusal. Nor
was he refused in this instance. The presence of
those we love makes us compassionate and gener-
ous. Flemming gave him a piece of gold ; and,
after a short conversation, he seated himself at a
little distance on the grass, and began to play and
sing. Wonderful and many were the soft accords
and plaintive sounds that came from that little
instrument, touched by the clever hand. Every
feeling of the human heart seemed to find an ex-
pression there, and awaken a kindred feeling in
the hearts of those who heard him. He sang
strange German songs, so full of longing, and of
pleasing sadness, and hope, and fear, and passion-
ate desire, and soul-subduing sorrow, that the tears
came into Mary Ashburton's eyes, though she
understood not the words he sang. Then his
countenance glowed with triumph, and he beat the
strings like a drum, and sang : —

> Oh, how the drum beats so loud!
> Close beside me in the fight,
> . My dying brother says, Good Night!
> And the cannon's awful breath
> Screams the loud halloo of Death!
> And the drum,
> And the drum,
> Beats so loud!

Many were the words of praise when the young
musician ended ; and, as he rose to depart, they
still entreated for one song more. Whereupon he
played a lively prelude, and, looking full into Flem-
ming's face, sang, with a pleasant smile and still in
German, this little song : —

I know a maiden fair to see ;
 Take care !
She can both false and friendly be.
 Beware ! Beware !
 Trust her not,
 She is fooling thee !

She has two eyes, so soft and brown ;
 Take care !
She gives a side-glance and looks down.
 Beware ! Beware !
 Trust her not,
 She is fooling thee !

And she has hair of a golden hue ;
 Take care !
And what she says, it is not true.
 Beware ! Beware !
 Trust her not,
 She is fooling thee !

She has a bosom as white as snow ;
 Take care !
She knows how much it is best to show.
 Beware ! Beware !
 Trust her not,
 She is fooling thee !

She gives thee a garland woven fair ;
 Take care !
It is a fool's-cap for thee to wear.
 Beware ! Beware !
 Trust her not,
 She is fooling thee !

The last stanza he sung in a laughing, triumphant tone, which resounded above the loud clang of his guitar like the jeering laugh of Till Eulenspiegel. Then, slinging his guitar over his shoulder, he took off his green cap, and made a leg to the ladies, in the style of Gil Blas ; waved his

hand in the air, and walked quickly down the valley, singing, " Adé! Adé! Adé! "

CHAPTER VIII.

THE FOUNTAIN OF OBLIVION.

The power of magic in the Middle Ages created monsters who followed the unhappy magician everywhere. The power of love in all ages creates angels, who likewise follow the happy or unhappy lover everywhere, even in his dreams. By such an angel was Paul Flemming now haunted, both when he waked and when he slept. He walked as in a dream, and was hardly conscious of the presence of those around him. A sweet face looked at him from every page of every book he read ; and it was the face of Mary Ashburton! — a sweet voice spake to him in every sound he heard ; and it was the voice of Mary Ashburton! Day and night succeeded each other, with pleasant interchange of light and darkness; but to him the passing of time was only as a dream. When he arose in the morning, he thought only of her, and wondered if she were yet awake; and when he lay down at night, he thought only of her, and how, like the Lady Christabel,

> Her gentle limbs she did undress,
> And lay down in her loveliness!

And the livelong day he was with her, either in reality or in day-dreams hardly less real ; for in each delirious vision of his waking hours, her beauteous form passed like the form of Beatrice through

Dante's heaven; and, as he lay in the summer
afternoon, and heard at times the sound of the
wind in the trees, and the sound of Sabbath bells
ascending up to heaven, holy wishes and prayers
ascended with them from his inmost soul, beseech-
ing that he might not love in vain! And when-
ever, in silence and alone, he looked into the silent,
lonely countenance of Night, he recalled the im-
passioned lines of Plato: —

> Lookest thou at the stars? If I were heaven,
> With all the eyes of heaven would I look down on thee!

Oh, how beautiful it is to love! Even thou, that
sneerest at this page, and laughest in cold indiffer-
ence or scorn, if others are near thee, — thou too
must acknowledge its truth, when thou art alone;
and confess that a foolish world is prone to laugh
in public at what in private it reveres, as one
of the highest impulses of our nature, — namely,
Love!

One by one the objects of our affection depart
from us. But our affections remain, and like vines
stretch forth their broken, wounded tendrils for
support. The bleeding heart needs a balm to heal
it; and there is none but the love of its kind, —
none but the affection of a human heart! Thus
the wounded, broken affections of Flemming began
to lift themselves from the dust and cling around
this new object. Days and weeks passed, and,
like the student Crisostomo, he ceased to love, be-
cause he began to adore. And with this adoration
mingled the prayer, that, in that hour when the
world is still, and the voices that praise are mute,
and reflection cometh like twilight, and the maiden,

in her day-dreams, counted the number of her friends, some voice in the sacred silence of her thoughts might whisper his name!

They were sitting together one morning, on the green, flowery meadow, under the ruins of Burg Unspunnen. She was sketching the ruins. The birds were singing, one and all, as if there were no aching hearts, no sin nor sorrow in the world. So motionless was the bright air, that the shadow of the trees lay engraven on the grass. The distant snow-peaks sparkled in the sun, and nothing frowned, save the square tower of the old ruin above them.

" What a pity it is," said the lady, as she stopped to rest her weary fingers, " what a pity it is, that there is no old tradition connected with this ruin ! "

" I will make you one, if you wish," said Flemming.

" Can you make old traditions ? "

" Oh, yes ! I made three, the other day, about the Rhine, and one very old one about the Black Forest. A lady with dishevelled hair ; a robber with a horrible slouched hat ; and a night storm among the roaring pines."

" Delightful ! Do make one for me."

" With the greatest pleasure. Where will you have the scene ? Here, or in the Black Forest ? "

" In the Black Forest, by all means ! Begin."

" I will unite this ruin and the forest together. But first promise not to interrupt me. If you snap the golden threads of thought, they will float away on the air like the film of the gossamer, and I shall never be able to recover them."

" I promise."

" Listen, then, to the tradition of THE FOUN-
TAIN OF OBLIVION."

" Begin."

Flemming was reclining on the flowery turf, at
the lady's feet, looking up with dreamy eyes into
her sweet face, and then into the leaves of the lin-
den-trees overhead.

" Gentle lady ! Dost thou remember the linden-
trees of Bülach, — those tall and stately trees,
with velvet down upon their shining leaves, and
rustic benches underneath their overhanging eaves?
A leafy dwelling, fit to be the home of elf or fairy,
where first I told my love to thee, thou cold and
stately Hermione ! A little peasant-girl stood
near, and listened all the while, with eyes of won-
der and delight, and an unconscious smile, to hear
the stranger still speak on, in accents deep yet
mild, — none else was with us in that hour, save
God and that little child ! "

" Why, it is in rhyme ! "

" No, no ! the rhyme is only in your imagination.
You promised not to interrupt me, and you have
already snapped asunder the gossamer threads
of as sweet a dream as was ever spun from a poet's
brain."

" It certainly did rhyme ! "

" This was the reverie of the student Hierony-
mus, as he sat at midnight in a chamber of this
old tower, with his hands clasped together, and
resting upon an open volume, which he should
have been reading. His pale face was raised, and
the pupils of his eyes dilated, as if the spirit-world

were open before him, and some beauteous vision
were standing there, and drawing the student's
soul through his eyes up into heaven, — as the
evening sun, through parting summer-clouds, seems
to draw into its bosom the vapors of the earth.
Oh, it was a lovely vision! I can see it before me
now!

" Near the student stood an antique bronze
lamp, with strange figures carved upon it. It was
a magic lamp, which once belonged to the Arabian
astrologer El Geber, in Spain. Its light was beau-
tiful as the light of stars; and, night after night,
as the lonely wight sat alone and read in this lofty
tower, through the mist and murk and dropping
rain, it streamed out into the darkness, and was
seen by many wakeful eyes. To the poor student
Hieronymus it was a wonderful Aladdin's Lamp;
for in its flame a Divinity revealed herself unto
him, and showed him treasures. Whenever he
opened a ponderous, antiquated tome, it seemed as
if some angel opened for him the gates of Paradise;
and already he was known in the land as Hierony-
mus the Learned.

" But, alas! he could read no more. The charm
was broken. Hour after hour he passed with his
hands clasped before him, and his fair eyes gazing
at vacancy. What could so disturb the studies of.
this melancholy wight? Lady, he was in love!
Have you ever been in love? He had seen the
face of the beautiful Hermione; and as, when we
have thoughtlessly looked at the sun, our dazzled
eyes, though closed, behold it still, so he beheld by
day and by night the radiant image of her upon

whom he had too rashly gazed. Alas! he was un-
happy; for the proud Hermione disdained the
love of a poor student, whose only wealth was a
magic lamp. In marble halls, and amid the gay
crowd that worshipped her, she had almost forgot-
ten that such a being lived as the student Hierony-
mus. The adoration of his heart had been to her
only as the perfume of a wild-flower which she had
carelessly crushed with her foot in passing. But
he had lost all; for he had lost the quiet of his
thoughts; and his agitated soul reflected only
broken and distorted images of things. The world
laughed at the poor student, who, in his threadbare
cassock, dared to lift his eyes to the Lady Her-
mione, while he sat alone, in his desolate chamber,
and suffered in silence. He remembered many
things which he would fain have forgotten; but
which, if he had forgotten them, he would have
wished again to remember. Such were the linden-
trees of Bülach, under whose pleasant shades he
had told his love to Hermione. This was the scene
which he wished most to forget, yet loved most to
remember; and of this he was now dreaming, with
his hands clasped upon his book, and that music
in his thoughts, which you, lady, mistook for
rhyme.

"Suddenly, with a melancholy clang, the convent
clock struck twelve. It roused the student Hiero-
ymus from his dream, and rang in his ears, like
the iron hoofs of the steeds of Time. The magic
hour had come, when the Divinity of the lamp
most willingly revealed herself to her votary. The
bronze figures seemed alive; a white cloud rose

from the flame and spread itself through the chamber; the four walls dilated into magnificent cloud-vistas; a fragrance, as of wild-flowers, filled the air; and a dreamy music, like distant, sweet-chiming bells, announced the approach of the midnight Divinity. Through his streaming tears the heart-broken student beheld her once more descending a pass in the snowy cloud-mountains, as, at evening, the dewy Hesperus comes from the bosom of the mist, and assumes his station in the sky. At her approach, his spirit grew more calm; for her presence was, to his feverish heart, like a tropical night, — beautiful and soothing and invigorating. At length she stood before him, revealed in all her beauty; and he comprehended the visible language of her sweet but silent lips, which seemed to say, ' What would the student Hieronymus to-night?' — ' Peace!' he answered, raising his clasped hands, and smiling through his tears. ' The student Hieronymus imploreth peace! ' — ' Then go,' said the spirit, ' go to the Fountain of Oblivion in the deepest solitude of the Black Forest, and cast this scroll into its waters; and thou shalt be at peace once more.' Hieronymus opened his arms to embrace the Divinity, for her countenance assumed the features of Hermione; but she vanished away; the music ceased; the gorgeous cloud-land sank and fell asunder; and the student was alone within the four bare walls of his chamber. As he bowed his head downward, his eye fell upon a parchment scroll, which was lying beside the lamp. Upon it was written only the name of Hermione!

" The next morning Hieronymus put the scroll

into his bosom, and went his way in search of the
Fountain of Oblivion. A few days brought him
to the skirts of the Black Forest. He entered, not
without a feeling of dread, that land of shadows;
and passed onward, under melancholy pines and
cedars, whose branches grew abroad and mingled
together, and, as they swayed up and down, filled
the air with solemn twilight and a sound of sorrow.
As he advanced into the forest, the waving moss
hung, like curtains, from the branches overhead,
and more and more shut out the light of heaven;
and he knew that the Fountain of Oblivion was
not far off. Even then the sound of falling waters
was mingling with the roar of the pines above
him; and erelong he came to a river, moving in
solemn majesty through the forest, and falling with
a dull, leaden sound into a motionless and stagnant
lake, above which the branches of the forest met
and mingled, forming perpetual night. This was
the Fountain of Oblivion.

" Upon its brink the student paused, and gazed
into the dark waters with a steadfast look. They
were limpid waters, dark with shadows only. And
as he gazed, he beheld, far down in their silent
depths, dim and ill-defined outlines, wavering to
and fro, like the folds of a white garment in the
twilight. Then more distinct and permanent
shapes arose, — shapes familiar to his mind, yet
forgotten and remembered again, as the fragments
of a dream; till at length, far, far below him, he
beheld the great City of the Past, with silent
marble streets, and moss-grown walls, and spires
uprising with a wave-like, flickering motion.

" And amid the crowd that thronged those streets, he beheld faces once familiar and dear to him, and heard sorrowful, sweet voices singing, Oh, forget us not! forget us not! and then the distant, mournful sound of funeral bells, that were tolling below, in the City of the Past. But in the gardens of that city there were children playing, and among them one who wore his features, as they had been in childhood. He was leading a little girl by the hand, and caressed her often, and adorned her with flowers. Then, like a dream, the scene changed, and the boy had grown older, and stood alone, gazing into the sky; and as he gazed, his countenance changed again, and Hieronymus beheld him, as if it had been his own image in the clear water; and before him stood a beauteous maiden, whose face was like the face of Hermione, and he feared lest the scroll had fallen into the water, as he bent over it.

" Starting, as from a dream, he put his hand into his bosom, and breathed freely again, when he found the scroll still there. He drew it forth, and read the blessed name of Hermione, and the city beneath him vanished away, and the air grew fragrant as with the breath of May-flowers, and a light streamed through the shadowy forest, and gleamed upon the lake; and the student Hieronymus pressed the dear name to his lips, and exclaimed, with streaming eyes: ' Oh, scorn me as thou wilt, still, still will I love thee; and thy name shall irradiate the gloom of my life, and make the waters of Oblivion smile!' And the name was no longer Hermione, but was changed to Mary;

and the student Hieronymus — is lying at your feet! O gentle Lady,

> " I did hear you talk
> Far above singing; after you were gone,
> I grew acquainted with my heart, and searched
> What stirred it so! Alas! I found it love."

CHAPTER IX.

A TALK ON THE STAIRS.

No! I will not describe that scene; nor how pale the stately lady sat on the border of the green, sunny meadow! The hearts of some women tremble like leaves at every breath of love which reaches them, and then are still again. Others, like the ocean, are moved only by the breath of a storm, and not so easily lulled to rest. And such was the proud heart of Mary Ashburton. It had remained unmoved by the presence of this stranger; and the sound of his footsteps and his voice excited in it no emotion. He had deceived himself! Silently they walked homeward through the green meadow. The very sunshine was sad; and the rising wind, through the old ruin above them, sounded in his ears like a hollow laugh!

Flemming went straight to his chamber. On the way, he passed the walnut-trees under which he had first seen the face of Mary Ashburton. Involuntarily he closed his eyes. They were full of tears. Oh, there are places in this fair world which we never wish to see again, however dear they may be to us! The towers of the old Fran-

ciscan convent never looked so gloomily as then,
though the bright summer sun was shining full
upon them.

In his chamber he found Berkley. He was
looking out of the window, whistling.

"This evening I leave Interlachen forever,"
said Flemming, rather abruptly. Berkley stared.

"Indeed! Pray what is the matter? You look
as pale as a ghost!"

"And have good reason to look pale," replied
Flemming bitterly. "Hoffmann says, in one of
his note-books, that on the eleventh of March, at
half past eight o'clock, precisely, he was an ass.
That is what I was this morning, at half past ten
o'clock, precisely, and am now, and I suppose al-
ways shall be."

He tried to laugh, but could not. He then re-
lated to Berkley the whole story, from beginning
to end.

"This is a miserable piece of business!" ex-
claimed Berkley, when he had finished. "Strange
enough! And yet I have long ceased to marvel
at the caprices of women. Did not Pan captivate
the chaste Diana? Did not Titania love Nick
Bottom with his ass's head? Do you think that
maidens' eyes are no longer touched with the juice
of love-in-idleness? Take my word for it, she is
in love with somebody else. There must be some
reason for this. No; women never have any
reasons, except their will. But never mind. Keep
a stout heart. Care killed a cat. After all, —
what is she? Who is she? Only a " —

" Hush! hush! " exclaimed Flemming, in great

excitement. "Not one word more, I beseech you. Do not think to console me by depreciating her. She is very dear to me still; a beautiful, high-minded, noble woman."

"Yes," answered Berkley; "that is the way with you all, you young men. You see a sweet face, or a something, you know not what, and flickering reason says, Good night; amen to common sense! The imagination invests the beloved object with a thousand superlative charms; adorns her with all the purple and fine linen, all the rich apparel and furniture, of human nature. I did the same when I was young. I was once as desperately in love as you are now; and went through all the

> " Delicious deaths, soft exhalations
> Of soul, dear and divine annihilations;
> A thousand unknown rites
> Of joys, and rarefied delights.

I adored and was rejected. 'You are in love with certain attributes,' said the lady. 'Damn your attributes, Madam,' said I; 'I know nothing about attributes.' — 'Sir,' said she, with dignity, 'you have been drinking.' — So we parted. She was married afterwards to another, who knew something about attributes, I suppose. I have seen her once since, and only once. She had a baby in a yellow gown. I hate a baby in a yellow gown. How glad I am she did not marry me! One of these days, you will be glad you have been rejected. Take my word for it."

"All that does not prevent my lot from being a very melancholy one!" said Flemming sadly.

"Oh, never mind the lot," cried Berkley, laugh-

ing, "so long as you don't get Lot's wife. If the
cucumber is bitter, throw it away, as the philoso-
pher Marcus Antoninus says, in his Meditations.
Forget her, and all will be as if you had not known
her."

"I shall never forget her," replied Flemming,
rather solemnly. "Not my pride, but my affec-
tions are wounded; and the wound is too deep
ever to heal. I shall carry it with me always. I
enter no more into the world, but will dwell only
in the world of my own thoughts. All great and
unusual occurrences, whether of joy or sorrow, lift
us above this earth; and we should do well always
to preserve this elevation. Hitherto I have not
done so. But now I will no more descend; I will
sit apart and above the world, with my mournful,
yet holy thoughts."

"Whew! You had better go into society; the
whirl and delirium will cure you in a week. If
you find a lady who pleases you very much, and
you wish to marry her, and she will not listen to
such a horrid thing, I see but one remedy, which is
to find another, who pleases you more, and who
will listen to it."

"No, my friend; you do not understand my
character," said Flemming, shaking his head. "I
love this woman with a deep and lasting affection.
I shall never cease to love her. This may be mad-
ness in me; but so it is. Alas and alas! Para-
celsus of old wasted life in trying to discover its
elixir, which, after all, turned out to be alcohol;
and instead of being made immortal upon earth,
he died drunk on the floor of a tavern. The like

happens to many of us. We waste our best years in distilling the sweetest flowers of life into love-potions, which after all do not immortalize, but only intoxicate us. By Heaven! we are all of us mad."

"But are you sure the case is utterly hope-less?"

"Utterly! utterly!"

"And yet I perceive you have not laid aside all hope. You still flatter yourself that the lady's heart may change. The great secret of happiness consists not in enjoying, but in renouncing. But it is hard, very hard. Hope has as many lives as a cat or a king. I dare say you have heard the old proverb, 'The king never dies.' But perhaps you have never heard that, at the court of Naples, when the dead body of a monarch lies in state, his dinner is carried up to him as usual, and the court physician tastes it, to see that it be not poisoned, and then the servants bear it out again, saying, 'The king does not dine to-day.' Hope in our souls is king; and we also say, 'The king never dies.' Even when in reality he lies dead within us, in solemn mockery we offer him his accustomed food, but are constrained to say, 'The king does not dine to-day.' It must be an evil day, indeed, when a king of Naples has no heart for his dinner! but you yourself are a proof that the king never dies. You are feeding your king, although you say he is dead."

"To show you that I do not wish to cherish hope," replied Flemming, "I shall leave Inter-lachen to-morrow morning. I am going to the Tyrol."

" You are right," said Berkley ; " there is nothing
so good for sorrow as rapid motion in the open air.
I shall go with you; though probably your conver-
sation will not be very various; nothing but Ed-
ward and Kunigunde."

" What do you mean by that? "

" Go to Berlin, and you will find out. However,
jesting apart, I will do all I can to cheer you, and
make you forget the Dark Ladie, and this untó-
ward accident."

" Accident! " said Flemming. " This is no ac-
cident, but God's providence, which brought us to-
gether, to punish me for my sins."

" Oh, my friend," interrupted Berkley, " if you
see the finger of Providence so distinctly in every
act of your life, you will end by thinking your-
self an Apostle and Envoy Extraordinary. I see
nothing so very uncommon in what has happened
to you."

" What! not when our souls are so akin to each
other ? when we seemed so formed to be together,
— to be one ? "

" I have often observed," replied Berkley coldly,
" that those who are of kindred souls rarely wed
together; almost as rarely as those who are akin
by blood. Therefore, mad lover, do not think to
persuade thyself and thy scornful lady that you
have kindred souls ; but rather the contrary, —
that you are much unlike, and each wanting in
those qualities which most mark and distinguish
the other. Trust me, thy courtship will then be
more prosperous. But good morning. I must
prepare for this sudden journey."

On the following morning, Flemming and Berkley started on their way to Innsbruck, like Huon of Bordeaux and Scherasmin on their way to Babylon. Berkley's self-assumed duty was to console his companion ; a duty which he performed like an ancient Spanish Despenadora, whose business was to attend the sick, and put her elbow into the stomach of the dying, to shorten their agony.

BOOK THE FOURTH

Mortal, they softly say,
 Peace to thy heart !
We too, yes, mortal,
 Have been as thou art ;
Hope-lifted, doubt-depressed,
 Seeing in part,
Tried, troubled, tempted,
 Sustained, — as thou art.

CAROLINE SOUTHEY.

CHAPTER I.

A MISERERE.

In the Orlando Innamorato, Malagigi, the necromancer, puts all the company to sleep by reading to them from a book. Some books have this power of themselves and need no necromancer. Fearing, Gentle Reader, that mine may be of this kind, I have provided these introductory chapters from time to time, like stalls or Misereres in a church, with flowery canopies and poppy-heads over them, where thou mayest sit down and sleep.

No, — the figure is not a bad one. This book does somewhat resemble a minster, in the Romanesque style, with pinnacles, and flying buttresses, and roofs,

> Gargoyled with greyhounds, and with many lions
> Made of fine gold, with divers sundry dragons.

You step into its shade and coolness out of the hot
streets of life; a mysterious light streams through
the painted glass of the marigold windows, stain-
ing the cusps and crumpled leaves of the window-
shafts, and the cherubs and holy-water-stoups be-
low. Here and there is an image of the Virgin
Mary; and other images, "in divers vestures,
called weepers, stand in housings made about the
tomb;" and above all swells the vast dome of
heaven, with its star-mouldings, and the flaming
constellations, like the mosaics in the dome of St.
Peter's. Have you not heard funeral psalms from
the chantry? Have you not heard the sound of
church-bells, as I promised, — mysterious sounds
from the Past and Future, as from the belfries out-
side the cathedral, — even such a mournful, mel-
low, watery peal of bells, as is heard sometimes at
sea, from cities afar off below the horizon?

I know not how this Romanesque, and at times
flamboyant, style of architecture may please the
critics. They may wish, perhaps, that I had
omitted some of my many ornaments, my ara-
besques, and roses, and fantastic spouts, and Holy-
Roods and Galilee-steeples. But would it then
have been Romanesque?

But perhaps, Gentle Reader, thou art one of
those who think the days of romance gone forever.
Believe it not! Oh, believe it not! Thou hast
at this moment in thy heart as sweet a romance
as was ever written. Thou art not less a woman,
because thou dost not sit aloft in a tower, with a
tassel-gentle on thy wrist. Thou art not less a
man, because thou wearest no hauberk, nor mail-

sark, and goest not on horseback after foolish ad-
ventures. Every one has a romance in his own
heart. All that has blessed or awed the world lies
there; and

> The oracle within him, that which lives,
> He must invoke and question, — not dead books,
> Not ordinances, not mould-rotted papers.

Sooner or later, some passages of every one's
romance must be written, either in words or ac-
tions. They will proclaim the truth, for Truth is
thought which has assumed its appropriate gar-
ments, either of words or actions; while Falsehood
is thought which, disguised in words or actions not
its own, comes before the blind old world, as
Jacob came before the patriarch Isaac, clothed
in the goodly raiment of his brother Esau. And
the world, like the patriarch, is often deceived;
for though the voice is Jacob's voice, yet the
hands are the hands of Esau, and the False takes
away the birthright and the blessing from the
True. Hence it is that the world so often lifts up
its voice and weeps.

That very pleasing and fanciful Chinese ro-
mance, the Shadow in the Water, ends with the
hero's marrying both the heroines. I hope my
gentle reader feels curious to know the end of this
romance, which is a shadow upon the earth, and
see whether there be any marriage at all in it.

That is the very point I am now thinking of, as
I sit here at my pleasant chamber-window, and en-
joy the balmy air of a bright summer morning,
and watch the motions of the golden robin that
sits on its swinging nest on the outermost pendu-

lous branch of yonder elm. The broad meadows
and the steel-blue river remind me of the meadows
of Unterseen and the river Aar ; and beyond them
rise magnificent snow-white clouds, piled up like
Alps. Thus the shades of Washington and Wil-
liam Tell seem to walk together on these Elysian
Fields, for it was here that, in days long gone, our
great patriot dwelt ; and yonder clouds so much
resemble the snowy Alps, that they remind me
irresistibly of the Swiss. Noble examples of a
high purpose and a fixed will! Do they not move,
Hyperion-like, on high? Were they not, likewise,
sons of Heaven and Earth?

Nothing can be more lovely than these summer
mornings, nor than the southern window at which
I sit and write, in this old mansion, which is like
an Italian villa. But oh, this lassitude, — this wea-
riness, — when all around me is so bright! I have
this morning a singular longing for flowers, a wish
to stroll among the roses and carnations, and inhale
their breath, as if it would revive me. I wish I
knew the man who called flowers "the fugitive po-
etry of Nature." From this distance, from these
scholastic shades, — from this leafy, blossoming,
and beautiful Cambridge, — I stretch forth my
hand to grasp his, as the hand of a poet ! — Yes ;
this morning I would rather stroll with him among
the gay flowers, than sit here and write. I feel so
weary !

Old men with their staves, says the Spanish
poet, are ever knocking at the door of the grave.
But I am not old. The Spanish poet might have
included the young also. — No matter! Courage,

and forward ! The romance must be finished, and finished soon.

O thou poor authorling ! Reach a little deeper into the human heart ! Touch those strings, — touch those deeper strings, and more boldly, or the notes will die away like whispers, and no ear shall hear them, save thine own ! And, to cheer thy solitary labor, remember that the secret studies of an author are the sunken piers upon which is to rest the bridge of his fame, spanning the dark waters of Oblivion. They are out. of sight ; but without them no superstructure can stand secure !

And now, Reader, since the sermon is over, and we are still sitting here in this Miserere, let us read aloud a page from the old parchment manuscript on the lettern before us ; let us sing it through these dusky aisles, like a Gregorian chant, and startle the sleeping congregation !

"I have read of the great river Euripus, which ebbeth and floweth seven times a day, and with such violence that it carrieth ships upon it with full sail directly against the wind. Seven times in an hour ebbeth and floweth rash opinion in the torrent of indiscreet and troublesome apprehensions, carrying critic calumny and squint - eyed detraction mainly against the wind of wisdom and judgment."

In secula seculorum ! Amen !

CHAPTER II.

CURFEW BELLS.

Welcome, Disappointment! Thy hand is cold and hard, but it is the hand of a friend! Thy voice is stern and harsh, but it is the voice of a friend! Oh, there is something sublime in calm endurance, something sublime in the resolute, fixed purpose of suffering without complaining, which makes disappointment oftentimes better than success!

The Emperor Isaac Angelus made a treaty with Saladin, and tried to purchase the Holy Sepulchre with gold. Richard Lion-heart scorned such alliance, and sought to recover it by battle. Thus do weak minds make treaties with the passions they cannot overcome, and try to purchase happiness at the expense of principle. But the resolute will of a strong man scorns such means, and struggles nobly with his foe to achieve great deeds. Therefore, whosoever thou art that sufferest, try not to dissipate thy sorrow by the breath of the world, nor drown its voice in thoughtless merriment. It is a treacherous peace that is purchased by indulgence. Rather take this sorrow to thy heart, and make it a part of thee, and it shall nourish thee till thou art strong again.

The shadows of the mind are like those of the body. In the morning of life, they all lie behind us; at noon, we trample them under foot; and in the evening, they stretch long, broad, and deepening before us. Are not, then, the sorrows of child-

hood as dark as those of age? Are not the morning shadows of life as deep and broad as those of its evening? . Yes; but morning shadows soon fade away, while those of evening reach forward into the night, and mingle with the coming darkness. Man is begotten in delight and born in pain ; and in these are the rapture and labor of his life foreshadowed from the beginning. But the life of man upon this fair earth is made up, for the most part, of little pains and little pleasures. The great wonder-flowers bloom but once in a lifetime.

A week had already elapsed since the events recorded in the last chapter. Paul Flemming went his way, a melancholy man, " drinking the sweet wormwood of his sorrow." He did not rail at Providence and call it fate, but suffered and was silent. It is a beautiful trait in the lover's character, that he thinks no evil of the object loved. What he suffered was no swift storm of feeling, that passes away with a noise, and leaves the heart clearer ; but a dark phantom had risen up in the clear night, and, like that of Adamastor, hid the stars ; and if it ever vanished away for a season, still the deep sound of the moaning main would be heard afar, through many a dark and lonely hour. And thus he journeyed on, wrapped in desponding gloom, and mainly heedless of all things around him. His mind was distempered. That one face was always before him ; that one voice was forever saying : —

" You are not the Magician."

Painful indeed it is to be misunderstood and undervalued by those we love. But this, too, in our

life, must we learn to bear without a murmur; for it is a tale often repeated.

There are persons in this world to whom all local associations are naught. The genius of the place speaks not to them. Even on battle-fields, where the voice of this genius is loudest, they hear only the sound of their own voices; they meet there only their own dull and pedantic thoughts, as the old grammarian Brunetto Latini met on the plain of Roncesvalles a poor student riding on a bay mule. This was not always the case with Paul Flemming, but it had become so now. He felt no interest in the scenery around him. He hardly looked at it. Even the difficult mountain-passes, where, from his rocky eyrie, the eagle-eyed Tyrolese peasant had watched his foe, and the roaring, turbid torrent underneath, which had swallowed up the bloody corse, that fell from the rocks like a crushed worm, awakened no lively emotion in his breast. All around him seemed dreamy and vague; all within dim, as in a sun's eclipse. As the moon, whether visible or invisible, has power over the tides of the ocean, so the face of that lady, whether present or absent, had power over the tides of his soul, both by day and night, both waking and sleeping. In every pale face and dark eye he saw a resemblance to her; and what the day denied him in reality the night gave him in dreams.

" This is a strange, fantastic world," said Berkley, after a very long silence, during which the two travellers had been sitting each in his corner of the travelling-carriage, wrapped in his own reflections. " A very strange, fantastic world, where each one

pursues his own golden bubble, and laughs at his neighbor for doing the same. I have been thinking how a moral Linnæus would classify our race. I think he would divide it, — not as Lord Byron did, into two great classes, the bores and those who are bored, — but into three, namely, Happy Men, Lucky Dogs, and Miserable Wretches. This is more true and philosophical, though perhaps not quite so comprehensive. He is the Happy Man who, blessed with modest ease, a wife and children, sits enthroned in the hearts of his family, and knows no other ambition than that of making those around him happy. But the Lucky Dog is he who, free from all domestic cares, saunters up and down his room, in morning gown and slippers; drums on the window, of a rainy day; and, as he stirs his evening fire, snaps his fingers at the world, and says, ' I have no wife nor children, good or bad, to provide for.' I had a friend who is now no more. He was taken away in the bloom of life, by a very rapid —— widow. He was by birth and by profession a beau, — born with a quizzing-glass and a cane. Cock of the walk, he flapped his wings, and crowed among the feathered tribe. But, alas! a fair, white partlet has torn his crest out, and he shall crow no more. In the evening he rocks the cradle, and gets up in the night when the child cries. Like a Goth of the Dark Ages, he consults his wife on all mighty matters, and looks upon her as a being of more than human goodness and wisdom. In short, the women all say he is a very domestic man, and makes a good husband; which, under the rose, is only a more polite way of saying he is hen-

pecked. He is a Happy Man. I have another
dear friend, who is a sexagenary bachelor. He has
one of those well-oiled dispositions which turn upon
the hinges of the world without creaking. The
heyday of life is over with him, but his old age is
sunny and chirping, and a merry heart still nestles
in his tottering frame, like a swallow that builds in
a tumble-down chimney. He is a professed Squire
of Dames. The rustle of a silk gown is music to
his ears, and his imagination is continually lantern-
led by some will-with-a-wisp in the shape of a
lady's stomacher. In his devotion to the fair sex
— the muslin, as he calls it — he is the gentle
flower of chivalry. It is amusing to see how quick
he strikes into the scent of a lady's handkerchief.
When once fairly in pursuit, there is no such thing
as throwing him off. His heart looks out at his
eye; and his inward delight tingles down to the
tail of his coat. He loves to bask in the sunshine
of a smile; when he can breathe the sweet at-
mosphere of kid gloves and cambric handker-
chiefs, his soul is in its element, and his supreme
delight is to pass the morning, to use his own
quaint language, in making dodging calls, and
wriggling round among the ladies! He is a Lucky
Dog."

"And as a specimen of the class of Miserable
Wretches, I suppose you will take me," said Flem-
ming, making an effort to enter into his friend's
humor. "Certainly I am wretched enough. You
may make me the stuffed bear, — the specimen of
this class."

"By no means," replied Berkley; "you are not

reduced so low. He only is utterly wretched who
is the slave of his own passions, or those of others.
This, I trust, will never be your condition. Why
so wan and pale, fond lover? Do you remember
Sir John Suckling's song?

> "Why so wan and pale, fond lover?
> Pr'ythee why so pale?
> Will, if looking well can't move her,
> Looking ill prevail?
> Pr'ythee why so pale?
>
> "Why so dull and mute, young sinner?
> Pr'ythee why so mute?
> Will, if speaking well can't win her,
> Saying nothtng do 't?
> Pr'ythee why so mute?
>
> "Quit, quit, for shame! this cannot move,
> This cannot take her!
> If of herself she do not love,
> Nothing will make her!
> The devil take her!

How do you like that?"

"To you I say quit, quit for shame!" replied
Flemming. "Why quote the songs of that witty
and licentious age? Have you no better consola-
tion to offer me? How many, many times must I
tell you that I bear the lady no ill-will? I do not
blame her for not loving me. I desire her happi-
ness, even at the sacrifice of my own."

"That is generous in you, and deserves a better
fate. But you are so figurative in all you say, that
a stranger would think you had no real feeling, and
only fancied yourself in love."

"Expression of feeling is different with different
minds. It is not always simple. Some minds,

when excited, naturally speak in figures and si-
militudes. They do not on that account feel less
deeply. This is obvious in our most common
modes of speech. It depends upon the individ-
ual."

" Kyrie Eleyson ! "

" Well, abuse my figures of speech as much as
you please. What I insist upon is, that you shall
not abuse the lady. When did you ever hear me
breathe a whisper against her ? "

"Oho ! Now you speak like Launce to his
dog ! "

Their conversation, which had begun so merrily,
was here suddenly interrupted by a rattling peal
of thunder, that announced a near-approaching
storm. It was late in the afternoon, and the whole
heaven black with low, trailing clouds. Still black-
er the storm came sailing up majestically from the
southwest, with almost unbroken volleys of dis-
tant thunder. The wind seemed to be storming
a cloud-redoubt, and marched onward with dust,
and the green banners of the trees flapping in
the air, and heavy cannonading, and occasionally
an explosion, like the blowing up of a powder-
wagon. Mingled with this was the sound of
thunder-bells from a village not far off. They
were all ringing dolefully to ward off the thunder-
bolt. At the entrance of the village stood a large
wooden crucifix, around which was a crowd of
priests and peasants, kneeling in the wet grass, by
the roadside, with their hands and eyes lifted to
heaven, and praying for rain. Their prayer was
soon answered.

The travellers drove on with the driving wind and rain. They had come from Landeck, and hoped to reach Innsbruck before midnight. Night closed in, and Flemming fell asleep with the loud storm overhead, and at his feet the roaring Inn, a mountain torrent leaping onward as wild and restless as when it first sprang from its cradle in the solitudes of Engaddin; meet emblem of himself, thus rushing through the night. His slumber was long, but broken; and at length he awoke in terror; for he heard a voice pronounce in his ear distinctly these words : —

" They have brought the dead body."

They were driving by a churchyard at the entrance of a town; and among the tombs a dim lamp was burning before an image of the Virgin. It had a most unearthly appearance. Flemming almost feared to see the congregation of the dead go into the church and sing their midnight mass. He spoke to Berkley, but received no answer; he was in a deep sleep.

" Then it was only a dream," said he to himself; " yet how distinct the voice was! Oh, if we had spiritual organs, to see and hear things now invisible and inaudible to us, we should behold the whole air filled with the departing souls of that vast multitude which every moment dies, — should behold them streaming up like thin vapors heavenward, and hear the startling blast of the archangel's trump sounding incessant through the universe, and proclaiming the awful judgment-day! Truly, the soul departs not alone on its last journey, but spirits of its kind attend it, when not ministering

angels, and they go in families to the unknown
land! Neither in life nor in death are we alone."

He slept again at intervals; and at length,
though long after midnight, reached Innsbruck
between sleeping and waking, his mind filled with
dim recollections of the unspeakably dismal night
journey; — the climbing of hills, and plunging
into dark ravines; the momentary rattling of the
wheels over paved streets of towns, and the suc-
ceeding hollow rolling and tramping on the wet
earth; the blackness of the night; the thunder and
lightning and rain; the roar of waters, leaping
through deep chasms by the roadside; and the
wind through the mountain-passes, sounding loud
and long, like the inextinguishable laughter of
the gods.

The travellers on the morrow lingered not long
in Innsbruck. They did not fail, however, to visit
the tomb of Maximilian in the Franciscan Church
of the Holy Cross, and gaze with some admiration
upon the twenty-eight gigantic bronze statues
of Godfrey of Bouillon, and King Arthur, and
Ernest the Iron-man, and Frederick of the Empty
Pockets, kings and heroes, and others, which stand
leaning on their swords between the columns of
the church, as if guarding the tomb of the dead.
These statues reminded Flemming of the bronze
giants which strike the hours on the belfry of San
Basso, in Venice, and of the flail-armed monsters
that guarded the gateway of Angulaffer's castle in
Oberon. After gazing awhile at these motionless
sentinels, they went forth, and strolled through the
public gardens, with the jagged mountains right

over their heads, and all around them tall, melancholy pines, like Tyrolese peasants, with shaggy hair; and at their feet the mad torrent of the Inn, sweeping with turbid waves through the midst of the town. In the afternoon, they drove on towards Salzburg, through the magnificent mountain-passes of Waidering and Unken.

CHAPTER III.

SHADOWS ON THE WALL.

On the following morning, Flemming awoke in a chamber of the Golden Ship at Salzburg, just as the clock in the cathedral opposite was striking ten. The window-shutters were closed, and the room was nearly dark. He was lying with his hands crossed upon his breast, and his eyes looking up at the white curtains overhead. He thought them the white marble canopy of a tomb, and himself the marble statue lying beneath. When the clock ceased striking, the eight-and-twenty gigantic bronze statues from the Church of Holy Rood in Innsbruck stalked into the chamber, and arranged themselves along the walls, which spread into dimly lighted aisles and arches. On the painted windows he saw Interlachen, with its Franciscan cloister, and the Square Tower of the ruins. In a pendant, overhead, stood the German mechanic, as Saint Vitus; and on a lavatory, below, sat a cherub, with the form and features of Berkley. Then the organ-pipes began to blow, and he heard the voices of an invisible choir chanting. And

anon the gilded gates in the bronze screen before
the chancel opened, and a bridal procession passed
through. The bride was clothed in the garb of
the Middle Ages, and held a book in her hand,
with velvet covers, and golden clasps. It was
Mary Ashburton. She looked at him as she passed.
Her face was pale, and there were tears in her
sweet eyes. Then the gates closed again, and one
of the oaken poppy-heads over a carved stall, in
the shape of an owl, flapped its broad wings, and
hooted, " To-whit! to-who! " Then the whole
scene changed, and he thought himself a monk's-
head on a gutter-spout; and it rained dismally,
and Berkley was standing underneath with an um-
brella, laughing!

In other words, Flemming was in a raging fever,
and delirious. He remained in this state for a
week. The first thing he was conscious of was
hearing the doctor say to Berkley : —

" The crisis is passed. I now consider him out
of danger."

He then fell into a sweet sleep; the wild fever
had swept away like an angry, red cloud, and the
refreshing summer rain began to fall like dew
upon the parched earth. Still another week, and
Flemming was " sitting clothed, and in his right
mind." Berkley had been reading to him, and
still held the book in his hand, with his fore-finger
between the leaves. It was a volume of Hoff-
mann's writings.

" How very strange it is," said he, " that you
can hardly open the biography of any German
author, but you will find it begin with an account

of his grandfather! It will tell you how the venerable old man walked up and down the garden among the gay flowers, wrapped in his morning gown, which is likewise covered with flowers, and perhaps wearing on his head a little velvet cap. Or you will find him sitting by the chimney-corner in the great chair, smoking his ancestral pipe, with shaggy eyebrows, and eyes like bird's-nests under the eaves of a house, and a mouth like a Nuremberg nutcracker's. The future poet climbs upon the old man's knees. His genius is not recognized yet. He is thought for the most part a dull boy. His father is an austere man, or perhaps dead. But the mother is still there, a sickly, saint-like woman, with knitting-work; and an elder sister, who has already been in love, and wears rings on her fingers : —

> " Death's heads, and such mementoes,
> Her grandmother and worm-eaten aunts left to her,
> To tell her what her beauty must arrive at."

" But this is not the case with the life of Hoffmann, if I recollect right."

" No, not precisely. Instead of the grandfather, we have the grandmother, a stately dame, who has long since shaken hands with the vanities of life. The mother, separated from her husband, is sick in mind and body, and flits to and fro like a shadow. Then there is an affectionate maiden aunt; and an uncle, a retired judge, the terror of little boys, — the Giant Despair of this Doubting Castle in Königsberg; and occasionally the benign countenance of a venerable grand-uncle, whom La Motte Fouqué called a hero of the olden time in morning

gown and slippers, looks in at the door and smiles.
In the upper story of the same house lived a poor
boy with his mother, who was so far crazed as to
believe herself to be the Virgin Mary, and her son
the Saviour of the world. Wild fancies, likewise,
were to sweep through the brain of that child.
He was to meet Hoffmann elsewhere and be his
friend in after years, though as yet they knew
nothing of each other. This was Werner, who has
made some noise in German literature as the author
of many wild Destiny-Dramas."

"Hoffmann died, I believe, in Berlin."

"Yes. He left Königsberg at twenty years of
age, and passed the next eight years of his life in
the Prussian-Polish provinces, where he held some
petty office under government, and took to himself
many bad habits and a Polish wife. After this he
was Music-Director at various German theatres,
and led a wandering, wretched life for ten years.
He then went to Berlin as Clerk of the Exchange,
and there remained till his death, which took place
some seven or eight years afterward."

"Did you ever see him ?"

"I was in Berlin during his lifetime, and saw
him frequently. I shall never forget the first time.
It was at one of the Æsthetic Teas given by a lit-
erary lady *unter den Linden,* where the lions were
fed with convenient food, from tea and bread and
butter up to oysters and Rhine-wine. During the
evening, my attention was arrested by the entrance
of a strange little figure, with a wild head of brown
hair. His eyes were bright gray, and his thin
lips closely pressed together with an expression of

not unpleasing irony. This strange-looking personage began to bow his way through the crowd, with quick, nervous, hinge-like motions, much resembling those of a marionnette. He had a hoarse voice, and such a rapid utterance that, although I understand German well enough for ordinary purposes, I could not make out one half he said. Erelong he had seated himself at the piano-forte, and was improvising such wild, sweet fancies, that the music of one's dreams is not more sweet and wild. Then suddenly some painful thought seemed to pass over his mind, as if he imagined that he was there to amuse the company. He rose from the piano-forte, and seated himself in another part of the room, where he began to make grimaces, and talk loud while others were singing. Finally he disappeared like a hobgoblin, laughing, ' Ho ! ho ! ho ! ' I asked a person beside me who this strange being was. ' That is Hoffmann,' was the answer. ' The Devil ! ' said I. ' Yes,' continued my informant, ' and if you should follow him now, you would see him plunge into an obscure and unfrequented wine-cellar, and there, amid boon companions, with wine and tobacco-smoke, and quirks and quibbles, and quaint, witty sayings, turn the dim night into glorious day.' "

" What a strange being ! "

" I once saw him at one of his night-carouses. He was sitting in his glory, at the head of the table ; not stupidly drunk, but warmed with wine, which made him madly eloquent, as the Devil's Elixir did the monk Medardus. There, in the full tide of witty discourse, or, if silent, his gray hawk-

eye flashing from beneath his matted hair, and
taking note of all that was grotesque in the com-
pany round him, sat this unfortunate genius, till
the day began to dawn. Then he found his way
homeward, having, like the souls of the envious in
Purgatory, his eyelids sewed together with iron
wire ; — though his was from champagne bottles.
At such hours he wrote his wild, fantastic tales.
To his excited fancy everything assumed a spectral
look. The shadows of familiar things about him
stalked like ghosts through the haunted chambers
of his soul ; and the old portraits on the walls
winked at him, and seemed stepping down from
their frames ; till, aghast at the spectral throng
about him, he would call his wife from her bed, to
sit by him while he wrote."

" No wonder he died in the prime of life ! "

" No. The only wonder is, that he could have
followed this course of life for six years. I am
astonished that it did not kill him sooner."

" But death came at last in an appalling shape."

"Yes ; his forty-sixth birthday found him sitting
at home in his arm-chair, with his friends around
him. But the rare old wine — he always drank
the best — touched not the sick man's lips that
night. His wonted humor was gone. Of all his
' jibes, his gambols, his songs, his flashes of mer-
riment, that were wont to set the table on a roar,
not one now, to mock his own grinning ! — quite
chapfallen.' The conversation was of death and
the grave. And when one of his friends said that
life was not the highest good, Hoffmann interrupted
him, exclaiming, with a startling earnestness, ' No,

no! Life, life, only life! on any condition what-
soever!' Five months after this he had ceased to
suffer, because he had ceased to live. He died
piecemeal. His feet and hands, his legs and arms,
gradually, and in succession, became motionless,
dead. But his spirit was not dead, nor motionless;
and, through the solitary day or sleepless night,
lying in his bed, he dictated to an amanuensis his
last stories. Strange stories, indeed, were they for
a dying man to write! Yet such delight did he
take in dictating them, that he said to his friend
Hitzig, that, upon the whole, he was willing to give
up forever the use of his hands, if he could but
preserve the power of writing by dictation. Such
was his love of life, — of what he called the sweet
habitude of being!' "

" Was it not he, who in his last hours expressed
such a longing to behold the green fields once more,
and exclaimed, 'Heaven! it is already summer,
and I have not yet seen a single green tree'?' "

"Yes, that was Hoffmann. Soon afterwards he
died. The closing scene was striking. He grad-
ually lost all sensation, though his mind remained
vigorous. Feeling no more pain, he said to his
physician: 'It will soon be over now. I feel no
more pain.' He thought himself well again; but
the physician knew that he was dying, and said,
'Yes, it will soon be over!' The next morning
he called his wife to his bedside, and begged her
to fold his motionless hands together. Then, as
he raised his eyes to heaven, she heard him say,
'We must, then, think of God, also!' More sor-
rowful words than these have seldom fallen from

the lips of man. Shortly afterwards the flame of life glared up within him; he said he was well again; that in the evening he should go on with the story he was writing; and wished that the last sentence might be read over to him. Shortly after this they turned his face to the wall, and he died."

"And thus passed to its account a human soul, after much self-inflicted suffering. Let us tread lightly upon the poet's ashes. For my part, I confess that I have not the heart to take him from the general crowd of erring, sinful men, and judge him harshly. The little I have seen of the world, and know of the history of mankind, teaches me to look upon the errors of others in sorrow, not in anger. When I take the history of one poor heart that has sinned and suffered, and represent to myself the struggles and temptations it has passed, — the brief pulsations of joy, the feverish inquietude of hope and fear, the tears of regret, the feebleness of purpose, the pressure of want, the desertion of friends, the scorn of a world that has little charity, the desolation of the soul's sanctuary, and threatening voices within, — health gone, happiness gone, — even hope, that stays longest with us, gone, — I have little heart for aught else than thankfulness that it is not so with me, and would fain leave the erring soul of my fellow-man with Him from whose hands it came,

"Even as a little girl,
Weeping and laughing in her childish sport."

"You are right. And it is worth a student's while to observe calmly how tobacco, wine, and midnight did their work like fiends upon the deli-

cate frame of Hoffmann ; and no less thoroughly upon his delicate mind. He who drinks beer thinks beer ; and he who drinks wine thinks wine ; and he who drinks midnight thinks midnight. He was a man of rare intellect. He was endowed with racy humor, and sarcastic wit, and a glorious imagination. But the fire of his genius burned not peacefully and with a steady flame upon the hearth of his home. It was a glaring and irregular flame ; for the branches that he fed it with were not branches from the Tree of Life, but from another tree that grew in Paradise, and they were wet with the unhealthy dews of night, and more unhealthy wine ; and thus, amid smoke and ashes, the fire burned fitfully, and went out with a glare which leaves the beholder blind."

"This fire within him was a Meleager's firebrand ; and when it burned out, he died. And, as you say, marks of all this are clearly visible in Hoffmann's writings. Indeed, when I read his strange fancies, it is with me as when in the summer night I hear the rising wind among the trees, and the branches bow, and beckon with their long fingers, and voices go gibbering and mocking through the air. A feeling of awe and mysterious dread comes over me. I wish to hear the sound of living voice or footstep near me, — to see a friendly and familiar face. In truth, if it be late at night, the reader as well as the writer of these unearthly fancies would fain have a patient, meek-eyed wife, with her knitting-work, at his elbow."

Berkley smiled ; but Flemming continued without noticing the smile, though he knew what was passing in the mind of his friend : —

" The life and writings of this singular being interest me in a high degree. Sometimes we may learn more from a man's errors than from his virtues. Moreover, from the common sympathies of our nature, souls that have struggled and suffered are dear to me. Willingly do I recognize their brotherhood. Scars upon their foreheads do not so deform them that they cease to interest. They are always signs of struggle, though, alas! too often, likewise, of defeat. Seasons of unhealthy, dreamy, vague delight are followed by seasons of weariness and darkness. Where are then the bright fancies, that, amid the great stillness of the night, arise like stars in the firmament of our souls? The morning dawns, the light of common day shines in upon us, and the heavens are without a star! From the lives of such men we learn that mere pleasant sensations are not happiness; that sensual pleasures are to be drunk sparingly, and, as it were, from the palm of the hand; and that those who bow down upon their knees to drink of these bright streams that water life are not chosen of God either to overthrow or overcome! "

" I think you are very lenient in your judgment. This is not the usual defect of critics. Like Shakespeare's samphire-gatherer, they have a dreadful trade! and, to make the simile complete, they ought to hang for it! "

" Methinks it would be hard to hang a man for the sake of a simile. But now go on with the Phantasy-Pieces in Callot's manner."

" By the way, who was this Callot? "

" He was a Lorraine painter, of the seventeenth

century, celebrated for his wild and grotesque con-
ceptions. These sketches of Hoffmann are imita-
tions of his style."

" And which of them shall I read to you next?
The Ritter Glück; or the Musical Sufferings of
John Kreisler; or that exquisite story of the
Golden Jar, wherein is depicted the life of Poesy
in this commonplace world of ours?"

" Read the shortest. Read Kreisler. That
will amuse me. It is a picture of his own suffer-
ings at the Æsthetic Teas in Berlin, supposed to be
written in pencil on the blank leaves of a music-
book."

Thereupon Berkley leaned back in his easy-
chair, and read as follows.

CHAPTER IV.

MUSICAL SUFFERINGS OF JOHN KREISLER.

" They are all gone! I might have known it
by the whispering, shuffling, coughing, humming
through all the notes of the gamut. It was a true
swarm of bees, leaving the old hive. Gottlieb has
lighted fresh candles for me, and placed a bottle of
Burgundy on the piano-forte. I can play no more,
I am perfectly exhausted. My glorious old friend
here on the music-stand is to blame for that. Again
he has borne me away through the air, as Mephis-
topheles did Faust, and so high, that I took not the
slightest notice of the little men under me, though
I dare say they made noise enough. A rascally,
worthless, wasted evening! But now I am well

and merry! However, while I was playing, I took out my pencil, and on page sixty-three, under the last staff, noted down a couple of good flourishes in cipher with my right hand, while the left was struggling away in the torrent of sweet sounds. Upon the blank page at the end I go on writing. I leave all ciphers and sweet sounds, and with true delight, like a sick man restored to health, who can never stop relating what he has suffered, I note down here circumstantially the dire agonies of this evening's tea-party. And not for myself alone, but likewise for all those who from time to time may amuse and edify themselves with my copy of John Sebastian Bach's Variations for the Piano-forte, published by Nägeli in Zürich, and who find my marks at the end of the thirtieth variation, and, led on by the great Latin *Verte* (I will write it down the moment I get through this doleful statement of grievances) turn over the leaf and read.

"They will at once see the connection. They know that the Geheimerath Rödelein's house is a charming house to visit in, and that he has two daughters, of whom the whole fashionable world proclaims with enthusiasm that they dance like goddesses, speak French like angels, and play and sing and draw like the Muses. The Geheimerath Rödelein is a rich man. At his quarterly dinners he sends up the most delicious wines and richest dishes. All is established on a footing of the greatest elegance ; and whoever at his tea-parties does not amuse himself heavenly, has no *ton*, no *esprit*, and particularly no taste for the fine arts. It is with an eye to these that, with the tea, punch,

wine, ices, etc., a little music is always served up, which, like the other refreshments, is very quietly swallowed by the fashionable world.

" The arrangements are as follows. After every guest has had time enough to drink as many cups of tea as he may wish, and punch and ices have been handed round twice, the servants wheel out the card-tables for the elder and more solid part of the company, who had rather play cards than any musical instrument ; and, in fact, this kind of playing does not make such a useless noise as the other, and you hear only the clink of money.

" This is a hint for the younger part of the company to pounce upon the Misses Rödelein. A great tumult ensues ; in the midst of which you can distinguish these words : —

" ' *Schönes Fräulein !* do not refuse us the gratification of your heavenly talent ! Oh, sing something ! that 's a good dear ! — impossible, — bad cold, — the last ball ! have not practised anything. — Oh, do, do, we beg of you,' etc.

" Meanwhile Gottlieb has opened the pianoforte, and placed the well-known music-book on the stand ; and from the card-table cries the respectable mamma, —

" ' *Chantez donc, mes enfants !* '

" That is the cue of *my* part. I place myself at the piano-forte, and the Rödeleins are led up to the instrument in triumph.

" And now another difficulty arises. Neither wishes to sing first.

" ' You know, dear Nanette, how dreadfully hoarse I am.'

" ' Why, my dear Marie, I am as hoarse as you are.'

" ' I sing so badly ! ' —

" ' Oh, my dear child ; *do* begin ! '

" My suggestion, (I always make the same !) that they should both begin together with a duet, is loudly applauded ; — the music-book is thumbed over, and the leaf, carefully folded down, is at length found, and away we go with *Dolce dell' anima*, etc.

" To tell the truth, the talent of the Misses Rödelein is not the smallest. I have been an instructor here only five years, and little short of two years in the Rödelein family. In this short time, Fräulein Nanette has made such progress, that a tune, which she has heard at the theatre only ten times, and has played on the piano-forte, at farthest, ten times more, she will sing right off, so that you know in a moment what it is. Fräulein Marie catches it at the eighth time; and if she is sometimes a quarter of a note lower than the piano-forte, after all it is very tolerable, considering her pretty little doll-face, and very passable rosy lips.

" After the duet, a universal chorus of applause! And now ariettas and duettinos succeed each other, and right merrily I hammer away at the thousand-times-repeated accompaniments. During the singing, the Finanzräthin Eberstein, by coughing and humming, has given us to understand that she also sings. Fräulein Nanette says : —

" ' But, my dear Finanzräthin, now you must let us hear *your* exquisite voice.'

" A new tumult arises. She has a bad cold in her head, — she does not know anything by heart! Gottlieb brings straightway two armfuls of music-books; and the leaves are turned over again and again. First she thinks she will sing *Der Hölle Rache*, etc., then *Hebe sich*, etc., then *Ach, Ich liebte*, etc. In this embarrassment, I propose, *Ein Veilchen auf der Wiese*, etc. But she is for the heroic style; she wants to make a display, and finally selects *Constanze*.

" Oh, scream, squeak, mew, gurgle, groan, ago-nize, quiver, quaver, just as much as you please, Madam, I have my foot on the fortissimo pedal, and thunder myself deaf! O Satan, Satan! which of thy goblins damned has got into this throat, pinching, and kicking, and cuffing the tones about so! Four strings have snapped already, and one hammer is lamed for life. My ears ring again, — my head hums, — my nerves tremble! Have all the harsh notes from the cracked trumpet of a mountebank been imprisoned in this little throat! (But this excites me, — I must drink a glass of Burgundy.)

" The applause was unbounded, and some one observed, that the Finanzräthin and Mozart had put me quite into a blaze. I smiled with downcast eyes, very stupidly. I could but acknowledge it. And now all talents, which hitherto had bloomed unseen, were in motion, wildly flitting to and fro. They were bent upon a surfeit of music; tuttis, finales, choruses, must be performed. The Canon-icus Kratzer sings, you know, a heavenly bass, as was observed by the gentleman yonder, with the

head of Titus Andronicus, who modestly remarked also, that he himself was properly only a second-rate tenor ; but, though he said it who should not say it, he was nevertheless member of several academies of music. Forthwith preparations are made for the first chorus in the opera of Titus. It went off gloriously. The Canonicus, standing close behind me, thundered out the bass over my head, as if he were singing with bass-drums and trumpet *obligato* in a cathedral. He struck the notes gloriously ; but in his hurry he got the *tempo* about twice too slow. However, he was true to himself at least in this, that through the whole piece he dragged along just half a beat behind the rest. The others showed a most decided *penchant* for the ancient Greek music, which, as is well known, having nothing to do with harmony, ran on in *unison* or monotone. They all sang treble, with slight variations, caused by accidental rising or falling of the voice, say some quarter of a note.

" This somewhat noisy affair produced a universal tragic state of feeling, namely a kind of terror, even at the card-tables, which for the moment could no longer, as before, chime in melodramatically, by weaving into the music sundry exclamations ; as, for instance : —

" ' Oh ! I loved, — eight and forty, — was so happy, — I pass, — then I knew not, — whist, — pangs of love, — follow suit,' etc. — It has a very pretty effect. (I fill my glass.)

" That was the highest point of the musical exhibition this evening. ' Now it is all over,' thought

I to myself. I shut the book, and got up from the piano-forte. But the Baron, my ancient tenor, came up to me and said : —

"'My dear Herr Capellmeister, they say you play the most exquisite voluntaries! Now do play us one; only a short one, I entreat you!'

" I answered very dryly, that to-day my fantasies had all gone a wool-gathering; and while we are talking about it, a devil, in the shape of a dandy, with two waistcoats, had smelt out Bach's Variations, which were lying under my hat in the next room. He thinks they are merely little variations, such as *Nel cor mio non più sento*, or *Ah vous dirai-je, maman*, etc., and insists upon it that I *shall* play them. I try to excuse myself, but they all attack me. So then, ' Listen, and burst with ennui,' think I to myself, and begin to work away.

" When I had got to variation number three, several ladies departed, followed by the gentleman with the Titus-Andronicus head. The Rödeleins, as their teacher was playing, stood it out, though not without difficulty, to number twelve. Number fifteen made the man with two waistcoats take to his heels. Out of most excessive politeness, the Baron stayed till number thirty, and drank up all the punch which Gottlieb placed on the piano-forte for me.

" I should have brought all to a happy conclusion, but, alas! this number thirty — the theme — tore me irresistibly away. Suddenly the quarto leaves spread out to a gigantic folio, on which a thousand imitations and developments of the theme stood written, and I could not choose but play

them. The notes became alive, and glimmered and hopped all round about me, — an electric fire streamed through the tips of my fingers into the keys, — the spirit from which it gushed forth spread his broad wings over my soul, the whole room was filled with a thick mist, in which the candles burned dim, — and through which peered forth now a nose, and anon a pair of eyes, and then suddenly vanished away again. And thus it came to pass that I was left alone with my Sebastian Bach, by Gottlieb attended, as by a familiar spirit. (Your good health, Sir.)

"Is an honest musician to be tormented with music, as I have been to-day, and am so often tormented? Verily, no art is so damnably abused as this same glorious, holy Musica, who, in her delicate being, is so easily desecrated. Have you real talent, — real feeling for art? Then study music, — do something worthy of the art, — and dedicate your whole soul to the beloved saint. If without this you have a fancy for quavers and demi-semiquavers, practise for yourself and by yourself, and torment not therewith the Capellmeister Kreisler and others.

"Well, now I might go home, and put the finishing touch to my sonata for the piano-forte; but it is not yet eleven o'clock, and, withal, a beautiful summer night. I will lay any wager that at my neighbor's, the Oberjägermeister, the young ladies are sitting at the window, screaming down into the street, for the twentieth time, with harsh, sharp, piercing voices, 'When thine eye is beaming, love,' — but only the first stanza, over and over again.

Obliquely across the way, some one is murdering
the flute, and has, moreover, lungs like Rameau's
nephew; and, in notes of 'linked sweetness long
drawn out,' his neighbor is trying acoustic experi-
ments on the French horn. The numerous dogs
of the neighborhood are growing unquiet, and my
landlord's cat, inspired by that sweet duet, is mak-
ing, by my window (for, of course, my musico-
poetic laboratory is an attic) certain tender con-
fessions, upward through the whole chromatic
scale, soft complaining, to the neighbor's tabby,
with whom he has been in love since March last!
Till this is all fairly over, I think I will sit quietly
here. Besides, there is still blank paper and Bur-
gundy left, of which I forthwith take a sip.

"There is, as I have heard, an ancient law, for-
bidding those who follow any noisy handicraft from
living near literary men. Should not then musi-
cal composers, poor and hard beset, and who,
moreover, are forced to coin their inspiration into
gold to spin out the thread of life withal, be al-
lowed to apply this law to themselves, and banish
out of the neighborhood all ballad-singers and bag-
pipers? What would a painter say, while trans-
ferring to his canvas a form of ideal beauty, if
you should hold up before him all manner of wild
faces and ugly masks? He might shut his eyes,
and in this way, at least, quietly follow out the
images of fancy. Cotton, in one's ears, is of no
use; one still hears the dreadful massacre. And
then the idea, — the bare idea, 'Now they are
going to sing, — now the horn strikes up,' — is
enough to send one's sublimest thoughts to the
very Devil."

CHAPTER V.

SAINT GILGEN.

It was a bright Sunday morning when Flemming and Berkley left behind them the cloud-capped hills of Salzburg, and journeyed eastward towards the lakes. The landscape around them was one to attune their souls to holy musings. Field, forest, hill and vale, fresh air, and the perfume of clover-fields and new-mown hay, birds singing, and the sound of village bells, and the moving breeze among the branches, — no laborers in the fields, but peasants on their way to church, coming across the green pastures, with roses in their hats, — the beauty and quiet of the holy day of rest, — all, all in earth and air breathed upon the soul like a benediction.

They stopped to change horses at Hof, a handful of houses on the brow of a breezy hill, the church and inn standing opposite to each other, and nothing between them but the dusty road, and the churchyard with its iron crosses and the fluttering tinsel of the funeral garlands. In the churchyard, and at the inn-door, were groups of peasants, waiting for divine service to begin. They were clothed in their holiday dresses. The men wore breeches and long boots and frock-coats with large metal buttons; the women, straw hats and gay calico gowns with short waists and scant folds. They were adorned with a profusion of great trumpery ornaments, and reminded Flemming of the Indians in the frontier villages of America. Near the church-

yard-gate was a booth, filled with flaunting cali-
coes ; and opposite sat an old woman behind a
table, which was loaded with gingerbread. She
had a roulette at her elbow, where the peasants
risked a kreutzer for a cake. On other tables,
cases of knives, scythes, reaping-hooks, and other
implements of husbandry were offered for sale.

The travellers continued their journey, without
stopping to hear mass. In the course of the fore-
noon, they came suddenly in sight of the beautiful
lake of Saint Wolfgang, lying deep beneath them
in the valley. On its shore, under them, sat the
white village of Saint Gilgen, like a swan upon its
reedy nest. They seemed to have taken it un-
awares, and, as it were, clapped their hands upon
it in its sleep, and almost expected to see it spread
its broad snow-white wings and fly away. The
whole scene was one of surpassing beauty.

They drove leisurely down the steep hill, and
stopped at the village inn. Before the door was a
magnificent broad-armed tree, with benches and
tables beneath its shadow. On the front of the
house was written in large letters, " Post-Tavern
by Franz Schöndorfer ; " and over this was a large
sun-dial, and a half-effaced painting of a bear-
hunt, covering the whole side of the house, and
mostly red. As they drove up, a procession of
priests with banners, and peasants with their hats
in their hands, passed by towards the church.
They were singing a solemn psalm. At the same
moment, a smart servant-girl, with a black straw
hat set coquettishly on her flaxen hair, and a large
silver spoon in her girdle, came out of the inn, and

asked Flemming what he would please to order for
breakfast.

Breakfast was soon ready, and was served at the
head of the stairs, on an old-fashioned oaken table
in the great hall, into which the chambers opened.
Berkley ordered at the same time a tub of cold
water, in which he seated himself, with his coat on,
and a bed-quilt thrown round his knees. Thus he
sat for an hour; ate his breakfast, and smoked a
pipe, and laughed a good deal. He then went to
bed and slept till dinner-time. Meanwhile Flem-
ming sat in his chamber and read. It was a large
room in the front of the house, looking upon the
village and the lake. The windows were latticed,
with small panes, and the window-sills filled with
fragrant flowers.

At length the heat of noon was over. Day, like
a weary pilgrim, had reached the western gate of
heaven, and Evening stooped down to unloose the
latchets of his sandal-shoon. Flemming and Berk-
ley sallied forth to ramble by the borders of the
lake. Down the cool green glades and alleys, be-
neath the illuminated leaves of the forest, over the
rising grounds in the glimmering fretwork of sun-
shine and leaf-shadow, — an exhilarating walk!
The cool evening air by the lake was like a bath.
They drank the freshness of the hour in thirsty
draughts, and their breasts heaved rejoicing and
revived, after the feverish, long confinement of the
sultry summer day. And there, too, lay the lake,
so beautiful and still! Did it not recall, think ye,
the lake of Thun?

On their return homeward, they passed near the
village churchyard.

"Let us go in and see how the dead rest," said
Flemming, as they passed beneath the belfry of
the church; and they went in, and lingered among
the tombs and the evening shadows.

How peaceful is the dwelling-place of those who
inhabit the green hamlets and populous cities of
the dead! They need no antidote for care, — no
armor against fate. No morning sun shines in at
the closed windows and awakens them, nor shall
until the last great day. At most, a straggling
sunbeam creeps in through the crumbling wall of
an old, neglected tomb, — a strange visitor, that
stays not long. And there they all sleep, the holy
ones, with their arms crossed upon their breasts,
or lying motionless by their sides, — not carved in
marble by the hand of man, but formed in dust by
the hand of God. God's peace be with them! No
one comes to them now, to hold them by the hand,
and with delicate fingers to smooth their hair.
They heed no more the blandishments of earthly
friendship. They need us not, however much we
may need them. And yet they silently await our
coming.

Beautiful is that season of life, when we can
say, in the language of Scripture, "Thou hast the
dew of thy youth." But of these flowers Death
gathers many. He places them upon his bosom,
and he is transformed into something less terrific
than before. We learn to gaze and shudder not;
for he carries in his arms the sweet blossoms of
our earthly hopes. We shall see them all again,
blooming in a happier land.

Yes, Death brings us again to our friends. They

are waiting for us, and we shall not long delay. They have gone before us, and are like the angels in heaven. They stand upon the borders of the grave to welcome us, with the countenance of affection which they wore on earth ; yet more lovely, more radiant, more spiritual ! He spake well who said that graves are the footprints of angels !

Death has taken thee, too, and thou hast the dew of thy youth. He has placed thee upon his bosom, and his stern countenance wears a smile. The far country, toward which we journey, seems nearer to us, and the way less dark ; for thou hast gone before, passing so quietly to thy rest, that day itself dies not more calmly !

It was in an hour of blessed communion with the souls of the departed, that the sweet poet Henry Vaughan wrote those few lines which have made death lovely.

> They are all gone into a world of light,
> And I alone sit lingering here !
> Their very memory is fair and bright,
> And my sad thoughts doth clear.
>
> It glows and glitters in my cloudy breast,
> Like stars upon some gloomy grove,
> Or those faint beams in which the hill is dressed
> After the sun's remove.
>
> I see them walking in an air of glory,
> Whose light doth trample on my days,
> My days, which are at best but dull and hoary,
> Mere glimmerings and decays.
>
> O holy hope, and high humility,
> High as the heavens above !
> These are your walks, and ye have showed them me,
> To kindle my cold love.

Dear, beauteous Death! the jewel of the just!
 Shining nowhere but in the dark!
What mysteries do lie beyond thy dust,
 Could man outlook that mark!

He that hath found some fledged bird's nest may know,
 At first sight, if the bird be flown;
But what fair field or grove he sings in now,
 That is to him unknown.

And yet as angels, in some brighter dreams,
 Call to the soul when man doth sleep,
So some strange thoughts transcend our wonted themes,
 And into glory peep.

If a star were confined into a tomb,
 Her captive flame must needs burn there,
But when the hand that locked her up gave room
 She'd shine through all the sphere.

O Father of eternal life, and all
 Created glories under thee!
Resume thy spirit from this world of thrall
 Into true liberty.

Either disperse these mists, which blot and fill
 My perspective, still as they pass,
Or else remove me hence unto that hill
 Where I shall need no glass.

Such were Flemming's thoughts, as he stood among the tombs at evening in the churchyard of Saint Gilgen. A holy calm stole over him. The fever of his heart was allayed. He had a moment's rest from pain, and went back to his chamber in peace. Whence came this holy calm, this long-desired tranquillity? He knew not; yet the place seemed consecrated. He resolved to linger there beside the lake, which was a Pool of Bethesda for him; and let Berkley go on alone to the baths

of Ischel. He would wait for him there in the solitude of Saint Gilgen. Long after they had parted for the night, he sat in his chamber, and thought of what he had suffered, and enjoyed the silence within and without. Hour after hour slipped by unheeded, as he sat lost in his reverie. At length, his candle sank in its socket, gave one flickering gleam, and expired with a sob. This aroused him.

He went to the window, and peered out into the dark night. It was very late. Twice already since midnight had the great pulpit-orator Time, like a preacher in the days of the Puritans, turned the hour-glass on his high pulpit, the church-belfry, and still went on with his sermon, thundering downward to the congregation in the churchyard and in the village. But they heard him not. They were all asleep in their narrow pews, namely, in their beds and in their graves. Soon afterward the cock crew; and the cloudy heaven, like the Apostle who denied his Lord, wept bitterly.

CHAPTER VI.

SAINT WOLFGANG.

The morning is lovely beyond expression. The heat of the sun is great; but a gentle wind cools the air. Birds never sang more loud and clear. The flowers, too, on the window-sill, and on the table, rose, geranium, and the delicate crimson cactus, are all so beautiful, that we think the German poet right, when he calls the flowers "stars in the

firmament of the earth." Out of doors all is quiet.
Opposite the window stands the village school-
house. There are two parasite trees, with their
outspread branches nailed against the white walls,
like the wings of culprit kites. There the rods
grow. Under them, on a bench at the door, sit
school-girls; and barefoot urchins in breeches are
spelling out their lessons. The clock strikes twelve,
and one by one they disappear, and go into the
hive, like bees at the sound of a brass pan. At
the door of the next house sits a poor woman, knit-
ting in the shade ; and in front of her is an aque-
duct, pouring its cool, clear water into a rough,
wooden trough. A travelling-carriage, without
horses, stands at the inn-door, and a postilion in
red jacket is talking with a blacksmith, who wears
blue woollen stockings and a leather apron. Be-
yond is a stable, and still farther a cluster of houses
and the village church. They are repairing the
belfry and the bulbous steeple. A little farther,
over the roofs of the houses, you can see Saint
Wolfgang's lake. Water so bright and beautiful
hardly flows elsewhere. Green and blue and sil-
ver-white run into each other, with almost imper-
ceptible change. And above are the pinnacles
of the mountains ; some bald, and rocky, and
cone-shaped, and others bold, and broad, and dark
with pines.

Such was the scene which Paul Flemming be-
held from his window a few mornings after
Berkley's departure. The quiet of the place had
soothed him. He had become more calm. His
heart complained less loudly in the holy village

silence, as we are wont to lower our voices when those around us speak in whispers. He began to feel at times an interest in the lowly things about him. The face of the landscape pleased him, but more than this the face of the poor woman who sat knitting in the shade. It was a pale, meek countenance, with more delicacy in its features than is usual among peasantry. It wore also an expression of patient suffering. As he was looking at her, a deformed child came out of the door and hung upon her knees. She caressed it affectionately. It was her child, in whom she beheld her own fair features distorted and hardly to be recognized, as one sometimes sees one's face reflected from the bowl of a spoon.

The child's deformity and the mother's tenderness interested the feelings of Flemming. The landlady told him something of the poor woman's history. She was the widow of a blacksmith, who had died soon after their marriage. But she survived to become a mother, as, in oaks, immediately after fecundation, the male flower fades and falls, while the female continues and ripens into perfect fruit. Alas! her child was deformed. Yet she looked upon him with eyes of maternal fondness and pity, loving him still more for his deformity. And in her heart she said, as the Mexicans say to their new-born offspring, — " Child, thou art come into the world to suffer. Endure, and hold thy peace." Though poor, she was not entirely destitute; for her husband had left her, besides the deformed child, a life estate in a tomb in the churchyard of Saint Gilgen. During the week

she labored for other people, and on Sundays for herself, by going to church and reading the Bible. On one of the blank leaves she had recorded the day of her birth, and that of her child's, likewise her marriage and her husband's death. Thus she lived, poor, patient, and resigned. Her heart was a passion-flower, bearing within it the crown of thorns and the cross of Christ. Her ideas of heaven were few and simple. She rejected the doctrine that it was a place of constant activity, and not of repose, and believed that, when she at length reached it, she should work no more, but sit always in a clean white apron, and sing psalms.

As Flemming sat meditating on these things, he paid new homage in his heart to the beauty and excellence of the female character. He thought of the absent and the dead ; and said, with tears in his eyes : —

" Shall I thank God for the green summer, and the mild air, and the flowers, and the stars, and all that makes this world so beautiful, and not for the good and beautiful beings I have known in it? Has not their presence been sweeter to me than flowers ? Are they not higher and holier than the stars ? Are they not more to me than all things else ? "

Thus the morning passed away in musings ; and in the afternoon, when Flemming was preparing to go down to the lake, as his custom was, a carriage drew up before the door, and, to his great astonishment, out jumped Berkley. The first thing he did was to give the postmaster, who stood near

the door, a smart cut with his whip. The sufferer
gently expostulated, saying, —

"Pray, Sir, don't; I am lame."

Whereupon Berkley desisted, and began instead
to shake the postmaster's wife by the shoulders,
and order his dinner in English. But all this was
done so good-naturedly, and with such a rosy,
laughing face, that no offence was taken.

"So you have returned much sooner than you
intended," said Flemming, after the first friendly
salutations.

"Yes," replied Berkley; "I became tired of
Ischel, — very tired. I did not find there the
friends I expected. Now I am going back to
Salzburg, and then to Gastein. There I shall cer-
tainly find them. You must go with me."

Flemming declined the invitation; and proposed
to Berkley that he should join him in his excur-
sion on the lake.

"You shall hear the grand echo of the Falken-
stein," said he, "and behold the scene of the Bridal
Tragedy; and then we will go on as far as the
village of Saint Wolfgang, which you have not yet
seen, except across the lake."

"Well, this afternoon I devote to you; for to-
morrow we part once more, and who knows when
we shall meet again?"

They went down to the water's side without
further delay; and, taking a boat with two oars,
struck across an elbow of the lake towards a barren
rock by the eastern shore, from which a small white
monument shone in the sun.

"That monument," said one of the boatmen,

a stout young lad in leather breeches, " was built
by a butcher, to the glory of Saint Wolfgang, who
saved him from drowning. He was one day riding
an ox to market along the opposite bank; when
the animal, taking fright, sprang into the water,
and swam over to this place, with the butcher on
his back."

" And do you think he could have done this,"
asked Berkley, " if Saint Wolfgang had not helped
him ? "

" Of course not! " answered leather-breeches ;
and the Englishman laughed.

From this point they rowed along under the
shore to a low promontory, upon which stood an-
other monument, commemorating a more tragical
event.

" This is the place I was speaking of," said
Flemming, as the boatmen rested on their oars.
" The melancholy and singular event it commem-
orates happened more than two centuries ago.
There was a bridal party here upon the ice, one
winter ; and in the midst of the dance the ice
broke, and the whole merry company were drowned
together, except the fiddlers, who were sitting on
the shore."

They looked in silence at the monument, and at
the blue quiet water, under which the bones of the
dancers lay buried, hand in hand. The monument
is of stone, painted white, with an overhanging
roof to shelter it from storms. In a niche in front
is a small image of the Saviour, in a sitting pos-
ture ; and an inscription upon a marble tablet
below says that it was placed there by Longinus

Walther, and his wife, Barbara Juliana von Hain-
berg; themselves long since peacefully crumbled
to dust, side by side, in some churchyard.

"That was breaking the ice with a vengeance!"
said Berkley, as they pushed out into the lake
again; and erelong they were floating beneath the
mighty precipice of Falkenstein; a steep wall of
rock, crowned with a chapel and a hermitage,
where in days of old lived the holy Saint Wolfgang.
It is now haunted only by an echo, so distinct and
loud, that one might imagine the ghost of the de-
parted saint to be sitting there, and repeating the
voices from below, — not word by word, but sen-
tence by sentence, as if he were passing them up
to the recording angel.

"Ho! ho! ho!" shouted Berkley; and the
sound seemed to strike the wall of stone, like the
flapping of steel plates; — "Ho! ho! ho! How
are you to-day, Saint Wolfgang? You infernal
old rascal! How is the Frau von Wolfgang? —
God save great George, our king! Damn your
eyes! Hold your tongue! Ho! ho! ha! ha!
hi!"

And the words were recorded above; and a voice
repeated them with awful distinctness in the blue
depths overhead; and Flemming felt in his inmost
soul the contrast between the holy heavens, and
the mockery of laughter, and the idle words, which
fall back from the sky above us and soil not its
purity.

In half an hour they were at the village of Saint
Wolfgang, threading a narrow street, above which
the roofs of quaint, picturesque old houses almost

met. It led them to a Gothic church ; a magnificent one for a village ; — in front of which was a small court, shut in by Italian-looking houses, with balconies, and flowers at the windows. Here a bronze fountain of elaborate workmanship was playing in the shade. On its summit stood an image of the patron saint of the village ; and, running round the under lip of the water-basin below, they read this inscription in old German rhymes : —

" I am in the honor of Saint Wolfgang raised. Abbot Wolfgang Habel of Emensee, he hath made me for the use and delight of poor pilgrim wight. Neither gold nor wine hath he ; at this water shall he merry be. In the year of the Lord fifteen hundred and fifteen hath the work completed been. God be praised ! "

As they were deciphering the rude characters of this pious inscription, a village priest came down a high flight of steps from the parsonage near the church, and courteously saluted the strangers. After returning the salutation, the mad Englishman, without preface, asked him how many natural children were annually born in the parish. The question seemed to astonish the good father ; but he answered it civilly, as he did several other questions, which Flemming thought rather indiscreet, to say the least.

" You will excuse our curiosity," said he to the priest, by way of apology. " We are strangers from distant countries. My friend is an Englishman, and I an American."

Berkley, however, was not so easily silenced. After a few moments' conversation, he broke out

into most audacious Latin, in which the only
words clearly intelligible were : —

" Plurimum reverende, in Christo religiosissime
ac clarissime Domine, necnon et amice observan-
dissime ! Petrus sic est locutus : ' Nec argentum
mihi, nec aurum est ; sed quod habeo, hoc tibi do ;
surge et ambula.' "

He seemed to be speaking of the fountain. The
priest answered meekly, —

" Non intellexi, Domine ! "

But Berkley continued with great volubility to
speak of his being a stranger in the land, and all
men being strangers upon earth, and hoping to
meet the good priest hereafter in the kingdom
of heaven. The priest seemed confounded and
abashed. Through the mist of a strange pronun-
ciation, he could recognize only here and there a
familiar word. He took out his snuff-box ; and
tried to quote a passage from Saint Paul : —

" Ut dixit Sanctus Paulus : Qui bene facit " —

Here his memory failed him, or, as the French
say, he was at the end of his Latin, and, stretch-
ing forth his long forefinger, he concluded in Ger-
man : —

" Yes ; — I don't — so clearly remember — what
he did say."

The Englishman helped him through with a
moral phrase ; and then, pulling off his hat, ex-
claimed very solemnly : —

" Vale, Domine doctissime et reverendissime ! "

And the Dominie, as if pursued by a demon,
made a sudden and precipitate retreat down a
flight of steps into the street.

" There ! " said Berkley, laughing, " I beat him at his own weapons. What do you say of my Latin ? "

" I say of it," replied Flemming, " what Holofernes said of Sir Nathaniel's : — ' Priscian a little scratched ; 't will serve.' I think I have heard better. But what a whim ! I thought I should have laughed aloud."

They were still sitting by the bronze fountain, when the priest returned, accompanied by a short man, with large feet, and a long blue surtout, so greasy that it reminded one of Polilla's in the Spanish play, which was lined with slices of pork. His countenance was broad and placid, but his blue eyes gleamed with a wild, mysterious, sorrowful expression. Flemming thought the Latin contest was to be renewed, with more powder and heavier guns. He was mistaken. The stranger saluted him in German, and said, that, having heard he was from America, he had come to question him about that distant country, for which he was on the point of embarking. There was nothing peculiar in his manner, nor in the questions he asked, nor the remarks he made. They were the usual questions and remarks about cities and climate and sailing the sea. At length Flemming asked him the object of his journey to America. The stranger came close to him, and, lowering his voice, said very solemnly : —

" That holy man, Frederick Baraga, missionary among the Indians at Lacroix, on Lake Superior, has returned to his fatherland, Krain ; and I am chosen by Heaven to go forth as Minister Extraor-

dinary of Christ, to unite all nations and people in one church ! "

Flemming almost started at the singular earnestness with which he uttered these words; and looked at him attentively, thinking to see the face of a madman. But the modest, unassuming look of that placid countenance was unchanged ; only in the eyes burned a mysterious light, as if candles had been lighted in the brain, to magnify the daylight there.

" It is truly a high vocation," said he, in reply. " But are you sure that this is no hallucination ? Are you certain that you have been chosen by Heaven for this great work ? "

" I am certain," replied the German, in a tone of great calmness and sincerity ; " and if Saint Peter and Saint Paul should come down from heaven to assure me of it, my faith would be no stronger than it now is. It has been declared to me by many signs and wonders. I can no longer doubt nor hesitate. I have already heard the voice of the Spirit, speaking to me at night ; and I know that I am an Apostle, and chosen for this work."

Such was the calm enthusiasm with which he spoke, that Flemming could not choose but listen. He felt interested in this strange being. There was something awe-inspiring in the spirit that possessed him. After a short pause, he continued : —

" If you wish to know who I am, I can tell you in few words. I think you will not find the story without interest."

He then went on to relate the circumstances recorded in the following chapter.

CHAPTER VII.

THE STORY OF BROTHER BERNARDUS.

" I was born in the city of Stein, in the land of Krain. My pious mother, Gertrude, sang me psalms and spiritual songs in childhood; and often, when I awoke in the night, I saw her still sitting patiently at her work, by the stove, and heard her singing those hymns of heaven, or praying in the midnight darkness when her work was done. It was for me she prayed. Thus, from my earliest childhood, I breathed the breath of pious aspirations. Afterwards I went to Laybach, as a student of theology; and, after the usual course of study, was ordained a priest. I went forth to the care of souls; my own soul filled with the faith that erelong all people would be united in one church. Yet at times my heart was heavy, to behold how many nations there are who have not heard of Christ; and how those who are called Christians are divided into numberless sects, and how among these are many who are Christians in name only. I determined to devote myself to the great work of the one Church Universal, and, for this purpose, to give myself wholly up to the study of the Evangelists and the Fathers. I retired to the Benedictine cloister of Saint Paul in the valley of Lavant. The father-confessor in the nunnery of Laak, where I then lived, strengthened me in this resolve. I had long walked with this angel of God in a human form, and his parting benediction sank deep into my soul. The Prince-Abbot

Berthold, of blessed memory, was then head of the Benedictine convent. He received me kindly, and led me to the library, where I gazed with secret rapture on the vast folios of the Christian Fathers, from which, as from an arsenal, I was to draw the weapons of holy warfare. In the study of these the year of my novitiate passed. I became a Franciscan friar, and took the name of Brother Bernardus. Yet my course of life remained unchanged. I seldom left the cloister; but sat in my cell, and pored over those tomes of holy wisdom. About this time the aged confessor in Laak departed this life. His death was made known to me in a dream. It must have been after midnight, when I thought that I came into the church, which was brilliantly lighted up. The dead body of the venerable saint was brought in, attended by a great crowd. It seemed to me that I must go up into the pulpit and pronounce his funeral oration; and as I ascended the stairs the words of my text came into my mind, — ' Blessed in the sight of the Lord is the death of his saints.' My funeral sermon ended in a strain of exultation; and I awoke with ' Amen! ' upon my lips. A few days afterwards, I heard that on that night the old man died. After this event, I became restless and melancholy. I strove in vain to drive away my gloomy thoughts. I could no longer study. I was no longer contented in the cloister. I even thought of leaving it.

" One night, I had gone to bed early, according to my custom, and had fallen asleep. Suddenly I was awakened by a bright and wonderful light,

which shone all about me, and filled me with
heavenly rapture. Shortly after, I heard a voice,
which pronounced distinctly these words, in the
Sclavonian tongue: — 'Remain in the cloister!'
It was the voice of my departed mother. I was
fully awake, yet saw nothing but the bright light,
which disappeared when the words had been
spoken. Still it was broad daylight in my cham-
ber. I thought I had slept beyond my usual hour.
I looked at my watch. It was just one o'clock
after midnight. Suddenly the daylight vanished,
and it was dark. In the morning I arose, as if
new-born, through the wonderful light and the
words of my mother's voice. It was no dream.
I knew it was the will of God that I should stay,
and I could again give myself up to quiet study.
I read the whole Bible through once more in the
original text; and went on with the Fathers in
chronological order. Often, after the apparition
of the light, I awoke at the same hour, and though
I heard no voice and saw no light, yet was re-
freshed with heavenly consolation.

"Not long after this, an important event hap-
pened in the cloister. In the absence of the deacon
of the abbey, I was to preach the Thanksgiving
sermon of Harvest-home. During the week, the
Prince-Abbot Berthold gave up the ghost, and my
sermon became at once a thanksgiving and funeral
sermon. Perhaps it may not be unworthy of no-
tice, that I was thus called to pronounce the burial
discourse over the body of the last reigning spir-
itual Prince-Abbot in Germany. He was a man
of God, and worthy of this honor.

" One year after this event, I was appointed
Professor of Biblical Hermeneutics in Klagenfurt,
and left the abbey forever. In Klagenfurt I re-
mained ten years, dwelling in the same house, and
eating at the same table, with seventeen other Pro-
fessors. Their conversation naturally suggested
new topics of study, and brought to my notice
books which I had never before seen. One day I
heard at table that Maurus Cappellari, a monk of
Camaldoli, had been elected Pope, under the name
of Gregory Sixteenth. He was spoken of as a
very learned man, who had written many books.
At this time I was a firm believer in the Pope's
infallibility ; and when I heard these books men-
tioned, there arose in me an irresistible longing to
read them. I inquired for them ; but they were
nowhere to be had. At length I heard that his
most important work, ' The Triumph of the Holy
See and of the Church,' had been translated into
German and published in Augsburg. Erelong the
precious volume was in my hands. I began to
read it with the profoundest awe. The farther I
read, the more my wonder grew. The subject was
of the deepest interest to me. I could not lay the
book out of my hand, till I had read it through
with the closest attention. Now at length my
eyes were opened. I saw before me a monk who
had been educated in an Italian cloister ; who in-
deed had read much, and yet only what was calcu-
lated to strengthen him in the prejudices of his
childhood, and who had entirely neglected those
studies upon which a bishop should most rely, in
order to work out the salvation of man. I per-

ceived, at the same time, that this was the strongest instrument for battering down the walls which separate Christian from Christian. I saw, though as yet dimly, the way in which the union of Christians in the one true Church was to be accomplished. I knew not whether to be most astonished at my own blindness, that, in all my previous studies, I had not perceived what the reading of this single book made manifest to me; or at the blindness of the Pope, who had undertaken to justify such follies, without perceiving that at the same moment he was himself lying in fatal error. But since I have learned more thoroughly the ways of the Lord, I am now no more astonished at this, but pray only to Divine Providence, who so mysteriously prepares all people to be united in one true Church. I no longer believed in the Pope's infallibility; nay, I believed even, that, to the great injury of humanity, he lay in fatal error. I felt, moreover, that now the time had fully come when I should publicly show myself, and found in America a parish and a school, and become the spiritual guide of men and the schoolmaster of children.

" It was then, and on that account, that I wrote in the Latin tongue my great work on Biblical Hermeneutics. But in Germany it cannot be published. The Austrian censor of the press cannot find time to read it; though I think that, if I have spent so many laborious days and sleepless nights in writing it, this man ought likewise to find time enough not only to read it, but to examine all the grounds of my reasoning, and point out to me

my errors, if he can find any. Notwithstanding, the Spirit gave me no repose, but urged me ever mightily on to the perfection of my great work.

" One morning I sat writing, under peculiar influences of the Spirit, upon the Confusion of Tongues, the Division of the People, and the importance of the study of Comparative Philology, in reference to their union in one Church. So wrapped was I in the thought that I came late into my lecture-room ; and after lecture returned to my chamber, where I wrote till the clock struck twelve. At dinner, one of the Professors asked if any one had seen the star about which so much was said. The Professor of Physics said that the student Johannes Schminke had come to him in the greatest haste, and besought him to go out and see the wonderful star ; but, being incredulous about it, he made no haste, and when they came into the street the star had disappeared. When I heard the star spoken of, my soul was filled with rapture ; and a voice within me seemed to say, ' The great time is approaching ; labor unweariedly in thy work.' I sought out the student, and, like Herod, inquired diligently at what time the star appeared. He informed me that, just as the clock was striking eight in the morning, he went out of his house to go to the college, and saw on the square a crowd looking at a bright star. It was the very hour when I was writing alone in my chamber on the importance of Comparative Philology in bringing about the union of all nations. I felt that my hour had come. Strangely moved, I walked up and down my chamber. The evening

twilight came on. I lighted my lamp, and drew
the green curtains before the windows, and sat
down to read. · But hardly had I taken the book
into my hand, when the Spirit began to move me,
and urge me then to make my last decision and
resolve. I made a secret vow that I would under-
take the voyage to America. Suddenly my trou-
bled thoughts were still. An unwonted rapture
filled my heart. I sat and read till the supper-bell
rang. They were speaking at table of a red, glar-
ing meteor, which had just been seen in the air,
southeast from Klagenfurt, and had suddenly dis-
appeared with a dull, hollow sound. It was the
very moment at which I had taken my final reso-
lution to leave my native land. Every great pur-
pose and event of my life seemed heralded and
attended by divine messengers, — the voices of the
dead, the bright morning star shining in the clear
sunshine, and the red meteor in the evening twi-
light.

" I now began seriously to prepare for my de-
parture. The chamber I occupied had once been
the library of a Franciscan convent. Only a thick
wall separated it from the church. In this wall
was a niche, with heavy folding-doors, which had
served the Franciscans as a repository for pro-
hibited books. Here also I kept my papers and
my great work on Biblical Hermeneutics. The
inside of the doors was covered with horrible cari-
catures of Luther, Melancthon, Calvin, and other
great men. I used often to look at them with the
deepest melancholy, when I thought that these
great men likewise had labored upon earth, and

STORY OF BROTHER BERNARDUS 269

fought with Satan in the Church. But they were persecuted, denounced, condemned to die. So perhaps will it be with me. I thought of this often, and armed myself against the fear of death. I was in constant apprehension, lest the police should search my chamber during my absence, and, by examining my papers, discover my doctrine and designs. But the Spirit said to me : ' Be of good cheer; I will so blind the eyes of thy enemies, that it shall not once occur to them to think of thy writings.'

"At length, after many difficulties and temptations of the Devil, I am on my way to America. Yesterday I took leave of my dearest friend, Gregory Kuscher, in Hallstadt. He seemed filled with the Spirit of God, and has wonderfully strengthened me in my purpose. All the hosts of heaven looked on, and were glad. The old man kissed me, at parting ; and I ascended the mountain as if angels bore me up in their arms. Near the summit lay a newly fallen avalanche, over which, as yet, no footsteps had passed. This was my last temptation. ' Ha ! ' cried I aloud, ' Satan has prepared a snare for me ; but I will conquer him with godly weapons.' I sprang over the treacherous snow, with greater faith than St. Peter walked the waters of the Lake of Galilee ; and came down the valley, while the mountain peaks yet shone in the setting sun. God smiles upon me. I go forth full of hopeful courage. On Christmas next, I shall excommunicate the Pope."

Saying these words, he slowly and solemnly took his leave, like one conscious of the great

events which awaited him, and withdrew with the other priest into the church. Flemming could not smile as Berkley did ; for in the solitary, singular enthusiast, who had just left them, he saw only another melancholy victim to solitude and over-labor of the brain ; and felt how painful a thing it is thus to become unconsciously the almsman of other men's sympathies, a kind of blind beggar for the charity of a good wish or a prayer.

The sun was now setting. Silently they floated back to Saint Gilgen, amid the cool evening shadows. The village clock struck nine, as they landed ; and as Berkley was to depart early in the morning, he went to bed betimes. On bidding Flemming good night, he said : —

" I shall not see you in the morning ; so good by, and God bless you. Remember my parting words. Never mind trifles. In this world a man must either be anvil or hammer. Care killed a cat ! "

" I have heard you say that so often," replied Flemming, laughing, " that I begin to believe it. But I wonder if Care shaved his left eyebrow after doing the deed, as the ancient Egyptians used to do ! "

" Aha ! now you are sweeping cobwebs from the sky ! Good night ! Good night ! "

A sorrowful event happened in the neighborhood that night. The widow's child died suddenly. " Woe is me ! " — thus mourns the childless mother in one of the funeral songs of Greenland ; — " Woe is me, that I should gaze upon thy place and find it vacant ! In vain for thee thy mother dries the

sea-drenched garments ! " Not in these words, but in thoughts like these, did the poor mother bewail the death of her child, thinking mostly of the vacant place, and the daily cares and solicitudes of maternal love. Flemming saw a light in her chamber and shadows moving to and fro, as he stood by the window, gazing into the starry, silent sky. But he little thought of the awful domestic tragedy which was even then enacted behind those thin curtains !

CHAPTER VIII.

FOOTPRINTS OF ANGELS.

It was Sunday morning; and the church bells were all ringing together. From the neighboring villages came the solemn, joyful sounds, floating through the sunny air, mellow and faint and low, — all mingling into one harmonious chime, like the sound of some distant organ in heaven. Anon they ceased, and the woods, and the clouds, and the whole village, and the very air itself, seemed to pray, — so silent was it everywhere.

Two venerable old men — high-priests and patri-archs were they in the land — went up the pulpit stairs, as Moses and Aaron went up Mount Hor, in the sight of all the congregation, — for the pulpit stairs were in front, and very high.

Paul Flemming will never forget the sermon he heard that day, — no, not even if he should live to be as old as he who preached it. The text was, " I know that my Redeemer liveth." It was meant to

console the pious, poor widow, who sat right below
him at the foot of the pulpit stairs, all in black,
and her heart breaking. He said nothing of the
terrors of death, nor of the gloom of the narrow
house ; but, looking beyond these things, as mere
circumstances to which the imagination mainly
gives importance, he told his hearers of the in-
nocence of childhood upon earth, and the holiness
of childhood in heaven, and how the beautiful Lord
Jesus was once a little child, and now in heaven
the spirits of little children walked with him, and
gathered flowers in the fields of Paradise. Good
old man ! In behalf of humanity, I thank thee
for these benignant words ! And still more than
I, the bereaved mother thanked thee ; and from
that hour, though she wept in secret for her child,
yet

> She knew he was with Jesus
> And she asked him not again.

After the sermon, Paul Flemming walked forth
alone into the churchyard. There was no one
there, save a little boy, who was fishing with a pin
hook in a grave half full of water. But a few
moments afterward, through the arched gateway
under the belfry came a funeral procession. At
its head walked a priest in white surplice, chant-
ing. Peasants, old and young, followed him, with
burning tapers in their hands. A young girl car-
ried in her arms a dead child, wrapped in its little
winding-sheet. The grave was close under the
wall, by the church-door. A vase of holy water
stood beside it. The sexton took the child from
the girl's arms, and put it into a coffin ; and, as he

placed it in the grave, the girl held over it a cross wreathed with roses, and the priest and peasants sang a funeral hymn. When this was over, the priest sprinkled the grave and the crowd with holy water ; and then they all went into the church, each one stopping, as he passed the grave, to throw a handful of earth into it, and sprinkle it with the hyssop.

A few moments afterwards, the voice of the priest was heard saying mass in the church, and Flemming saw the toothless old sexton treading, with his clouted shoes, the fresh earth into the grave of the little child. He approached him, and asked the age of the deceased. The sexton leaned a moment on his spade, and, shrugging his shoulders, replied : —

"Only an hour or two. It was born in the night, and died this morning early."

"A brief existence," said Flemming. " The child seems to have been born only to be buried and have its name recorded on a wooden tombstone."

The sexton went on with his work, and made no reply. Flemming still lingered among the graves, gazing with wonder at the strange devices by which man has rendered death horrible and the grave loathsome.

In the temple of Juno at Elis, Sleep and his twin-brother, Death, were represented as children reposing in the arms of Night. On various funeral monuments of the ancients the Genius of Death is sculptured as a beautiful youth, leaning on an inverted torch, in the attitude of repose, his wings

folded and his feet crossed. In such peaceful and attractive forms did the imagination of ancient poets and sculptors represent death. And these were men in whose souls the religion of Nature was like the light of stars, beautiful, but faint and cold ! Strange, that, in later days, this angel of God, which leads us with a gentle hand into the "land of the great departed, into the silent land," should have been transformed into a monstrous and terrific thing ! Such is the spectral rider on the white horse ; — such the ghastly skeleton with scythe and hour-glass, — the Reaper, whose name is Death !

One of the most popular themes of poetry and painting in the Middle Ages, and continuing down even into modern times, was the Dance of Death. In almost all languages is it written, — the apparition of the grim spectre putting a sudden stop to all business, and leading men away into the "remarkable retirement" of the grave. It is written in an ancient Spanish poem, and painted on a wooden bridge in Switzerland. The designs of Holbein are well known. The most striking among them is that, where, from a group of children sitting round a cottage hearth, Death has taken one by the hand, and is leading it out of the door. Quietly and unresisting goes the little child, and in its countenance no grief, but wonder only ; while the other children are weeping and stretching forth their hands in vain towards their departing brother. It is a beautiful design, in all save the skeleton. An angel had been better, with folded wings, and torch inverted.

And now the sun was growing high and warm.
A little chapel, whose door stood open, seemed to
invite Flemming to enter and enjoy the grateful
coolness. He went in. There was no one there.
The walls were covered with paintings and sculp-
ture of the rudest kind, and with a few funeral
tablets. There was nothing there to move the
heart to devotion; but in that hour the heart of
Flemming was weak, — weak as a child's. He
bowed his stubborn knees, and wept. And, oh,
how many disappointed hopes, how many bitter
recollections, how much of wounded pride and un-
requited love, were in those tears through which
he read, on a marble tablet in the chapel wall oppo-
site, this singular inscription : —

" Look not mournfully into the Past. It comes
not back again. Wisely improve the Present. It
is thine. Go forth to meet the shadowy Future,
without fear, and with a manly heart."

It seemed to him as if the unknown tenant of
that grave had opened his lips of dust, and spoken
to him the words of consolation, which his soul
needed, and which no friend had yet spoken. In a
moment the anguish of his thoughts was still. The
stone was rolled away from the door of his heart ;
death was no longer there, but an angel clothed in
white. He stood up, and his eyes were no more
bleared with tears ; and, looking into the bright
morning heaven, he said : —

" I will be strong ! "

Men sometimes go down into tombs, with painful
longings to behold once more the faces of their de-
parted friends ; and as they gaze upon them, lying

there so peacefully with the semblance that they wore on earth, the sweet breath of heaven touches them, and the features crumble and fall together, and are but dust. So did his soul then descend for the last time into the great tomb of·the Past, with painful longings to behold once more the dear faces of those he had loved; and the sweet breath of heaven touched them, and they would not stay, but crumbled away and perished as he gazed. They, too, were dust. And thus, far-sounding, he heard the great gate of the Past shut behind him, as the divine poet did the gate of Paradise, when the angel pointed him the way up the Holy Mountain; and to him likewise was it forbidden to look back.

In the life of every man there are sudden transitions of feeling, which seem almost miraculous. At once, as if some magician had touched the heavens and the earth, the dark clouds melt into the air, the wind falls, and serenity succeeds the storm. The causes which produce these sudden changes may have been long at work within us; but the changes themselves are instantaneous, and apparently without sufficient cause. It was so with Flemming; and from that hour forth he resolved that he would no longer veer with every shifting wind of circumstance, — no longer be a child's plaything in the hands of Fate, which we ourselves do make or mar. He resolved henceforward not to lean on others, but to walk self-confident and self-possessed; no longer to waste his years in vain regrets, nor wait the fulfilment of boundless hopes and indiscreet desires, but to live in the Present

wisely, alike forgetful of the Past, and careless of
what the mysterious Future might bring. And
from that moment he was calm and strong; he was
reconciled with himself. His thoughts turned to
his distant home beyond the sea. An indescribable
sweet feeling rose within him.

" Thither will I turn my wandering footsteps,"
said he, "and be a man among men, and no longer
a dreamer among shadows. Henceforth be mine a
life of action and reality! I will work in my own
sphere, nor wish it other than it is. This alone is
health and happiness. This alone is Life, —

> " Life that shall send
> A challenge to its end,
> And when it comes, say, Welcome, friend!

Why have I not made these sage reflections, this
wise resolve, sooner? Can such a simple result
spring only from the long and intricate process of
experience? Alas! it is not till time, with reck-
less hand, has torn out half the leaves from the
Book of Human Life, to light the fires of passion
with, from day to day, that man begins to see that
the leaves which remain are few in number, and to
remember, faintly at first, and then more clearly,
that upon the earlier pages of that book was writ-
ten a story of happy innocence, which he would fain
read over again. Then come listless irresolution,
and the inevitable inaction of despair; or else the
firm resolve to record upon the leaves that still re-
main a more noble history than the child's story
with which the book began."

CHAPTER IX.

THE LAST PANG.

"Farewell to thee, Saint Gilgen!" said Flemming, as he turned on the brow of the hill, to take his last look at the lake and the village below, and felt that this was one of the few spots on the wide earth to which he could say farewell with regret. "Thy majestic hills have impressed themselves upon my soul, as a seal upon wax. The quiet beauty of thy lake shall be to me forever an image of peace and purity and stillness, and that inscription in thy little churchyard a sentence of wisdom for my after life."

Before the setting of the same sun which then shone on that fair landscape, he was far on his way towards Munich. He had left behind him the mountains of the Tyrol, and beheld them for the last time in the soft evening twilight, their bases green with forest-trees, and here and there a sharp rocky spire, and a rounded summit capped with snow. There they lay, their backs like the backs of camels; a mighty caravan, reposing at evening in its march across the desert.

From Munich he passed through Augsburg and Ulm, on his way to Stuttgard. At the entrances of towns and villages, he saw large crucifixes; and on the fronts of many houses, coarse paintings and images of saints. In Gunzburg three priests in black were slowly passing down the street, and women fell on their knees to receive a blessing. There were many beggars, too, in the streets; and

an old man who was making hay in a field by the roadside, when he saw the carriage approaching, threw down his rake, and came tumbling over the ditch, uttering the most dismal wail, with his hat held out in both hands. The next day, the bright yellow jackets of the postilions, and the two great tassels of their bugle-horns, dangling down their backs, like cauliflowers, told him he was in Würtemberg; and, late in the evening, he stopped at a hotel in Stuttgard, and from his chamber-window saw, in the bright moonlight, the old Gothic cathedral, with its narrow, lancet windows and jutting buttresses, right in front of him. Erelong he had forgotten all his cares and sorrows in sleep, and with them his hopes, and wishes, and good resolves.

He was still sitting at breakfast in his chamber, the next morning, when the great bell of the cathedral opposite began to ring, and reminded him that it was Sunday. Erelong the organ answered from within, and from its golden lips breathed forth a psalm. The congregation began to assemble, and Flemming went up with them to the house of the Lord. In the body of the church he found the pews all filled or locked; they seemed to belong to families. He went up into the gallery, and looked over the psalm-book of a peasant, while the congregation sang the sublime old hymn of Martin Luther, —

> Our God, he is a tower of strength,
> A trusty shield and weapon.

During the singing, a fat clergyman, clad in black, with a surplice thrown loosely about him, came

pacing along one of the aisles, from beneath the organ-loft, and ascended the pulpit. After the hymn, he read a portion of Scripture, and then said : —

"Let us unite in silent prayer."

And turning round, he knelt in the pulpit, while the congregation remained standing. For a while there was a breathless silence in the church, which to Flemming was more solemnly impressive than any audible prayer. The clergyman then arose, and began his sermon. His theme was the Reformation, and he attempted to prove how much easier it was to enter the kingdom of Heaven through the gateways of the Reformed Evangelical German Church, than by the aisles and penitential staircases of Saint Peter's. He then gave a history of the Reformation; and when Flemming thought he was near the end, he heard him say that he should divide his discourse into four heads. This reminded him of the sturdy old Puritan, Cotton Mather, who, after preaching an hour, would coolly turn the hour-glass on the pulpit, and say: "Now, my beloved hearers, let us take another glass." He stole out into the silent, deserted street, and went to visit the veteran sculptor Dannecker. He found him sitting alone, with his psalm-book, and the reminiscences of a life of eighty years. As Flemming entered, he arose from the sofa, and tottered towards him ; a venerable old man of low stature, dressed in a loose white jacket, with a face like Franklin's, a pale blue eye, and his white hair flowing over his shoulders.

"So you are from America," said he. "But

you have a German name. Paul Flemming was
one of our old poets. I have never been in Amer-
ica, and never shall go there. I am now too old.
I have been in Paris and in Rome. But that
was long ago. I am now eight-and-seventy years
old."

Here he took Flemming by the hand, and made
him sit down by his side, on the sofa. And Flem-
ming felt a mysterious awe creep over him, on
touching the hand of the good old man, who sat so
serenely amid the gathering shade of years, and
listened to life's curfew-bell, telling, with eight-
and-seventy solemn strokes, that the hour had
come when the fires of all earthly passion must be
quenched within, and man must prepare to lie
down and rest till the morning.

" You see," he continued, in a melancholy tone,
" my hands are cold; colder than yours. They
were warmer once. I am now an old man."

" Yet these are the hands," answered Flemming,
" that sculptured the beautiful Ariadne and the
Panther. The soul never grows old."

" Nor does Nature," said the old man, pleased
with this allusion to his great work, and pointing
to the green trees before his window. " This
pleasure I have left to me. My sight is still good.
I can even distinguish objects on the side of yonder
mountain. My hearing is also unimpaired. For
all which I thank God."

Then, directing Flemming's attention to a fine
engraving, which hung on the opposite wall of the
room, he continued : —

" That is an engraving of Canova's Religion.

I love to sit here and look at it, for hours together. It is beautiful. He made the statue for his native town, where they had no church until he built them one. He placed the statue in it. This engraving he sent me as a present. Ah, he was a dear, good man. The name of his native town I have forgotten. My memory fails me. I cannot remember names."

Fearful that he had disturbed the old man in his morning devotions, Flemming did not remain long, but took his leave with regret. There was something impressive in the scene he had witnessed; — this beautiful old age of the artist; sitting by the open window, in the bright summer morning, — the labor of life accomplished, the horizon reached, where heaven and earth meet, — thinking it was angel's music, when he heard the church-bells ring; himself too old to go. As he walked back to his chamber, he thought within himself whether he likewise might not accomplish something which should live after him, — might not bring something permanent out of this fast-fleeting life, and then sit down, like the artist, in serene old age, and fold his hands in silence. He wondered how a man felt when he grew so old that he could no longer go to church, but must sit at home and read the Bible in large print. His heart was full of indefinite longings, mingled with regrets; longings to accomplish something worthy of life; regret that as yet he had accomplished nothing, but had felt and dreamed only. Thus the warm days in spring bring forth passion-flowers and forget-me-nots. It is only after midsummer, when the days

grow shorter and hotter, that fruit begins to appear. Then the heat of the day brings forward the harvest, and after the harvest the leaves fall, and there is a gray frost. Much meditating upon these things, Paul Flemming reached his hotel. At that moment a person clad in green came down the church steps, and crossed the street. It was the German mechanic of Interlachen. Flemming started, as if a green snake had suddenly crossed his path. He took refuge in his chamber.

That night, as he was sitting alone, having made his preparations to depart the following morning, his attention was arrested by the sound of a female voice in the next room. A thin partition, with a door, separated it from his own. He had not before observed that the room was occupied. But, in the stillness of the night, the tones of that voice struck his ear. He listened. It was a lady, reading the prayers of the English Church. The tones were familiar, and awakened at once a thousand painfully sweet recollections. It was the voice of Mary Ashburton ! His heart could not be deceived ; and all its wounds began to bleed afresh, like those of a murdered man when the murderer approaches. His first impulse was of affection only, boundless, irrepressible, delirious, as of old in the green valley of Interlachen. He waited for the voice to cease, that he might go to her, and behold her face once more. And then his pride rose up within him, and rebuked this weakness. He remembered his firm resolve, and blushed to find himself so feeble. And the voice ceased, and yet he did not go. Pride had so far gained the

mastery over affection. He lay down upon his bed, like a child as he was. All about him was silence, and the silence was holy, for she was near; so near, that he could almost hear the beating of her heart. He knew now for the first time how weak he was, and how strong was his passion for that woman. His heart was like the altar of the Israelites of old ; and, though drenched with tears, as with rain, it was kindled at once by the holy fire from heaven !

Towards morning he fell asleep, exhausted with the strong excitement ; and, in that hour, when, sleep being " nigh unto the soul," visions are deemed prophetic, he dreamed. O·blessed vision of the morning, stay ! thou wast so fair ! He stood again on the green sunny meadow, beneath the ruined tower ; and she was by his side, with her pale, speaking countenance and holy eyes ; and he kissed her fair forehead ; and she turned her face towards him, beaming with affection, and said, " I confess it now; you are the Magician ! " and pressed him in a meek embrace, that he " might rather feel than see the swelling of her heart." And then she faded away from his arms, and her face became transfigured, and her voice like the voice of an angel in heaven ; — and he awoke, and was alone !

It was broad daylight, and he heard the postilion and the stamping of horses' hoofs on the pavement at the door. He did not dare to stay. But, throwing himself into the carriage, he cast one look towards the window of the Dark Ladie, and a moment afterwards had left her forever!

He had drunk the last drop of the bitter cup, and now laid the golden goblet gently down, knowing that he should behold it no more!

No more! Oh, how majestically mournful are those words! They sound like the roar of the wind through a forest of pines!

KAVANAGH

The flighty purpose never is o'ertook,
Unless the deed go with it.
SHAKESPEARE.

———◆———

INTRODUCTORY NOTE.

ON the day when Mr. Longfellow wrote the last lines of *Evangeline* he noted in his diary: "Now for a little prose; a romance which I have in my brain — *Kavanagh* by name." This was February 27, 1847, and the book was published May 12, 1849. At that time he wrote of it: "People think it is not long enough. But why beat out one's ideas into thin leaf?" It must not be supposed, however, that he was at work for two years on this slight romance. He began it, indeed, immediately after finishing *Evangeline*, but appears to have worked at it in a very desultory fashion until the autumn of 1848. He records in his diary under date of October 3, 1848: "Still the imprisoning rain; but to-day welcome, thrice welcome. Sat by the fireside in the library and wrote in *Kavanagh*, to my own great satisfaction and delight." On the 31st of the same month, he wrote: "*Kavanagh* is nearly completed. I have

written it *con amore*, and have had so much satis-
faction as this, whatsoever may be its fate here-
after;" on the 9th of November he finished the
book. Yet, in spite of the evident pleasure which
he took in his work, he was not over-confident of
success. Perhaps he was affected a little by the
cautious appreciation which the manuscript re-
ceived from his first audience of three, — his wife,
his brother, and Sumner; — "The general opinion
favorable, on the whole, though it did not awaken
any very lively enthusiasm." At any rate, he
wrote in his diary, February 13, 1849: "With
some doubts and misgivings I carried the first
sheets of *Kavanagh* to the printer. I have never
hesitated so much about any of my books, except
the first hexameters, *The Children of the Lord's
Supper*. Let us see how it will look in print.
I want to get this out of the way. Things lying
in manuscript incumber and impede me; hold me
back from working on to something better." His
hesitation continued after he had begun to see the
book in print, and on the 8th of March he wrote:
"My mind is perplexed about *Kavanagh*. The
title is better than the book, and suggests a differ-
ent kind of book. One more long, spiritual chap-
ter must be written for it. The thought struck
me last night. It must go into the book as the
keystone into the arch. An idea so very obvi-
ous, and yet coming so late!" The next day,
he recorded: "Longed to write the chapter for
Kavanagh, but was obliged to go to college. Ah,
me! and yet what a delight to begin every day
with Dante!"

The chapter which was thus written to give spiritual significance and unity to the book was the eighteenth, which can be removed without disturbing the flow of the narrative, and yet does perform just the function designed by the author, since it is, as it were, a brief history of the hero's spiritual experience.

As has been said before, the figure of a school-master was a favorite one with Mr. Longfellow, and he seems to have employed it finally in *Kavanagh* as the centre about which to group his thoughts respecting literature and scholarship, — thoughts which before he had given in fragmentary, note-book form. He made use also of his country rambles both in the Berkshire hills and in Maine for pictures of life and scenery. The time when the romance was written easily explains the freedom of reference to domestic life, and the little society of the household. Without regarding the interior of Mr. Churchill's home as in any direct sense a reproduction of the author's, it is fair to suppose that the scenes narrated of childish life have the same general relation to Mr. Longfellow's domestic experience that the scenes portrayed in *Hyperion* bear to his life before his marriage.

Although Mr. Longfellow kept no note-book in the manner of Hawthorne's, recording suggestions for stories and poems, he was in the habit, as the reader has seen, of setting down occasionally in his diary a half-formed plan, and he also kept for use such newspaper clippings as bore upon his work. He valued the real touch which he conceived that he thus secured, and sometimes incor-

porated this matter in his manuscript. Thus the announcement of Edward Dimple in the nineteenth chapter was a veritable advertisement, cut from some newspaper and attached in its place to the manuscript given to the printer.

The name of Kavanagh is that of an old Roman Catholic family of Maine, now extinct, and is perpetuated both by this book and by a school in Portland called the Kavanagh School. The Arthur Kavanagh of the story is, however, an entirely imaginary personage.

KAVANAGH

BOOK THE FIRST.

Who ne'er his bread in sorrow ate,
 Who ne'er the mournful midnight hours
Weeping upon his bed has sate,
 He knows you not, ye Heavenly Powers.

GOETHE.

I.

GREAT men stand like solitary towers in the
city of God, and secret passages running deep be-
neath external nature give their thoughts inter-
course with higher intelligences, which strengthens
and consoles them, and of which the laborers on
the surface do not even dream!

Some such thought as this was floating vaguely
through the brain of Mr. Churchill, as he closed
his school-house door behind him; and if in any
degree he applied it to himself, it may perhaps be
pardoned in a dreamy, poetic man like him; for
we judge ourselves by what we feel capable of
doing, while others judge us by what we have al-
ready done. And moreover his wife considered
him equal to great things. To the people in the
village he was the schoolmaster, and nothing more.
They beheld in his form and countenance no out-
ward sign of the divinity within. They saw him

daily moiling and delving in the common path, like a beetle, and little thought that underneath that hard and cold exterior lay folded delicate golden wings, wherewith, when the heat of day was over, he soared and revelled in the pleasant evening air.

To-day he was soaring and revelling before the sun had set; for it was Saturday. With a feeling of infinite relief he left behind him the empty school-house, into which the hot sun of a September afternoon was pouring. All the bright young faces were gone; all the impatient little hearts were gone; all the fresh voices, shrill, but musical with the melody of childhood were gone; and the lately busy realm was given up to silence, and the dusty sunshine, and the old gray flies, that buzzed and bumped their heads against the window-panes. The sound of the outer door, creaking on its hebdomadal hinges, was like a sentinel's challenge, to which the key growled responsive in the lock; and the master, casting a furtive glance at the last caricature of himself in red chalk on the wooden fence close by, entered with a light step the solemn avenue of pines that led to the margin of the river.

At first his step was quick and nervous; and he swung his cane as if aiming blows at some invisible and retreating enemy. Though a meek man, there were moments when he remembered with bitterness the unjust reproaches of fathers and their insulting words; and then he fought imaginary battles with people out of sight, and struck them to the ground, and trampled upon them; for Mr.

Churchill was not exempt from the weakness of human nature, nor the customary vexations of a schoolmaster's life. Unruly sons and unreasonable fathers did sometimes embitter his else sweet days and nights. But as he walked, his step grew slower, and his heart calmer. The coolness and shadows of the great trees comforted and satisfied him, and he heard the voice of the wind as it were the voice of spirits calling around him in the air. So that when he emerged from the black woodlands into the meadows by the river's side, all his cares were forgotten.

He lay down for a moment under a sycamore, and thought of the Roman Consul Licinius, passing a night with eighteen of his followers in the hollow trunk of the great Lycian plane-tree. From the branches overhead the falling seeds were wafted away through the soft air on plumy tufts of down. The continuous murmur of the leaves and of the swift-running stream seemed rather to deepen than disturb the pleasing solitude and silence of the place; and for a moment he imagined himself far away in the broad prairies of the West, and lying beneath the luxuriant trees that overhang the banks of the Wabash and the Kaskaskia. He saw the sturgeon leap from the river, and flash for a moment in the sunshine. Then a flock of wild-fowl flew across the sky towards the sea-mist that was rising slowly in the east; and his soul seemed to float away on the river's current, till he had glided far out into the measureless sea, and the sound of the wind among the leaves was no longer the sound of the wind, but of the sea.

Nature had made Mr. Churchill a poet, but destiny made him a schoolmaster. This produced a discord between his outward and his inward existence. Life presented itself to him like the Sphinx, with its perpetual riddle of the real and the ideal. To the solution of this dark problem he devoted his days and his nights. He was forced to teach grammar when he would fain have written poems; and from day to day, and from year to year, the trivial things of life postponed the great designs, which he felt capable of accomplishing, but never had the resolute courage to begin. Thus he dallied with his thoughts and with all things, and wasted his strength on trifles; like the lazy sea, that plays with the pebbles on its beach, but, under the inspiration of the wind might lift great navies on its outstretched palms, and toss them into the air as playthings.

The evening came. The setting sun stretched his celestial rods of light across the level landscape, and, like the Hebrew in Egypt, smote the rivers and the brooks and the ponds, and they became as blood.

Mr. Churchill turned his steps homeward. He climbed the hill with the old windmill on its summit, and below him saw the lights of the village; and around him the great landscape sinking deeper and deeper into the sea of darkness. He passed an orchard. The air was filled with the odor of the fallen fruit, which seemed to him as sweet as the fragrance of the blossoms in June. A few steps farther brought him to an old and neglected graveyard; and he paused a moment to look at

the white gleaming stone, under which slumbered the old clergyman, who came into the village in the time of the Indian wars, and on which was recorded that for half a century he had been "a painful preacher of the word." He entered the village street, and interchanged a few words with Mr. Pendexter, the venerable divine, whom he found standing at his gate. He met, also, an ill-looking man, carrying so many old boots that he seemed literally buried in them ; and at intervals encountered a stream of strong tobacco smoke, exhaled from the pipe of an Irish laborer, and pervading the damp evening air. At length he reached his own door.

II.

When Mr. Churchill entered his study, he found the lamp lighted, and his wife waiting for him. The wood fire was singing on the hearth like a grasshopper in the heat and silence of a summer noon ; and to his heart the chill autumnal evening became a summer noon. His wife turned towards him with looks of love in her joyous blue eyes ; and in the serene expression of her face he read the Divine beatitude, " Blessed are the pure in heart."

No sooner had he seated himself by the fireside than the door was swung wide open, and on the threshold stood, with his legs apart, like a miniature colossus, a lovely, golden boy, about three years old, with long, light locks, and very red cheeks. After a moment's pause, he dashed for-

ward into the room with a shout, and established himself in a large arm-chair, which he converted into a carrier's wagon, and over the back of which he urged forward his imaginary horses. He was followed by Lucy, the maid of all work, bearing in her arms the baby, with large, round eyes, and no hair. In his mouth he held an India-rubber ring, and looked very much like a street-door knocker. He came down to say good night, but after he got down, could not say it; not being able to say anything but a kind of explosive " Papa! " He was then a good deal kissed and tormented in various ways, and finally sent off to bed blowing little bubbles with his mouth, — Lucy blessing his little heart, and asseverating that nobody could feed him in the night without loving him ; and that if the flies bit him any more she would pull out every tooth in their heads !

Then came Master Alfred's hour of triumph and sovereign sway. The fire-light gleamed on his hard, red cheeks, and glanced from his liquid eyes, and small, white teeth. He piled his wagon full of books and papers, and dashed off to town at the top of his speed ; he delivered and received parcels and letters, and played the post-boy's horn with his lips. Then he climbed the back of the great chair, sang " Sweep ho ! " as from the top of a very high chimney, and, sliding down upon the cushion, pretended to fall asleep in a little white bed, with white curtains ; from which imaginary slumber his father awoke him by crying in his ear, in mysterious tones, —

" What little boy is this ! "

Finally he sat down in his chair at his mother's knee, and listened very attentively, and for the hundredth time, to the story of the dog Jumper, which was no sooner ended, than vociferously called for again and again. On the fifth repetition, it was cut as short as the dog's tail by Lucy, who, having put the baby to bed, now came for Master Alfred. He seemed to hope he had been forgotten, but was nevertheless marched off without any particular regard to his feelings, and disappeared in a kind of abstracted mood, repeating softly to himself his father's words, —

" Good night, Alfred ! "

His father looked fondly after him as he went up stairs, holding Lucy by one hand, and with the other rubbing the sleep out of his eyes.

" Ah ! these children, these children ! " said Mr. Churchill, as he sat down at the tea-table ; " we ought to love them very much now, for we shall not have them long with us ! "

" Good heavens ! " exclaimed his wife, " what do you mean ? Does anything ail them ? Are they going to die ? "

" I hope not. But they are going to grow up, and be no longer children."

" Oh, you foolish man ! You gave me such a fright ! "

" And yet it seems impossible that they should ever grow to be men, and drag the heavy artillery along the dusty roads of life."

" And I hope they never will. That is the last thing I want either of them to do."

" Oh, I do not mean literally, only figuratively.

By the way, speaking of growing up and growing old, I saw Mr. Pendexter this evening, as I came home."

"And what had he to say?"

"He told me he should preach his farewell sermon to-morrow."

"Poor old man! I really pity him."

"So do I. But it must be confessed he is a dull preacher; and I dare say it is as dull work for him as for his hearers."

"Why are they going to send him away?"

"Oh, there are a great many reasons. He does not give time and attention enough to his sermons and to his parish. He is always at work on his farm; always wants his salary raised; and insists upon his right to pasture his horse in the parish fields."

"Hark!" cried his wife, lifting up her face in a listening attitude.

"What is the matter?"

"I thought I heard the baby!"

There was a short silence. Then Mr. Churchill said, —

"It was only the cat in the cellar."

At this moment Lucy came in. She hesitated a little, and then, in a submissive voice, asked leave to go down to the village to buy some ribbon for her bonnet. Lucy was a girl of fifteen, who had been taken a few years before from an Orphan Asylum. Her dark eyes had a gypsy look, and she wore her brown hair twisted round her head after the manner of some of Murillo's girls. She had Milesian blood in her veins, and was impetuous and impatient of contradiction.

When she had left the room, the schoolmaster resumed the conversation by saying, —

"I do not like Lucy's going out so much in the evening. I am afraid she will get into trouble. She is really very pretty."

Then there was another pause, after which he added, —

"My dear wife, one thing puzzles me exceedingly."

"And what is that?"

"It is to know what that man does with all the old boots he picks up about the village. I met him again this evening. He seemed to have as many feet as Briareus had hands. He is a kind of centipede."

"But what has that to do with Lucy?"

"Nothing. It only occurred to me at the moment; and I never can imagine what he does with so many old boots."

III.

When tea was over, Mr. Churchill walked to and fro in his study, as his custom was. And as he walked, he gazed with secret rapture at the books, which lined the walls, and thought how many bleeding hearts and aching heads had found consolation for themselves and imparted it to others, by writing those pages. The books seemed to him almost as living beings, so instinct were they with human thoughts and sympathies. It was as if the authors themselves were gazing at him from the walls, with countenances neither sorrow-

ful nor glad, but full of calm indifference to fate, like those of the poets who appeared to Dante in his vision, walking together on the dolorous shore. And then he dreamed of fame, and thought that perhaps hereafter he might be in some degree, and to some one, what these men were to him ; and in the enthusiasm of the moment he exclaimed aloud,

"Would you have me be like these, dear Mary ?"

"Like these what ?" asked his wife, not comprehending him.

"Like these great and good men, — like these scholars and poets, — the authors of all these books ! "

She pressed his hand and said, in a soft, but excited tone, —

"Oh, yes ! Like them, only perhaps better ! "

"Then I will write a Romance ! "

"Write it ! " said his wife, like the angel. For she believed that then he would become famous forever ; and that all the vexed and busy world would stand still to hear him blow his little trumpet, whose sound was to rend the adamantine walls of time, and reach the ears of a far-off and startled posterity.

IV.

"I was thinking to-day," said Mr. Churchill a few minutes afterwards, as he took some papers from a drawer scented with a quince, and arranged them on the study table, while his wife as usual seated herself opposite to him with her work in her hand, — "I was thinking to-day how dull and

prosaic the study of mathematics is made in our
school-books ; as if the grand science of numbers
had been discovered and perfected merely to fur-
ther the purposes of trade.''

'' For my part,'' answered his wife, '' I do not see
how you can make mathematics poetical. There is
no poetry in them.''

'' Ah, that is a very great mistake ! There is
something divine in the science of numbers. Like
God, it holds the sea in the hollow of its hand. It
measures the earth ; it weighs the stars ; it illu-
mines the universe ; it is law, it is order, it is
beauty. And yet we imagine — that is, most of
us — that its highest end and culminating point is
book-keeping by double entry. It is our way of
teaching it that makes it so prosaic.''

So saying, he arose, and went to one of his
book-cases, from the shelf of which he took down
a little old quarto volume, and laid it upon the
table.

'' Now here,'' he continued, '' is a book of math-
ematics of quite a different stamp from ours.''

'' It looks very old. What is it ? ''

'' It is the Lilawati of Bhascara Acharya, trans-
lated from the Sanscrit.''

'' It is a pretty name. Pray what does it
mean ? ''

'' Lilawati was the name of Bhascara's daugh-
ter ; and the book was written to perpetuate it.
Here is an account of the whole matter.''

He then opened the volume, and read as fol-
lows : —

'' It is said that the composing of Lilawati was

occasioned by the following circumstance. Lila-
wati was the name of the author's daughter, con-
cerning whom it appeared, from the qualities of the
Ascendant at her birth, that she was destined to
pass her life unmarried, and to remain without
children. The father ascertained a lucky hour for
contracting her in marriage, that she might be
firmly connected, and have children. It is said
that, when that hour approached, he brought his
daughter and his intended son near him. He left
the hour-cup on the vessel of water, and kept in
attendance a time-knowing astrologer, in order
that, when the cup should subside in the water,
those two precious jewels should be united. But
as the intended arrangement was not according to
destiny, it happened that the girl, from a curiosity
natural to children, looked into the cup to observe
the water coming in at the hole ; when by chance
a pearl separated from her bridal dress, fell into
the cup, and, rolling down to the hole, stopped the
influx of the water. So the astrologer waited in
expectation of the promised hour. When the op-
eration of the cup had thus been delayed beyond
all moderate time, the father was in consterna-
tion, and examining, he found that a small pearl
had stopped the course of the water, and the long-
expected hour was passed. In short, the father,
thus disappointed, said to his unfortunate daugh-
ter, I will write a book of your name, which shall
remain to the latest times, — for a good name
is a second life, and the groundwork of eternal
existence."

As the schoolmaster read, the eyes of his wife
dilated and grew tender, and she said, —

"What a beautiful story! When did it happen?"

"Seven hundred years ago, among the Hindoos."

"Why not write a poem about it?"

"Because it is already a poem of itself, — one of those things of which the simplest statement is the best, and which lose by embellishment. The old Hindoo legend, brown with age, would not please me so well if decked in gay colors, and hung round with the tinkling bells of rhyme. Now hear how the book begins."

Again he read : —

"Salutation to the elephant-headed Being who infuses joy into the minds of his worshippers, who delivers from every difficulty those that call upon him, and whose feet are reverenced by the gods! — Reverence to Ganesa, who is beautiful as the pure purple lotos, and around whose neck the black curling snake winds itself in playful folds!"

"That sounds rather mystical," said his wife.

"Yes, the book begins with a salutation to the Hindoo deities, as the old Spanish Chronicles begin in the name of God and the Holy Virgin. And now see how poetical some of the examples are."

He then turned over the leaves slowly and read, —

"One third of a collection of beautiful water-lilies is offered to Mahadev, one fifth to Huri, one sixth to the Sun, one fourth to Devi, and six which remain are presented to the spiritual teacher. Required the whole number of water-lilies."

" That is very pretty," said the wife, " and would put it into the boys' heads to bring you pond-lilies." .

" Here is a prettier one still. One fifth of a hive of bees flew to the Kadamba flower ; one third flew to the Silandhara ; three times the difference of these two numbers flew to an arbor ; and one bee continued flying about, attracted on each side by the fragrant Ketaki and the Malati. What was the number of the bees? "

" I am sure I should never be able to tell."

" Ten times the square root of a flock of geese " —

Here Mrs. Churchill laughed aloud ; but he continued very gravely, —

" Ten times the square root of a flock of geese, seeing the clouds collect, flew to the Manus lake ; one eighth of the whole flew from the edge of the water amongst a multitude of water-lilies ; and three couple were observed playing in the water. Tell me my young girl with beautiful locks, what was the whole number of geese? "

" Well, what was it? "

" What should you think? "

" About twenty."

" No, one hundred and forty-four. Now try another. The square root of half a number of bees, and also eight ninths of the whole, alighted on the jasmines, and a female bee buzzed responsive to the hum of the male enclosed at night in a water-lily. Oh, beautiful damsel, tell me the number of bees."

" That is not there. You made it."

" No, indeed I did not. I wish I had made it. Look and see."

He showed her the book, and she read it herself. He then proposed some of the geometrical questions.

" In a lake the bud of a water-lily was observed, one span above the water, and when moved by the gentle breeze, it sank in the water at two cubits' distance. Required the depth of the water."

" That is charming, but must be very difficult. I could not answer it."

" A tree one hundred cubits high is distant from a well two hundred cubits ; from this tree one monkey descends and goes to the well ; another monkey takes a leap upwards, and then descends by the hypothenuse ; and both pass over an equal space. Required the height of the leap."

" I do not believe you can answer that question yourself, without looking into the book," said the laughing wife, laying her hand over the solution. " Try it."

" With great pleasure, my dear child," cried the confident schoolmaster, taking a pencil and paper. After making a few figures and calculations, he answered, —

" There, my young girl with beautiful locks, there is the answer, — forty cubits."

His wife removed her hand from the book, and then, clapping both in triumph, she exclaimed, —

" No, you are wrong, you are wrong, my beautiful youth with a bee in your bonnet. It is fifty cubits ! "

" Then I must have made some mistake."

" Of course you did. Your monkey did not jump high enough."

She signalized his mortifying defeat as if it had been a victory, by showering kisses, like roses, upon his forehead and cheeks, as he passed beneath the triumphal archway of her arms, trying in vain to articulate, —

" My dearest Lilawati, what is the whole number of the geese ? "

V.

After extricating himself from this pleasing dilemma, he said, —

" But I am now going to write. I must really begin in sober earnest, or I shall never get anything finished. And you know I have so many things to do, so many books to write, that really I do not know where to begin. I think I will take up the Romance first."

" It will not make much difference, if you only begin ! "

" That is true. I will not lose a moment."

" Did you answer Mr. Wainwright's letter about the cottage bedstead ? "

" Dear me, no ! I forgot it entirely. That must be done first, or he will make it all wrong."

" And the young lady who sent you the poetry to look over and criticise ? "

" No ; I have not had a single moment's leisure. And there is Mr. Hanson, who wants to know about the cooking-range. Confound it ! there is

always something interfering with my Romance. However, I will despatch those matters very speedily."

And he began to write with great haste. For a while nothing was heard but the scratching of his pen. Then he said, probably in connection with the cooking-range, —

" One of the most convenient things in house-keeping is a ham. It is always ready and always welcome. You can eat it with anything, and without anything. It reminds me always of the great wild boar Scrimner, in the Northern Mythology, who is killed every day for the gods to feast on in Valhalla, and comes to life again every night."

" In that case, I should think the gods would have the nightmare," said his wife.

" Perhaps they do."

And then another long silence, broken only by the skating of the swift pen over the sheet. Presently Mrs. Churchill said, — as if following out her own train of thought, while she ceased plying her needle to bite off the thread, which women will sometimes do in spite of all that is said against it, —

" A man came here to-day, calling himself the agent of an extensive house in the needle trade. He left this sample, and said the drill of the eye was superior to any other, and they are warranted not to cut the thread. He puts them at the whole-sale price ; and if I do not like the sizes, he offers to exchange them for others, either sharps or betweens."

To this remark the abstracted schoolmaster

vouchsafed no reply. He found his half-dozen letters not so easily answered, particularly that to the poetical young lady, and worked away busily at them. Finally they were finished and sealed, and he looked up to his wife. She turned her eyes dreamily upon him. Slumber was hanging in their blue orbs, like snow in the heavens, ready to fall. It was quite late, and he said to her, —

"I am too tired, my charming Lilawati, and you too sleepy, to sit here any longer to-night. And, as I do not wish to begin my Romance without having you at my side, so that I can read detached passages to you as I write, I will put it off till to-morrow or the next day."

He watched his wife as she went up stairs with the light. It was a picture always new and always beautiful, and like a painting of Gherardo della Notte. As he followed her, he paused to look at the stars. The beauty of the heavens made his soul overflow.

"How absolute," he exclaimed, "how absolute and omnipotent is the silence of the night! And yet the stillness seems almost audible! From all the measureless depths of air around us comes a half-sound, a half-whisper, as if we could hear the crumbling and falling away of earth and all created things, in the great miracle of nature, decay and reproduction, ever beginning, never ending, — the gradual lapse and running of the sand in the great hour-glass of Time!"

In the night, Mr. Churchill had a singular dream. He thought himself in school, where he was reading Latin to his pupils. Suddenly all the

genitive cases of the first declension began to make faces at him, and to laugh immoderately; and when he tried to lay hold of them, they jumped down into the ablative, and the circumflex accent assumed the form of a great moustache. Then the little village school-house was transformed into a vast and endless school-house of the world, stretching forward, form after form, through all the generations of coming time; and on all the forms sat young men and old, reading and transcribing his Romance, which now in his dream was completed, and smiling and passing it onward from one to another, till at last the clock in the corner struck twelve, and the weights ran down with a strange, angry whirr, and the school broke up; and the schoolmaster awoke to find this vision of fame only a dream, out of which his alarm clock had aroused him at an untimely hour.

VI.

Meanwhile, a different scene was taking place at the parsonage. Mr. Pendexter had retired to his study to finish his farewell sermon. Silence reigned through the house. Sunday had already commenced there. The week ended with the setting of the sun, and the evening and the morning were the first day.

The clergyman was interrupted in his labors by the old sexton, who called as usual for the key of the church. He was gently rebuked for coming so late, and excused himself by saying that his wife was worse.

" Poor woman ! " said Mr. Pendexter ; " has she her mind ? "

" Yes," answered the sexton, " as much as ever."

" She has been ill a long time," continued, the clergyman. " We have had prayers for her a great many Sundays."

" It is very true, sir," replied the sexton, mournfully ; " I have given you a great deal of trouble. But you need not pray for her any more. It is of no use."

Mr. Pendexter's mind was in too fervid a state to notice the extreme and hopeless humility of his old parishioner, and the unintentional allusion to the inefficacy of his prayers. He pressed the old man's hand warmly, and said, with much emotion, —

" To-morrow is the last time that I shall preach in this parish, where I have preached for twenty-five years. But it is not the last time I shall pray for you and your family."

The sexton retired also much moved ; and the clergyman again resumed his task. His heart glowed and burned within him. Often his face flushed and his eyes filled with tears, so that he could not go on. Often he rose and paced the chamber to and fro, and wiped away the large drops that stood on his red and feverish forehead.

At length the sermon was finished. He rose and looked out of the window. Slowly the clock struck twelve. He had not heard it strike before, since six. The moonlight silvered the distant hills, and lay, white almost as snow, on the frosty roofs of the village. Not a light could be seen at any window.

"Ungrateful people! Could you not watch with me one hour?" exclaimed he, in that excited and bitter moment; as if he had thought that on that solemn night the whole parish would have watched, while he was writing his farewell discourse. He pressed his hot brow against the window-pane to allay its fever, and across the tremulous wavelets of the river the tranquil moon sent towards him a silvery shaft of light, like an angelic salutation. And the consoling thought came to him that not only this river, but all rivers and lakes, and the great sea itself, were flashing with this heavenly light, though he beheld it as a single ray only; and that what to him were the dark waves were the dark providences of God, luminous to others, and even to himself should he change his position.

VII.

The morning came — the dear, delicious, silent Sunday; to the weary workman, both of brain and hand, the beloved day of rest. When the first bell rang, like a brazen mortar, it seemed from its gloomy fortress to bombard the village with bursting shells of sound, that exploded over the houses, shattering the ears of all the parishioners, and shaking the consciences of many.

Mr. Pendexter was to preach his farewell sermon. The church was crowded, and only one person came late. It was a modest, meek girl, who stole silently up one of the side aisles, — not so silently, however, but that the pew-door creaked a little as she opened it; and straightway a hundred

heads were turned in that direction, although it was in the midst of the prayer. Old Mrs. Fairfield did not turn round, but she and her daughter looked at each other, and their bonnets made a parenthesis in the prayer, within which one asked what that was, and the other replied, —

"It is only Alice Archer. She always comes late."

Finally the long prayer was ended, and the congregation sat down, and the weary children — who are always restless during prayers, and had been for nearly half an hour twisting and turning, and standing first on one foot and then on the other, and hanging their heads over the backs of the pews, like tired colts looking into neighboring pastures — settled suddenly down, and subsided into something like rest.

The sermon began, — such a sermon as had never been preached, or even heard of before. It brought many tears into the eyes of the pastor's friends, and made the stoutest hearts among his foes quake with something like remorse. As he announced the text, "Yea, I think it meet as long as I am in this tabernacle to stir you up, by putting you in remembrance," it seemed as if the apostle Peter himself, from whose pen the words first proceeded, were calling them to judgment.

He began by giving a minute sketch of his ministry and the state of the parish, with all its troubles and dissensions, social, political, and ecclesiastical. He concluded by thanking those ladies who had presented him with a black silk gown, and had been kind to his wife during her long illness;

by apologizing for having neglected his own business, which was to study and preach, in order to attend to that of the parish, which was to support its minister, — stating that his own shortcomings had been owing to theirs, which had driven him into the woods in winter and into the fields in summer; and finally by telling the congregation in general that they were so confirmed in their bad habits, that no reformation was to be expected in them under his ministry, and that to produce one would require a greater exercise of Divine power than it did to create the world; for in creating the world there had been no opposition, whereas, in their reformation, their own obstinacy and evil propensities, and self-seeking, and worldly-mindedness, were all to be overcome!

VIII.

When Mr. Pendexter had finished his discourse, and pronounced his last benediction upon a congregation to whose spiritual wants he had ministered for so many years, his people, now his no more, returned home in very various states of mind. Some were exasperated, others mortified, and others filled with pity.

Among the last was Alice Archer, — a fair, delicate girl, whose whole life had been saddened by a too sensitive organization and by somewhat untoward circumstances. She had a pale, transparent complexion and large gray eyes, that seemed to see visions. Her figure was slight, almost fragile; her hands white, slender, diaphanous. With

these external traits her character was in unison. She was thoughtful, silent, susceptible ; often sad, often in tears, often lost in reveries. She led a lonely life with her mother, who was old, querulous, and nearly blind. She had herself inherited a predisposition to blindness, and in her disease there was this peculiarity, that she could see in Summer, but in Winter the power of vision failed her.

The old house they lived in, with its four sickly Lombardy poplars in front, suggested gloomy and mournful thoughts. It was one of those houses that depress you as you enter, as if many persons had died in it, — sombre, desolate, silent. The very clock in the hall had a dismal sound, gasping and catching its breath at times, and striking the hour with a violent, determined blow, reminding one of Jael driving the nail into the head of Sisera.

One other inmate the house had, and only one. This was Sally Manchester, or Miss Sally Manchester, as she preferred to be called ; an excellent chambermaid and a very bad cook, for she served in both capacities. She was, indeed, an extraordinary woman, of large frame and masculine features ; — one of those who are born to work, and accept their inheritance of toil as if it were play, and who consequently, in the language of domestic recommendations, are usually styled " a treasure, if you can get her." A treasure she was to this family ; for she did all the housework, and in addition took care of the cow and the poultry, — occasionally venturing into the field of veterinary practice, and administering lamp-oil to the

cock, when she thought he crowed hoarsely. She
had on her forehead what is sometimes denomi-
nated a " widow's peak," — that is to say, her hair
grew down to a point in the middle ; and on Sun-
days she appeared at church in a blue poplin gown,
with a large pink bow on what she called " the
congregation side of her bonnet." Her mind was
strong, like her person ; her disposition not sweet,
but, as is sometimes said of apples by way of rec-
ommendation, a pleasant sour.

Such were the inmates of the gloomy house, —
from which the last-mentioned frequently expressed
her intention of retiring, being engaged to a trav-
elling dentist, who, in filling her teeth with amal-
gam, had seized the opportunity to fill a soft place
in her heart with something still more dangerous
and mercurial. The wedding-day had been from
time to time postponed, and at length the family
hoped and believed it never would come, — a wish
prophetic of its own fulfilment.

Almost the only sunshine that from without
shone into the dark mansion came from the face
of Cecilia Vaughan, the school-mate and bosom-
friend of Alice Archer. They were nearly of the
same age, and had been drawn together by that
mysterious power which discovers and selects
friends for us in our childhood. They sat together
in school; they walked together after school ; they
told each other their manifold secrets ; they wrote
long and impassioned letters to each other in the
evening; in a word, they were in love with each
other. It was, so to speak, a rehearsal in girlhood
of the great drama of woman's life.

IX.

The golden tints of Autumn now brightened the shrubbery around this melancholy house, and took away something of its gloom. The four poplar trees seemed all ablaze, and flickered in the wind like huge torches. The little border of box filled the air with fragrance, and seemed to welcome the return of Alice, as she ascended the steps, and entered the house with a lighter heart than usual. The brisk autumnal air had quickened her pulse and given a glow to her cheek.

She found her mother alone in the parlor, seated in her large arm-chair. The warm sun streamed in at the uncurtained windows, and lights and shadows from the leaves lay upon her face. She turned her head as Alice entered, and said, —

" Who is it ? Is it you, Alice ? "

" Yes, it is I, mother."

" Where have you been so long ? "

" I have been nowhere, dear mother. I have come directly home from church."

" How long it seems to me ! It is very late. It is growing quite dark. I was just going to call for the lights."

" Why, mother ! " exclaimed Alice, in a startled tone; " what do you mean ? The sun is shining directly into your face ! "

" Impossible, my dear Alice. It is quite dark. I cannot see you. Where are you ? "

She leaned over her mother and kissed her. Both were silent, — both wept. They knew that the hour, so long looked forward to with dismay, had suddenly come. Mrs. Archer was blind!

This scene of sorrow was interrupted by the abrupt entrance of Sally Manchester. She, too, was in tears; but she was weeping for her own affliction. In her hand she held an open letter, which she gave to Alice, exclaiming amid sobs, —

" Read this, Miss Archer, and see how false man can be! Never trust any man! They are all alike; they are all false — false — false!"

Alice took the letter and read as follows : —

"It is with pleasure, Miss Manchester, I sit down to write you a few lines. I esteem you as highly as ever, but Providence has seemed to order and direct my thoughts and affections to another, — one in my own neighborhood. It was rather unexpected to me. Miss Manchester, I suppose you are well aware that we, as professed Christians, ought to be resigned to our lot in this world. May God assist you, so that we may be prepared to join the great company in heaven. Your answer would be very desirable. I respect your virtue, and regard you as a friend.

"MARTIN CHERRYFIELD.

" P. S. The society is generally pretty good here, but the state of religion is quite low."

"That is a cruel letter, Sally," said Alice, as she handed it back to her. "But we all have our troubles. That man is unworthy of you. Think no more about him."

"What is the matter?" inquired Mrs. Archer, hearing the counsel given and the sobs with which it was received. "Sally, what is the matter?"

Sally made no answer; but Alice said, —

"Mr. Cherryfield has fallen in love with somebody else." .

"Is that all?" said Mrs. Archer, evidently relieved. "She ought to be very glad of it. Why does she want to be married? She had much better stay with us; particularly now that I am blind."

When Sally heard this last word, she looked up in consternation. In a moment she forgot her own grief to sympathize with Alice and her mother. She wanted to do a thousand things at once; to go here; to send there; to get this and that; and particularly to call all the doctors in the neighborhood. Alice assured her it would be of no avail, though she finally consented that one should be sent for.

Sally went in search of him. On her way, her thoughts reverted to herself; and, to use her own phrase, "she curbed in like a stage-horse," as she walked. This state of haughty and offended pride continued for some hours after her return home. Later in the day, she assumed a decent composure, and requested that the man — she scorned to name him — might never again be mentioned in her hearing. Thus was her whole dream of felicity swept away by the tide of fate, as the nest of a ground-swallow by an inundation. It had been built too low to be secure.

Some women, after a burst of passionate tears, are soft, gentle, affectionate; a warm and genial air succeeds the rain. Others clear up cold, and are breezy, bleak, and dismal. Of the latter class

was Sally Manchester. She became embittered against all men on account of one, and was often heard to say that she thought women were fools to be married, and that, for one, she would not marry any man, let him be who he might, — not she!

The village doctor came. He was a large man, of the cheerful kind; vigorous, florid, encouraging, and pervaded by an indiscriminate odor of drugs. Loud voice, large cane, thick boots — everything about him synonymous with noise. His presence in the sick-room was like martial music, — inspiriting, but loud. He seldom left it without saying to the patient, " I hope you will feel more comfortable to-morrow," or, " When your fever leaves you, you will be better." But, in this instance, he could not go so far. Even his hopefulness was not sufficient for the emergency. Mrs. Archer was blind, — beyond remedy, beyond hope, — irrevocably blind!

X.

On the following morning, very early, as the schoolmaster stood at his door, inhaling the bright, wholesome air, and beholding the shadows of the rising sun, and the flashing dew-drops on the red vine-leaves, he heard the sound of wheels, and saw Mr. Pendexter and his wife drive down the village street in their old-fashioned chaise, known by all the boys in town as " the ark." The old white horse, that for so many years had stamped at funerals, and gnawed the tops of so many posts, and imagined he killed so many flies because he

wagged the stump of a tail, and, finally, had been
the cause of so much discord in the parish, seemed
now to make common cause with his master, and
stepped as if endeavoring to shake the dust from
his feet as he passed out of the ungrateful village.
Under the axle-tree hung suspended a leather
trunk; and in the chaise, between the two occu-
pants, was a large bandbox which forced Mr. Pen-
dexter to let his legs hang out of the vehicle, and
gave him the air of imitating the Scriptural be-
havior of his horse. Gravely and from a distance
he saluted the schoolmaster, who saluted him in
return, with a tear in his eye, that no man saw,
but which, nevertheless, was not unseen.

"Farewell, poor old man!" said the school-
master within himself, as he shut out the cold
autumnal air, and entered his comfortable study.
"We are not worthy of thee, or we should have
had thee with us forever. Go back again to the
place of thy childhood, the scene of thine early
labors and thine early love; let thy days end
where they began, and, like the emblem of eter-
nity, let the serpent of life coil itself round and
take its tail into its mouth, and be still from all
its hissings forevermore! I would not call thee
back; for it is better thou shouldst be where thou
art, than amid the angry contentions of this little
town."

Not all took leave of the old clergyman in so
kindly a spirit. Indeed, there was a pretty gen-
eral feeling of relief in the village, as when one
gets rid of an ill-fitting garment, or old-fashioned
hat, which one neither wishes to wear, nor is quite
willing to throw away.

Thus Mr. Pendexter departed from the village. A few days afterwards he was seen at a fall training, or general muster of the militia, making a prayer on horseback, with his eyes wide open ; a performance in which he took evident delight, as it gave him an opportunity of going quite at large into some of the bloodiest campaigns of the ancient Hebrews.

XI.

For a while the schoolmaster walked to and fro, looking at the gleam of the sunshine on the carpet, and revelling in his day-dreams of unwritten books and literary fame. With these day-dreams mingled confusedly the pattering of little feet, and the murmuring and cooing of his children overhead. His plans that morning, could he have executed them, would have filled a shelf in his library with poems and romances of his own creation. But suddenly the vision vanished, and another from the actual world took its place. It was the canvas-covered cart of the butcher, that, like the flying wigwam of the Indian tale, flitted before his eyes. It drove up the yard and stopped at the back door ; and the poet felt that the sacred rest of Sunday, the God's-truce with worldly cares, was once more at an end. A dark hand passed between him and the land of light. Suddenly closed the ivory gate of dreams, and the horn gate of every-day life opened, and he went forth to deal with the man of flesh and blood.

"Alas ! " said he with a sigh ; "and must my

life, then, always be like the Sabbatical river of the
Jews, flowing in full stream only on the seventh
day, and sandy and arid all the rest?"

Then he thought of his beautiful wife and chil-
dren, and added, half aloud, —

"No; not so! Rather let me look upon the
seven days of the week as the seven magic rings of
Jarchas, each inscribed with the name of a separate
planet, and each possessing a peculiar power; —
or, as the seven sacred and mysterious stones which
the pilgrims of Mecca were forced to throw over
their shoulders in the valleys of Menah and Akbah,
cursing the devil and saying at each throw, 'God
is great!'"

He found Mr. Wilmerdings, the butcher, stand-
ing beside his cart, and surrounded by five cats,
that had risen simultaneously on their hind legs, to
receive their quotidian morning's meal. Mr. Wil-
merdings not only supplied the village with fresh
provisions daily, but he likewise weighed all the
babies. There was hardly a child in town that had
not hung beneath his steelyards, tied in a silk
handkerchief, the movable weight above. sliding
along the notched beam from eight pounds to
twelve. He was a young man with a very fresh
and rosy complexion, and every Monday morning
he appeared dressed in an exceedingly white frock.
He had lately married a milliner, who sold " Dun-
stable and eleven-braid, openwork and colored
straws," and their bridal tour had been to a neigh-
boring town to see a man hanged for murdering
his wife. A pair of huge ox-horns branched from
the gable of his slaughter-house, and near it stood

the great pits of the tannery, which all the school-
boys thought were filled with blood!

Perhaps no two men could be more unlike than
Mr. Churchill and Mr. Wilmerdings. Upon such
a grating iron hinge opened the door of his daily
life — opened into the school-room, the theatre of
those life-long labors, which theoretically are the
most noble, and practically the most vexatious in
the world. Toward this, as soon as breakfast was
over, and he had played a while with his children,
he directed his steps. On his way, he had many
glimpses into the lovely realms of Nature, and one
into those of Art, through the medium of a placard
pasted against a wall. It was as follows : —

"The subscriber professes to take profiles, plain
and shaded, which, viewed at right-angles with the
serious countenance, are warranted to be infallibly
correct.

"No trouble of adorning or dressing the per-
son is required. He takes infants and children
at sight, and has frames of all sizes to accommo-
date.

"A profile is a delineated outline of the exterior
form of any person's face and head, the use of
which when seen tends to vivify the affections of
those whom we esteem or love.

"WILLIAM BANTAM."

Erelong even this glimpse into the ideal world
had vanished ; and he felt himself bound to the
earth with a hundred invisible threads, by which
a hundred urchins were tugging and tormenting

him ; and it was only with considerable effort, and at intervals, that his mind could soar to the moral dignity of his profession.

Such was the schoolmaster's life, and a dreary, weary life it would have been, had not poetry from within gushed through every crack and crevice in it. This transformed it, and made it resemble a well, into which stones and rubbish have been thrown ; but underneath is a spring of fresh, pure water, which nothing external can ever check or defile.

XII.

Mr. Pendexter had departed. Only a few old and middle-aged people regretted him. To these few, something was wanting in the service ever afterwards. They missed the accounts of the Hebrew massacres, and the wonderful tales of the Zumzummims ; they missed the venerable gray hair, and the voice that had spoken to them in childhood, and forever preserved the memory of it in their hearts, as in the Russian Church the old hymns of the earliest centuries are still piously retained.

The winter came, with all its affluence of snows, and its many candidates for the vacant pulpit. But the parish was difficult to please, as all parishes are ; and talked of dividing itself, and building a new church, and other extravagances, as all parishes do. Finally it concluded to remain as it was, and the choice of a pastor was made.

The events of the winter were few in number,

and can be easily described. The following extract from a school-girl's letter to an absent friend contains the most important : —

" At school, things have gone on pretty much as usual. Jane Brown has grown very pale. They say she is in a consumption, but I think it is because she eats so many slate-pencils. One of her shoulders has grown a good deal higher than the other. Billy Wilmerdings has been turned out of school for playing truant. He promised his mother, if she would not whip him, he would experience religion. I am sure I wish he would; for then he would stop looking at me through the hole in the top of his desk. Mr. Churchill is a very curious man. To-day he gave us this question in arithmetic : ' One fifth of a hive of bees flew to the Kadamba flower; one third flew to the Silandhara; three times the difference of these two numbers flew to an arbor; and one bee continued flying about, attracted on each side by the fragrant Ketaki and the Malati. What was the number of bees ? ' Nobody could do the sum.

" The church has been repaired, and we have a new mahogany pulpit. Mr. Churchill bought the old one, and had it put up in his study. What a strange man he is ! A good many candidates have preached for us. The only one we like is Mr. Kavanagh. Arthur Kavanagh ! is not that a romantic name ? He is tall, very pale, with beautiful black eyes and hair ! Sally — Alice Archer's Sally — says ' he is not a man; he is a Thaddeus of Warsaw ! ' I think he is very handsome. And such sermons ! So beautifully written, so different

from old Mr. Pendexter's! He has been invited
to settle here, but he cannot come till Spring.
Last Sunday he preached about the ruling passion.
He said that once a German nobleman, when he
was dying, had his hunting-horn blown in his bed-
room, and his hounds let in, springing and howling
about him; and that so it was with the ruling pas-
sions of men; even around the death-bed, at the
well-known signal, they howled and leaped about
those that had fostered them! Beautiful, is it
not? and so original! He said in another sermon,
that disappointments feed and nourish us in the
desert places of life, as the ravens did the Prophet
in the wilderness; and that as, in Catholic coun-
tries, the lamps lighted before the images of saints,
in narrow and dangerous streets, not only served as
offerings of devotion, but likewise as lights to those
who passed, so, in the dark and dismal streets of
the city of Unbelief, every good thought, word, and
deed of a man, not only was an offering to heaven,
but likewise served to light him and others on their
way homeward! I have taken a good many notes
of Mr. Kavanagh's sermons, which you shall see
when you come back.

" Last week we had a sleigh-ride, with six white
horses. We went like the wind over the hollows
in the snow; — the driver called them ' thank-you-
ma'ams,' because they made everybody bow. And
such a frantic ball as we had at Beaverstock! I
wish you had been there! We did not get home
till two o'clock in the morning; and the next day
Hester Green's minister asked her if she did not
feel the fire of a certain place growing hot under
her feet, while she was dancing!

"The new fashionable boarding-school begins next week. The prospectus has been sent to our house. One of the regulations is, 'Young ladies are not allowed to cross their benders in school'! Papa says he never heard knees called so before. Old Mrs. Plainfield is gone at last. Just before she died, her Irish chambermaid asked her if she wanted to be buried with her false teeth! There has not been a single new engagement since you went away. But somebody asked me the other day if you were engaged to Mr. Pillsbury. I was very angry. Pillsbury, indeed! He is old enough to be your father!

"What a long, rambling letter I am writing you! — and only because you will be so naughty as to stay away and leave me all alone. If you could have seen the moon last night! But what a goose I am! — as if you did not see it! Was it not glorious? You cannot imagine, dearest, how every hour in the day I wish you were here with me. I know you would sympathize with all my feelings, which Hester does not at all. For, if I admire the moon, she says I am romantic, and, for her part, if there is anything she despises, it is the moon! and that she prefers a snug, warm bed (oh, horrible!) to all the moons in the universe!"

XIII.

The events mentioned in this letter were the principal ones that occurred during the winter. The case of Billy Wilmerdings grew quite desperate. In vain did his father threaten and the school-

master expostulate; he was only the more sullen and
stubborn. In vain did his mother represent to his
weary mind, that, if he did not study, the boys who
knew the dead languages would throw stones at
him in the street; he only answered that he should
like to see them try it. Till, finally, having lost
many of his illusions, and having even discovered
that his father was not the greatest man in the
world, on the breaking up of the ice in the river,
to his own infinite relief and that of the whole
village, he departed on a coasting trip in a fore-
and-aft schooner, which constituted the entire navi-
gation of Fairmeadow.

Mr. Churchill had really put up in his study
the old white pulpit, shaped like a wine-glass.
It served as a play-house for his children, who,
whether in it or out of it, daily preached to his
heart, and were a living illustration of the way to
enter into the kingdom of heaven. Moreover, he
himself made use of it externally as a note-book,
recording his many meditations with a pencil on
the white panels. The following will serve as a
specimen of this pulpit eloquence : —

Morality without religion is only a kind of dead-
reckoning, — an endeavor to find our place on
a cloudy sea by measuring the distance we have
run, but without any observation of the heavenly
bodies.

Many readers judge of the power of a book by
the shock it gives their feelings, — as some savage
tribes determine the power of muskets by their

recoil; that being considered best which fairly prostrates the purchaser.

Men of genius are often dull and inert in society; as the blazing meteor, when it descends to earth, is only a stone.

The natural alone is permanent. Fantastic idols may be worshipped for a while; but at length they are overturned by the continual and silent progress of Truth, as the grim statues of Copan have been pushed from their pedestals by the growth of forest-trees, whose seeds were sown by the wind in the ruined walls.

The every-day cares and duties, which men call drudgery, are the weights and counterpoises of the clock of time, giving its pendulum a true vibration, and its hands a regular motion; and when they cease to hang upon the wheels, the pendulum no longer swings, the hands no longer move, the clock stands still.

The same object, seen from the three different points of view, — the Past, the Present, and the Future, — often exhibits three different faces to us; like those sign-boards over shop doors, which represent the face of a lion as we approach, of a man when we are in front, and of an ass when we have passed.

In character, in manners, in style, in all things, the supreme excellence is simplicity.

With many readers, brilliancy of style passes for affluence of thought; they mistake buttercups in the grass for immeasurable gold mines under ground.

The motives and purposes of authors are not always so pure and high as, in the enthusiasm of youth, we sometimes imagine. To many the trumpet of fame is nothing but a tin horn to call them home, like laborers from the field, at dinner-time; and they think themselves lucky to get the dinner.

The rays of happiness, like those of light, are colorless when unbroken.

Critics are sentinels in the grand army of letters, stationed at the corners of newspapers and reviews, to challenge every new author.

The country is lyric, — the town dramatic. When mingled, they make the most perfect musical drama.

Our passions never wholly die; but in the last cantos of life's romantic epos, they rise up again and do battle, like some of Ariosto's heroes, who have already been quietly interred, and ought to be turned to dust.

This country is not priest-ridden, but press-ridden.

Some critics have the habit of rowing up the

Heliconian rivers with their backs turned, so as to see the landscape precisely as the poet did not see it. Others see faults in a book much larger than the book itself; as Sancho Panza, with his eyes blinded, beheld from his wooden horse the earth no larger than a grain of mustard-seed, and the men and women on it as large as hazel-nuts.

Like an inundation of the Indus is the course of Time. We look for the homes of our childhood, they are gone; for the friends of our childhood, they are gone. The loves and animosities of youth, where are they? Swept away like the camps that had been pitched in the sandy bed of the river.

As no saint can be canonized until the Devil's Advocate has exposed all his evil deeds, and showed why he should not be made a saint, so no poet can take his station among the gods until the critics have said all that can be said against him.

It is curious to note the old sea-margins of human thought! Each subsiding century reveals some new mystery; we build where monsters used to hide themselves.

XIV.

At length the Spring came, and brought the birds, and the flowers, and Mr. Kavanagh, the new clergyman, who was ordained with all the pomp and ceremony usual on such occasions. The open-

ing of the season furnished also the theme of his first discourse, which some of the congregation thought very beautiful, and others very incomprehensible.

Ah, how wonderful is the advent of the Spring! — the great annual miracle of the blossoming of Aaron's rod, repeated on myriads and myriads of branches! — the gentle progression and growth of herbs, flowers, trees, — gentle, and yet irrepressible, — which no force can stay, no violence restrain, like love, that wins its way and cannot be withstood by any human power, because itself is divine power. If Spring came but once a century, instead of once a year, or burst forth with the sound of an earthquake, and not in silence, what wonder and expectation would there be in all hearts to behold the miraculous change!

But now the silent succession suggests nothing but necessity. To most men, only the cessation of the miracle would be miraculous, and the perpetual exercise of God's power seems less wonderful than its withdrawal would be. We are like children who are astonished and delighted only by the second-hand of the clock, not by the hour-hand.

Such was the train of thought with which Kavanagh commenced his sermon. And then, with deep solemnity and emotion, he proceeded to speak of the Spring of the soul, as from its cheerless wintry distance it turns nearer and nearer to the great Sun, and clothes its dry and withered branches anew with leaves and blossoms, unfolded from within itself, beneath the penetrating and irresistible influence.

While delivering the discourse, Kavanagh had
not succeeded so entirely in abstracting himself
from all outward things as not to note in some
degree its effect upon his hearers. As in modern
times no applause is permitted in our churches,
however moved the audience may be, and, conse-
quently, no one dares wave his hat and shout, —
" Orthodox Chrysostom ! Thirteenth Apostle !
Worthy the Priesthood ! " — as was done in the
days of the Christian Fathers ; and, moreover, as
no one after church spoke to him of his sermon, or
of anything else, he went home with rather a
heavy heart, and a feeling of discouragement. One
thing had cheered and consoled him. It was the
pale countenance of a young girl, whose dark eyes
had been fixed upon him during the whole dis-
course with unflagging interest and attention. She
sat alone in a pew near the pulpit. It was Alice
Archer. Ah ! could he have known how deeply
sank his words into that simple heart, he might
have shuddered with another kind of fear than
that of not moving his audience sufficiently !

XV.

On the following morning Kavanagh sat musing
upon his worldly affairs, and upon various little
household arrangements which it would be neces-
sary for him to make. To aid him in these, he
had taken up the village paper, and was running
over the columns of advertisements, — those nar-
row and crowded thoroughfares, in which the
wants and wishes of humanity display themselves

like mendicants without disguise. His eye ran hastily over the advantageous offers of the cheap tailors and the dealers in patent medicines. He wished neither to be clothed nor cured. In one place he saw that a young lady, perfectly competent, desired to form a class of young mothers and nurses, and to instruct them in the art of talking to infants so as to interest and amuse them; and in another, that the firemen of Fairmeadow wished well to those hostile editors who had called them gamblers, drunkards, and rioters, and hoped that they might be spared from that great fire which they were told could never be extinguished! Finally, his eye rested on the advertisement of a carpet warehouse, in which the one-price system was strictly adhered to. It was farther stated that a discount would be made " to clergymen on small salaries, feeble churches, and charitable institutions." Thinking that this was doubtless the place for one who united in himself two of these qualifications for a discount, with a smile on his lips, he took his hat and sallied forth into the street.

A few days previous, Kavanagh had discovered in the tower of the church a vacant room, which he had immediately determined to take possession of, and to convert into a study. From this retreat, through the four oval windows, fronting the four corners of the heavens, he could look down upon the streets, the roofs and gardens of the village, — on the winding river, the meadows, the farms, the distant blue mountains. Here he could sit and meditate, in that peculiar sense of seclusion

and spiritual elevation, that entire separation from
the world below, which a chamber in a tower al-
ways gives. Here, uninterrupted and aloof from
all intrusion, he could pour his heart into those
discourses, with which he hoped to reach and move
the hearts of his parishioners.

It was to furnish this retreat, that he went forth
on the Monday morning after his first sermon. He
was not long in procuring the few things needed,
— the carpet, the table, the chairs, the shelves for
books ; and was returning thoughtfully homeward,
when his eye was caught by a sign-board on the
corner of the street, inscribed " Moses Merry-
weather, Dealer in Singing Birds, foreign and do-
mestic." He saw also a whole chamber-window
transformed into a cage, in which sundry canary-
birds, and others of a gayer plumage, were jargon-
ing together, like people in the market-places of
foreign towns. At the sight of these old favorites,
a long slumbering passion awoke within him, and
he straightway ascended the dark wooden stair-
case, with the intent of enlivening his solitary
room with the vivacity and songs of these captive
ballad-singers.

In a moment he found himself in a little room
hung round with cages, roof and walls ; full of
sunshine ; full of twitterings, cooings, and flutter-
ings ; full of downy odors, suggesting nests, and
dovecots, and distant islands inhabited only by
birds. The taxidermist — the Selkirk of the sunny
island — was not there ; but a young lady of noble
mien, who was looking at an English goldfinch in
a square cage with a portico, turned upon him, as

he entered, a fair and beautiful face, shaded by
long light locks, in which the sunshine seemed en-
tangled, as among the boughs of trees. That face
he had never seen before, and yet it seemed famil-
iar to him; and the added light in her large, celes-
tial eyes, and the almost imperceptible expression
that passed over her face, showed that she knew
who he was.

At the same moment the taxidermist presented
himself, coming from an inner room; — a little
man in gray, with spectacles upon his nose, holding
in his hands, with wings and legs drawn close and
smoothly together, like the green husks of the
maize ear, a beautiful carrier-pigeon, who turned
up first one bright eye and then the other, as if ask-
ing, "What are you going to do with me now?"
This silent inquiry was soon answered by Mr. Mer-
ryweather, who said to the young lady, —

"Here, Miss Vaughan, is the best carrier-pigeon
in my whole collection. The real Columba Ta-
bullaria. He is about three years old, as you can
see by his wattle."

"A very pretty bird," said the lady; "and how
shall I train it?"

"Oh, that is very easy. You have only to keep
it shut up for a few days, well fed and well
treated. Then take it in an open cage to the
place you mean it to fly to, and do the same thing
there. Afterwards it will give you no trouble; it
will always fly between those two places."

"That, certainly, is not very difficult. At all
events, I will make the trial. You may send the
bird home to me. On what shall I feed it?"

"On any kind of grain; barley and buckwheat are best; and remember to let it have a plenty of gravel in the bottom of its cage."

"I will not forget. Send me the bird to-day, if possible."

With these words she departed, much too soon for Kavanagh, who was charmed with her form, her face, her voice; and who, when left alone with the little taxidermist, felt that the momentary fascination of the place was gone. He heard no longer the singing of the birds; he saw no longer their gay plumage; and having speedily made the purchase of a canary and a cage, he likewise departed, thinking of the carrier-pigeons of Bagdad, and the columbaries of Egypt, stationed at fixed intervals as relays and resting-places for the flying post. With an indefinable feeling of sadness, too, came wafted like a perfume through his memory those tender, melancholy lines of Maria del Occidente : —

> And as the dove, to far Palmyra flying,
> From where her native founts of Antioch beam,
> Weary, exhausted, longing, panting, sighing,
> Lights sadly at the desert's bitter stream ;
>
> So many a soul, o'er life's drear desert faring, —
> Love's pure, congenial spring unfound, unquaffed, —
> Suffers, recoils, then, thirsty and despairing
> Of what it would, descends and sips the nearest draught.

Meanwhile, Mr. Merryweather, left to himself, walked about his aviary, musing, and talking to his birds. Finally he paused before the tin cage of a gray African parrot, between which and himself there was a strong family likeness, and, giving

it his finger to peck and perch upon, conversed with it in that peculiar dialect with which it had often made vocal the distant groves of Zanguebar. He then withdrew to the inner room, where he resumed his labor of stuffing a cardinal grossbeak, saying to himself between whiles, —

"I wonder what Miss Cecilia Vaughan means to do with a carrier-pigeon!"

Some mysterious connection he had evidently established already between this pigeon and Mr. Kavanagh; for, continuing his revery, he said, half aloud, —

"Of course she would never think of marrying a poor clergyman!"

XVI.

The old family mansion of the Vaughans stood a little out of town, in the midst of a pleasant farm. The county road was not near enough to annoy, and the rattling wheels and little clouds of dust seemed like friendly salutations from travellers as they passed. They spoke of safety and companionship, and took away all loneliness from the solitude.

On three sides, the farm was enclosed by willow and alder hedges, and the flowing wall of a river; nearer the house were groves clear of all underwood, with rocky knolls, and breezy bowers of beech; and afar off the blue hills broke the horizon, creating secret longings for what lay beyond them, and filling the mind with pleasant thoughts of Prince Rasselas and the Happy Valley.

The house was one of the few old houses still standing in New England, — a large, square building, with a portico in front, whose door in Summer time stood open from morning until night. A pleasing stillness reigned about it, and soft gusts of pine-embalmed air, and distant cawings from the crow-haunted mountains, filled its airy and ample halls.

In this old-fashioned house had Cecilia Vaughan grown up to maidenhood. The travelling shadows of the clouds on the hillsides, — the sudden Summer wind, that lifted the languid leaves, and rushed from field to field, from grove to grove, the forerunner of the rain, — and, most of all, the mysterious mountain, whose coolness was a perpetual invitation to her, and whose silence a perpetual fear, — fostered her dreamy and poetic temperament. Not less so did the reading of poetry and romance in the long, silent, solitary winter evenings. Her mother had been dead for many years, and the memory of that mother had become almost a religion to her. She recalled it incessantly, and the reverential love which it inspired completely filled her soul with melancholy delight. Her father was a kindly old·man, a judge in one of the courts; dignified, affable, somewhat bent by his legal erudition, as a shelf is by the weight of the books upon it. His papers encumbered the study table, — his law books, the study floor. They seemed to shut out from his mind the lovely daughter, who had grown up to womanhood by his side, but almost without his recognition. Always affectionate, always indulgent, he left her to walk alone,

without his stronger thought and firmer purpose to lean upon; and though her education had been, on this account, somewhat desultory, and her imagination indulged in many dreams and vagaries, yet, on the whole, the result had been more favorable than in many cases where the process of instruction has been too diligently carried on, and where, as sometimes on the roofs of farm-houses and barns, the scaffolding has been left to deform the building.

Cecilia's bosom-friend at school was Alice Archer; and, after they left school, the love between them, and consequently the letters, rather increased than diminished. These two young hearts found not only a delight, but a necessity, in pouring forth their thoughts and feelings to each other; and it was to facilitate this intercommunication, for whose exigencies the ordinary methods were now found inadequate, that the carrier-pigeon had been purchased. He was to be the flying post; their bedrooms the dovecots, the pure and friendly columbaria.

Endowed with youth, beauty, talent, fortune, and, moreover, with that indefinable fascination which has no name, Cecilia Vaughan was not without lovers, avowed and unavowed; — young men, who made an ostentatious display of their affection; — boys, who treasured it in their bosoms, as something indescribably sweet and precious, perfuming all the chambers of the heart with its celestial fragrance. Whenever she returned from a visit to the city, some unknown youth of elegant manners and varnished leather boots was sure to hover round the village inn for a few days, — was

known to visit the Vaughans assiduously, and then silently to disappear, and be seen no more. Of course, nothing could be known of the secret history of such individuals, but shrewd surmises were formed as to their designs and their destinies; till finally, any well-dressed stranger, lingering in the village without ostensible business, was set down as " one of Miss Vaughan's lovers."

In all this, what a contrast was there between the two young friends! The wealth of one and the poverty of the other were not so strikingly at variance, as this affluence and refluence of love. To the one, so much was given that she became regardless of the gift; from the other, so much withheld, that, if possible, she exaggerated its importance.

XVII.

In addition to these transient lovers, who were but birds of passage, winging their way, in an incredibly short space of time, from the torrid to the frigid zone, there was in the village a domestic and resident adorer, whose love for himself, for Miss Vaughan, and for the beautiful, had transformed his name from Hiram A. Hawkins to II. Adolphus Hawkins. He was a dealer in English linens and carpets — a profession which of itself fills the mind with ideas of domestic comfort. His waistcoats were made like Lord Melbourne's in the illustrated English papers, and his shiny hair went off to the left in a superb sweep, like the hand-rail of a banister. He wore many rings on his fingers,

and several breastpins and gold chains disposed
about his person. On all his bland physiognomy
was stamped, as on some of his linens,. " Soft finish
for family use." Everything about him spoke the
lady's man. He was, in fact, a perfect ring-dove ;
and, like the rest of his species, always walked
up to the female, and, bowing his head, swelled
out his white crop, and uttered a very plaintive
murmur.

Moreover, Mr. H. Adolphus Hawkins was a
poet, — so much a poet, that, as his sister frequently
remarked, he " spoke blank verse in the bosom of
his family." The general tone of his productions
was sad, desponding, perhaps slightly morbid.
How could it be otherwise with the writings of one
who had never been the world's friend, nor the
world his ? who looked upon himself as "a pyramid
of mind on the dark desert of despair " ? and who,
at the age of twenty-five, had drunk the bitter
draught of life to the dregs, and dashed the goblet
down ? His productions were published in the
Poet's Corner of the Fairmeadow Advertiser, and
it was a relief to know, that, in private life, as his
sister remarked, he was " by no means the censo-
rious and moody person some of his writings might
imply."

Such was the personage who assumed to himself
the perilous position of Miss Vaughan's permanent
lover. He imagined that it was impossible for
any woman to look upon him and not love him.
Accordingly, he paraded himself at his shop-door
as she passed ; he paraded himself at the corners
of the streets ; he paraded himself at the church·

steps on Sunday. He spied her from the window ;
he sallied from the door ; he followed her with his
eyes ; he followed her with his whole august per-
son ; he passed her and repassed her, and turned
back to gaze ; he lay in wait with dejected counte-
nance and desponding air ; he persecuted her with
his looks ; he pretended that their souls could
comprehend each other without words ; and when-
ever her lovers were alluded to in his presence, he
gravely declared, as one who had reason to know,
that, if Miss Vaughan ever married, it would be
some one of gigantic intellect !

Of these persecutions Cecilia was for a long
time the unconscious victim. She saw this indi-
vidual, with rings and strange waistcoats, perform-
ing his gyrations before her, but did not suspect .
that she was the centre of attraction, — not imag-
ining that any man would begin his wooing with
such outrages. Gradually the truth dawned upon
her, and became the source of indescribable annoy-
ance, which was augmented by a series of anony-
mous letters, written in a female hand, and setting
forth the excellences of a certain mysterious rela-
tive, — his modesty, his reserve, his extreme deli-
cacy, his talent for poetry, — rendered authentic
by extracts from his papers, made, of course, with-
out the slightest knowledge or suspicion on his
part. Whence came these sibylline leaves ? At
first Cecilia could not divine ; but, erelong, her
woman's instinct traced them to the thin and ner-
vous hand of the poet's sister. This surmise was
confirmed by her maid, who asked the boy that
brought them.

It was with one of these missives in her hand that Cecilia entered Mrs. Archer's house, after purchasing the carrier-pigeon. Unannounced she entered, and walked up the narrow and imperfectly lighted stairs to Alice's bedroom, — that little sanctuary draped with white, — that columbarium lined with warmth, and softness, and silence. Alice was not there ; but the chair by the window, the open volume of Tennyson's poems on the table, the note to Cecilia by its side, and the ink not yet dry in the pen, were like the vibration of a bough, when the bird has just left it, — like the rising of the grass, when the foot has just pressed it. In a moment she returned. She had been down to her mother, who sat talking, talking, talking, with an old friend in the parlor below, even as these young friends were talking together, in the bedroom above. Ah, how different were their themes! Death and Love, — apples of Sodom, that crumble to ashes at a touch, — golden fruits of the Hesperides, — golden fruits of Paradise, fragrant, ambrosial, perennial !

"I have just been writing to you," said Alice ; "I wanted so much to see you this morning !"

"Why this morning in particular? Has anything happened?"

"Nothing, only I had such a longing to see you!"

And, seating herself in a low chair by Cecilia's side, she laid her head upon the shoulder of her friend, who, taking one of her pale, thin hands in both her own, silently kissed her forehead again and again.

Alice was not aware, that, in the words she uttered, there was the slightest shadow of untruth. And yet had nothing happened? Was it nothing, that among her thoughts a new thought had risen, like a star, whose pale effulgence, mingled with the common daylight, was not yet distinctly visible even to herself, but would grow brighter as the sun grew lower, and the rosy twilight darker? Was it nothing, that a new fountain of affection had suddenly sprung up within her, which she mistook for the freshening and overflowing of the old fountain of friendship, that hitherto had kept the lowland landscape of her life so green, but now, being flooded by more affection, was not to cease, but only to disappear in the greater tide, and flow unseen beneath it? Yet so it was; and this stronger yearning — this unappeasable desire for her friend — was only the tumultuous swelling of a heart, that as yet knows not its own secret.

"I am so glad to see you, Cecilia!" she continued. "You are so beautiful! I love so much to sit and look at you! Ah, how I wish Heaven had made me as tall, and strong, and beautiful as you are!"

"You little flatterer! What an affectionate, lover-like friend you are! What have you been doing all the morning?"

"Looking out of the window, thinking of you, and writing you this letter, to beg you to come and see me."

"And I have been buying a carrier-pigeon, to fly between us, and carry all our letters."

"That will be delightful."

" He is to be sent home to-day ; and after he gets accustomed to my room, I shall send him here, to get acquainted with yours ; — an Iachimo in my Imogen's bedchamber, to spy out its secrets."

" If he sees Cleopatra in these white curtains, and silver Cupids in these andirons, he will have your imagination."

" He will see the book with the leaf turned down, and you asleep, and tell me all about you."

" A carrier-pigeon! What a charming idea! and how like you to think of it! "

" But to-day I have been obliged to bring my own letters. I have some more sibylline leaves from my anonymous correspondent, in laud and exaltation of her modest relative, who speaks blank verse in the bosom of his family. I have brought them to read you some extracts, and to take your advice; for, really and seriously, this must be stopped. It has grown too annoying."

" How much love you have offered you! " said Alice, sighing.

" Yes, quite too much of this kind. On my way here, I saw the modest relative, standing at the corner of the street, hanging his head in this way."

And she imitated the melancholy Hiram Adolphus, and the young friends laughed.

" I hope you did not notice him? " resumed Alice.

" Certainly not. But what do you suppose he did? As soon as he saw me, he began to walk backward down the street only a short distance in

front of me, staring at me most impertinently.
Of course, I took no notice of this strange con-
duct. I felt myself blushing to the eyes with in-
dignation, and yet could hardly suppress my desire
to laugh."

" If you had laughed, he would have taken it
for an encouragement, and I have no doubt it
would have brought on the catastrophe."

" And that would have ended the matter. I half
wish I had laughed."

" But think of the immortal glory of marrying
a poet ! "

" And of inscribing on my cards, Mrs. H. Adol-
phus Hawkins ! "

" A few days ago, I went to buy something at
his shop ; and, leaning over the counter, he asked
me if I had seen the sun set the evening before, —
adding, that it was gorgeous, and that the grass and
trees were of a beautiful Paris green ! "

And again the young friends gave way to their
mirth.

" One thing, dear Alice, you must consent to do
for me. You must write to Miss Martha Amelia,
the author of all these epistles, and tell her very
plainly how indelicate her conduct is, and how
utterly useless all such proceedings will prove in
effecting her purpose."

" I will write this very day. You shall be no
longer persecuted."

" And now let me give you a few extracts from
these wonderful epistles."

So saying, Cecilia drew forth a small package
of three-cornered billets, tied with a bit of pink

ribbon. Taking one of them at random, she was on the point of beginning, but paused, as if her attention had been attracted by something out of doors. The sound of passing footsteps was heard on the gravel walk.

"There goes Mr. Kavanagh," said she, in a half-whisper.

Alice rose suddenly from her low chair at Cecilia's side, and the young friends looked from the window to see the clergyman pass.

"How handsome he is!" said Alice, involuntarily.

"He is, indeed."

At that moment Alice started back from the window. Kavanagh had looked up in passing, as if his eye had been drawn by some secret magnetism. A bright color flushed the cheek of Alice; her eyes fell, but Cecilia continued to look steadily into the street. Kavanagh passed on, and in a few moments was out of sight.

The two friends stood silent, side by side.

XVIII.

Arthur Kavanagh was descended from an ancient Catholic family. His ancestors had purchased from the Baron Victor of St. Castine a portion of his vast estates, lying upon that wild and wonderful sea-coast of Maine, which, even upon the map, attracts the eye by its singular and picturesque indentations, and fills the heart of the beholder with something of that delight which throbbed in the veins of Pierre du Gast, when,

with a royal charter of the land from the Atlantic
to the Pacific, he sailed down the coast in all the
pride of one who is to be prince of such a vast
domain. Here, in the bosom of the solemn for-
ests, they continued the practice of that faith
which had first been planted there by Rasle and
St. Castine; and the little church where they wor-
shipped is still standing, though now as closed and
silent as the graves which surround it, and in
which the dust of the Kavanaghs lies buried.

In these solitudes, in this faith, was Kavanagh
born, and grew to childhood, a feeble, delicate boy,
watched over by a grave and taciturn father, and
a mother who looked upon him with infinite ten-
derness, as upon a treasure she should not long
retain. She walked with him by the seaside, and
spake to him of God, and the mysterious majesty
of the ocean, with its tides and tempests. She sat
with him on the carpet of golden threads beneath
the aromatic pines, and, as the perpetual melan-
choly sound ran along the rattling boughs, his soul
seemed to rise and fall, with a motion and a
whisper like those in the branches over him. She
taught him his letters from the Lives of the
Saints, — a volume full of wondrous legends, and
illustrated with engravings from pictures by the
old masters, which opened to him at once the
world of spirits and the world of art; and both
were beautiful. She explained to him the pic-
tures; she read to him the legends, — the lives of
holy men and women, full of faith and good works,
— things which ever afterward remained associ-
ated together in his mind. Thus holiness of life,

and self-renunciation, and devotion to duty, were early impressed upon his soul. To his quick imagination, the spiritual world became real; the holy company of the saints stood round about the solitary boy; his guardian angels led him by the hand by day, and sat by his pillow at night. At times, even, he wished to die, that he might see them and talk with them, and return no more to his weak and weary body.

Of all the legends of the mysterious book, that which most delighted and most deeply impressed him was the legend of St. Christopher. The picture was from a painting of Paolo Farinato, representing a figure of gigantic strength and stature, leaning upon a staff, and bearing the infant Christ on his bending shoulders across the rushing river. The legend related, that St. Christopher, being of huge proportions and immense strength, wandered long about the world before his conversion, seeking for the greatest king, and willing to obey no other. After serving various masters, whom he in turn deserted, because each recognized by some word or sign another greater than himself, he heard by chance of Christ, the king of heaven and earth, and asked of a holy hermit where he might be found, and how he might serve him. The hermit told him he must fast and pray, but the giant replied that if he fasted he should lose his strength, and that he did not know how to pray. Then the hermit told him to take up his abode on the banks of a dangerous mountain torrent, where travellers were often drowned in crossing, and to rescue any that might be in peril. The giant obeyed, and tear-

ing up a palm-tree by the roots for a staff, he took his station by the river's side, and saved many lives. And the Lord looked down from heaven and said, " Behold this strong man, who knows not yet the way to worship, but has found the way to serve me ! " And one night he heard the voice of a child, crying in the darkness and saying, " Christopher ! come and bear me over the river ! " And he went out, and found the child sitting alone on the margin of the stream ; and taking him upon his shoulders, he waded into the water. Then the wind began to roar, and the waves to rise higher and higher about him, and his little burden, which at first had seemed so light, grew heavier and heavier as he advanced, and bent his huge shoulders down, and put his life in peril ; so that, when he reached the shore, he said, " Who art thou, O child, that hast weighed upon me with a weight, as if I had borne the whole world upon my shoulders ? " And the little child answered, " Thou hast borne the whole world upon thy shoulders, and Him who created it. I am Christ, whom thou by thy deeds of charity wouldst serve. Thou and thy service are accepted. Plant thy staff in the ground, and it shall blossom and bear fruit ! " With these words, the child vanished away.

There was something in this beautiful legend that entirely captivated the heart of the boy, and a vague sense of its hidden meaning seemed at times to seize him and control him. Later in life it became more and more evident to him, and remained forever in his mind as a lovely allegory of

active charity and a willingness to serve. Like the giant's staff, it blossomed and bore fruit.

But the time at length came, when his father decreed that he must be sent away to school. It was not meet that his son should be educated as a girl. He must go to the Jesuit college in Canada. Accordingly, one bright summer morning, he departed with his father, on horseback, through those majestic forests that stretch with almost unbroken shadows from the sea to the St. Lawrence, leaving behind him all the endearments of home, and a wound in his mother's heart that never ceased to ache, — a longing, unsatisfied and insatiable, for her absent Arthur, who had gone from her perhaps forever.

At college he distinguished himself by his zeal for study, by the docility, gentleness, and generosity of his nature. There he was thoroughly trained in the classics, and in the dogmas of that august faith, whose turrets gleam with such crystalline light, and whose dungeons are so deep, and dark, and terrible. The study of philosophy and theology was congenial to his mind. Indeed, he often laid aside Homer for Parmenides, and turned from the odes of Pindar and Horace to the mystic hymns of Cleanthes and Synesius.

The uniformity of college life was broken only by the annual visit home in the summer vacation ; the joyous meeting, the bitter parting ; the long journey to and fro through the grand, solitary, mysterious forest. To his mother these visits were even more precious than to himself ; for ever more and more they added to her boundless affection

the feeling of pride and confidence and satisfaction, — the joy and beauty of a youth unspotted from the world, and glowing with the enthusiasm of virtue.

At length his college days were ended. He returned home full of youth, full of joy and hope; but it was only to receive the dying blessings of his mother, who expired in peace, having seen his face once more. Then the house became empty to him. Solitary was the sea-shore, solitary were the woodland walks. But the spiritual world seemed nearer and more real. For affairs he had no aptitude; and he betook himself again to his philosophic and theological studies. He pondered with fond enthusiasm on the rapturous pages of Molinos and Madame Guyon; and in a spirit akin to that which wrote, he read the writings of Santa Theresa, which he found among his mother's books, — the Meditations, the Road to Perfection, and the Moradas, or Castle of the Soul. She, too, had lingered over those pages with delight, and there were many passages marked by her own hand. Among them was this, which he often repeated to himself in his lonely walks: "O Life, Life! how canst thou sustain thyself, being absent from thy Life? In so great a solitude, in what shalt thou employ thyself? What shalt thou do, since all thy deeds are faulty and imperfect?"

In such meditations passed many weeks and months. But mingled with them, continually and ever with more distinctness, arose in his memory from the days of childhood the old tradition of St. Christopher, — the beautiful allegory of hu-

mility and labor. He and his service had been accepted, though he would not fast, and had not learned to pray! It became more and more clear to him, that the life of man consists not in seeing visions, and in dreaming dreams, but in active charity and willing service.

Moreover, the study of ecclesiastical history awoke within him many strange and dubious thoughts. The books taught him more than their writers meant to teach. It was impossible to read of Athanasius without reading also of Arius; it was impossible to hear of Calvin without hearing of Servetus. Reason began more energetically to vindicate itself; that Reason, which is a light in darkness, not that which is "a thorn in Revelation's side." The search after Truth and Freedom, both intellectual and spiritual, became a passion in his soul, and he pursued it until he had left far behind him many dusky dogmas, many antique superstitions, many time-honored observances, which the lips of her alone, who first taught them to him in his childhood, had invested with solemnity and sanctity.

By slow degrees, and not by violent spiritual conflicts, he became a Protestant. He had but passed from one chapel to another in the same vast cathedral. He was still beneath the same ample roof, still heard the same divine service chanted in a different dialect of the same universal language. Out of his old faith he brought with him all he had found in it that was holy and pure and of good report. Not its bigotry, and fanaticism, and intolerance; but its zeal, its self-devotion, its

heavenly aspirations, its human sympathies, its endless deeds of charity. Not till after his father's death, however, did he become a clergyman. Then his vocation was manifest to him. He no longer hesitated, but entered upon its many duties and responsibilities, its many trials and discouragements, with the zeal of Peter and the gentleness of John.

XIX.

A week later, and Kavanagh was installed in his little room in the church-tower. A week later, and the carrier-pigeon was on the wing. A week later, and Martha Amelia's anonymous epistolary eulogies of her relative had ceased forever.

Swiftly and silently the summer advanced, and the following announcement in the Fairmeadow Advertiser proclaimed the hot weather and its alleviations : —

"I have the pleasure of announcing to the Ladies and Gentlemen of Fairmeadow and its vicinity, that my Bath House is now completed, and ready for the reception of those who are disposed to regale themselves in a luxury peculiar to the once polished Greek and noble Roman.

"To the Ladies I will say, that Tuesday of each week will be appropriated to their exclusive benefit ; the white flag will be the signal ; and I assure the Ladies, that due respect shall be scrupulously observed, and that they shall be guarded from each vagrant foot and each licentious eye.

"EDWARD DIMPLE."

Moreover, the village was enlivened by the usual travelling shows, — the wax-work figures representing Eliza Wharton and the Salem Tragedy, to which clergymen and their families were "respectfully invited, free on presenting their cards"; a stuffed shark, that had eaten the exhibitor's father in Lynn Bay; the menagerie, with its loud music and its roars of rage; the circus, with its tan and tinsel, — its faded Columbine and melancholy Clown; and, finally, the standard drama, in which Elder Evans, like an ancient Spanish Bululú, impersonated all the principal male characters, and was particularly imposing in Iago and the Moor, having half his face lamp-blacked, and turning now the luminous, now the eclipsed side to the audience, as the exigencies of the dialogue demanded.

There was also a great Temperance Jubilee, with a procession, in which was conspicuous a large horse, whose shaven tail was adorned with gay ribbons, and whose rider bore a banner with the device, "Shaved in the Cause!" Moreover, the Grand Junction Railroad was opened through the town, running in one direction to the city, and in the other into unknown northern regions, stringing the white villages like pearls upon its black thread. By this, the town lost much of its rural quiet and seclusion. The inhabitants became restless and ambitious. They were in constant excitement and alarm, like children in story-books hidden away somewhere by an ogre, who visits them regularly every day and night, and occasionally devours one of them for a meal.

Nevertheless, most of the inhabitants considered

the railroad a great advantage to the village. Several ladies were heard to say that Fairmeadow had grown quite metropolitan; and Mrs. Wilmerdings, who suffered under a chronic suspension of the mental faculties, had a vague notion, probably connected with the profession of her son, that it was soon to become a seaport.

In the fields and woods, meanwhile, there were other signs and signals of the summer. The darkening foliage; the embrowning grain; the golden dragon-fly haunting the blackberry-bushes; the cawing crows, that looked down from the mountain on the cornfield, and waited day after day for the scarecrow to finish his work and depart; and the smoke of far-off burning woods, that pervaded the air and hung in purple haze about the summits of the mountains, — these were the vaunt-couriers and attendants of the hot August.

Kavanagh had now completed the first great cycle of parochial visits. He had seen the Vaughans, the Archers, the Churchills, and also the Hawkinses and the Wilmerdingses, and many more. With Mr. Churchill he had become intimate. They had many points of contact and sympathy. They walked together on leisure afternoons; they sat together through long summer evenings; they discoursed with friendly zeal on various topics of literature, religion, and morals.

Moreover, he worked assiduously at his sermons. He preached the doctrines of Christ. He preached holiness, self-denial, love; and his hearers remarked that he almost invariably took his texts from the Evangelists, as much as possible from the words of

Christ, and seldom from Paul, or the Old Testament. He did not so much denounce vice, as inculcate virtue; he did not deny, but affirm; he did not lacerate the hearts of his hearers with doubt and disbelief, but consoled, and comforted, and healed them with faith.

The only danger was that he might advance too far, and leave his congregation behind him; as a piping shepherd, who, charmed with his own music, walks over the flowery mead, not perceiving that his tardy flock is lingering far behind, more intent upon cropping the thymy food around them, than upon listening to the celestial harmonies that are gradually dying away in the distance.

His words were always kindly; he brought no railing accusation against any man; he dealt in no exaggerations nor over-statements. But while he was gentle, he was firm. He did not refrain from reprobating intemperance because one of his deacons owned a distillery; nor war, because another had a contract for supplying the army with muskets; nor slavery, because one of the great men of the village slammed his pew-door, and left the church with a grand air, as much as to say, that all that sort of thing would not do, and the clergy had better confine themselves to abusing the sins of the Hindoos, and let our domestic institutions alone.

In affairs ecclesiastical he had not suggested many changes. One that he had much at heart was, that the partition wall between parish and church should be quietly taken down, so that all should sit together at the Supper of the Lord. He

also desired that the organist should relinquish
the old and pernicious habit of preluding with tri-
umphal marches, and running his fingers at random
over the keys of his instrument, playing scraps of
secular music very slowly to make them sacred,
and substitute instead some of the beautiful sym-
phonies of Pergolesi, Palestrina, and Sebastian
Bach.

He held that sacred melodies were becoming to
sacred themes ; and did not wish, that, in his
church, as in some of the French Canadian
churches, the holy profession of religion should be
sung to the air of " When one is dead 't is for a
long time," — the commandments, aspirations for
heaven, and the necessity of thinking of one's sal-
vation, to "The Follies of Spain," "Louisa was
sleeping in a grove," or a grand " March of the
French Cavalry."

The study in the tower was delightful. There
sat the young apostle, and meditated the great de-
sign and purpose of his life, the removal of all
prejudice, and uncharitableness, and persecution,
and the union of all sects into one church univer-
sal. Sects themselves he would not destroy, but
sectarianism ; for sects were to him only as sepa-
rate converging roads, leading all to the same ce-
lestial city of peace. As he sat alone, and thought
of these things, he heard the great bell boom above
him, and remembered the ages when in all Chris-
tendom there was but one Church ; when bells
were anointed, baptized, and prayed for, that,
wheresoever those holy bells should sound, all de-
ceits of Satan, all danger of whirlwinds, thunders,

lightnings, and tempests might be driven away, — that devotion might increase in every Christian when he heard them, — and that the Lord would sanctify them with his Holy Spirit, and infuse into them the heavenly dew of the Holy Ghost. He thought of the great bell Guthlac, which an abbot of Croyland gave to his monastery, and of the six others given by his successor, — so musical, that, when they all rang together, as Ingulphus affirms, there was no ringing in England equal to it. As he listened, the bell seemed to breathe upon the air such clangorous sentences as,

Laudo Deum verum, plebem voco, congrego clerum,
Defunctos ploro, nimbum fugo, festaque honoro.

Possibly, also, at times, it interrupted his studies and meditations with other words than these. Possibly it sang into his ears, as did the bells of Varennes into the ears of Panurge, — " Marry thee, marry thee, marry, marry ; if thou shouldst marry, marry, marry, thou shalt find good therein, therein, therein, so marry, marry."

From this tower of contemplation he looked down with mingled emotions of joy and sorrow on the toiling world below. The wide prospect seemed to enlarge his sympathies and his charities, and he often thought of the words of Plato : " When we consider human life, we should view as from a high tower all things terrestrial ; such as herds, armies, men employed in agriculture, in marriages, divorces, births, deaths ; the tumults of courts of justice ; desolate lands ; various barbarous nations ; feasts, wailings, markets ; a medley of all things, in a system adorned by contrarieties."

On the outside of the door Kavanagh had written the vigorous line of Dante,

Think that To-day will never dawn again!

that it might always serve as a salutation and memento to him as he entered. On the inside, the no less striking lines of a more modern bard, —

Lose this day loitering, 't will be the same story
To-morrow, and the next more dilatory ;
For indecision brings its own delays,
And days are lost, lamenting o'er lost days.
Are you in earnest ? Seize this very minute !
What you can do or think you can, begin it !
Boldness has genius, power, and magic in it !
Only engage, and then the mind grows heated :
Begin it, and the work will be completed.

Once, as he sat in this retreat near noon, enjoying the silence, and the fresh air that visited him through the oval windows, his attention was arrested by a cloud of dust, rolling along the road, out of which soon emerged a white horse, and then a very singular, round-shouldered, old-fashioned chaise, containing an elderly couple, both in black. What particularly struck him was the gait of the horse, who had a very disdainful fling to his hind legs. The slow equipage passed, and would have been forever forgotten, had not Kavanagh seen it again at sunset, stationary at Mr. Churchill's door, towards which he was directing his steps.

As he entered, he met Mr. Churchill, just taking leave of an elderly lady and gentleman in black, whom he recognized as the travellers in the old chaise. Mr. Churchill looked a little flushed and disturbed, and bade his guests farewell with a constrained air. On seeing Kavanagh, he saluted

him, and called him by name ; whereupon the lady
pursed up her mouth, and, after a quick glance,
turned away her face ; and the gentleman passed
with a lofty look, in which curiosity, reproof, and
pious indignation were strangely mingled. They
got into the chaise, with some such feelings as
Noah and his wife may be supposed to have had
on entering the ark ; the whip descended upon the
old horse with unusual vigor, accompanied by a
jerk of the reins that caused him to say within
himself, " What is the matter now ? " He then
moved off at his usual pace, and with that peculiar
motion of the hind legs which Kavanagh had per-
ceived in the morning.

Kavanagh found his friend not a little disturbed,
and evidently by the conversation of the departed
guests.

" That old gentleman," said Mr. Churchill, " is
your predecessor, Mr. Pendexter. He thinks we
are in a bad way since he left us. He considers
your liberality as nothing better than rank Arian-
ism and infidelity. The fact is, the old gentleman
is a little soured ; the vinous fermentation in
his veins is now over, and the acetous has com-
menced."

Kavanagh smiled, but made no answer.

" I, of course, defended you stoutly," continued
Mr. Churchill ; " but if he goes about the village
sowing such seed, there will be tares growing with
the wheat."

" I have no fears," said Kavanagh, very quietly.

Mr. Churchill's apprehensions were not, how-
ever, groundless ; for in the course of the week it

came out that doubts, surmises, and suspicions of Kavanagh's orthodoxy were springing up in many weak but worthy minds. And it was ever after observed, that, whenever that fatal, apocalyptic white horse and antediluvian chaise appeared in town, many parishioners were harassed with doubts and perplexed with theological difficulties and uncertainties.

Nevertheless, the main current of opinion was with him ; and the parish showed their grateful acknowledgment of his zeal and sympathy, by requesting him to sit for his portrait to a great artist from the city, who was passing the summer months in the village for recreation, using his pencil only on rarest occasions and as a particular favor. To this martyrdom the meek Kavanagh submitted without a murmur. During the progress of this work of art, he was seldom left alone ; some one of his parishioners was there to enliven him ; and most frequently it was Miss Martha Amelia Hawkins, who had become very devout of late, being zealous in the Sunday School, and requesting her relative not to walk between churches any more. She took a very lively interest in the portrait, and favored with many suggestions the distinguished artist, who found it difficult to obtain an expression which would satisfy the parish, some wishing to have it grave, if not severe, and others with " Mr. Kavanagh's peculiar smile." Kavanagh himself was quite indifferent about the matter, and met his fate with Christian fortitude, in a white cravat and sacerdotal robes, with one hand hanging down from the back of his chair, and the other holding

a large book with the fore-finger between its leaves, reminding Mr. Churchill of Milo with his fingers in the oak. The expression of the face was exceedingly bland and resigned; perhaps a little wanting in strength, but on the whole satisfactory to the parish. So was the artist's price; nay, it was even held by some persons to be cheap, considering the quantity of background he had put in.

XX.

Meanwhile, things had gone on very quietly and monotonously in Mr. Churchill's family. Only one event, and that a mysterious one, had disturbed its serenity. It was the sudden disappearance of Lucy, the pretty orphan girl; and, as the booted centipede, who had so much excited Mr. Churchill's curiosity, disappeared at the same time, there was little doubt that they had gone away together. But whither gone, and wherefore, remained a mystery.

Mr. Churchill, also, had had his profile, and those of his wife and children, taken, in a very humble style, by Mr. Bantam, whose advertisement he had noticed on his way to school nearly a year before. His own was considered the best, as a work of art. The face was cut out entirely; the collar of the coat velvet; the shirt-collar very high and white; and the top of his head ornamented with a crest of hair turning up in front, though his own turned down, — which slight deviation from nature was explained and justified by the painter as a license allowable in art.

One evening, as he was sitting down to begin, for at least the hundredth time, the great Romance, — subject of so many resolves and so much remorse, so often determined upon but never begun, — a loud knock at the street-door, which stood wide open, announced a visitor. Unluckily, the study-door was likewise open; and consequently, being in full view, he found it impossible to refuse himself; nor, in fact, would he have done so, had all the doors been shut and bolted, — the art of refusing one's self being at that time but imperfectly understood in Fairmeadow. Accordingly, the visitor was shown in.

He announced himself as Mr. Hathaway. Passing through the village, he could not deny himself the pleasure of calling on Mr. Churchill, whom he knew by his writings in the periodicals, though not personally. He wished, moreover, to secure the coöperation of one, already so favorably known to the literary world, in a new Magazine he was about to establish, in order to raise the character of American literature, which, in his opinion, the existing reviews and magazines had entirely failed to accomplish. A daily increasing want of something better was felt by the public, and the time had come for the establishment of such a periodical as he proposed. After explaining, in rather a florid and exuberant manner, his plan and prospects, he entered more at large into the subject of American literature, which it was his design to foster and patronize.

"I think, Mr. Churchill," said he, "that we want a national literature commensurate with our

mountains and rivers, — commensurate with Niagara, and the Alleghanies, and the Great Lakes! "

" Oh ! "

" We want a national epic that shall correspond to the size of the country ; that shall be to all other epics what Banvard's Panorama of the Mississippi is to all other paintings, — the largest in the world ! "

" Ah ! "

" We want a national drama in which scope enough shall be given to our gigantic ideas, and to the unparalleled activity and progress of our people ! "

" Of course."

" In a word, we want a national literature altogether shaggy and unshorn, that shall shake the earth, like a herd of buffaloes thundering over the prairies ! "

" Precisely," interrupted Mr. Churchill ; " but excuse me ! — are you not confounding things that have no analogy ? Great has a very different meaning when applied to a river, and when applied to a literature. Large and shallow may perhaps be applied to both. Literature is rather an image of the spiritual world, than of the physical, is it not ? — of the internal, rather than the external. Mountains, lakes, and rivers are, after all, only its scenery and decorations, not its substance and essence. A man will not necessarily be a great poet because he lives near a great mountain. Nor, being a poet, will he necessarily write better poems than another, because he lives nearer Niagara."

" But, Mr. Churchill, you do not certainly mean to deny the influence of scenery on the mind ? "

" No, only to deny that it can create genius. At best, it can only develop it. Switzerland has produced no extraordinary poet ; nor, as far as I know, have the Andes, or the Himalaya mountains, or the Mountains of the Moon in Africa."

" But, at all events," urged Mr. Hathaway, " let us have our literature national. If it is not national, it is nothing."

" On the contrary, it may be a great deal. Nationality is a good thing to a certain extent, but universality is better. All that is best in the great poets of all countries is not what is national in them, but what is universal. Their roots are in their native soil ; but their branches wave in the unpatriotic air, that speaks the same language unto all men, and their leaves shine with the illimitable light that pervades all lands. Let us throw all the windows open ; let us admit the light and air on all sides ; that we may look towards the four corners of the heavens, and not always in the same direction."

" But you admit nationality to be a good thing ? "

" Yes, if not carried too far ; still, I confess, it rather limits one's views of truth. I prefer what is natural. Mere nationality is often ridiculous. Every one smiles when he hears the Icelandic proverb, ' Iceland is the best land the sun shines upon.' Let us be natural, and we shall be national enough. Besides, our literature can be strictly national only so far as our character and modes of thought differ from those of other nations. Now, as we are very like the English, —

are, in fact, English under a different sky, — I do not see how our literature can be very different from theirs. Westward from hand to hand we pass the lighted torch, but it was lighted at the old domestic fireside of England."

"Then you think our literature is never to be anything but an imitation of the English?"

"Not at all. It is not an imitation, but, as some one has said, a continuation."

"It seems to me that you take a very narrow view of the subject."

"On the contrary, a very broad one. No literature is complete until the language in which it is written is dead. We may well be proud of our task and of our position. Let us see if we can build in any way worthy of our forefathers."

"But I insist upon originality."

"Yes; but without spasms and convulsions. Authors must not, like Chinese soldiers, expect to win victories by turning somersets in the air."

"Well, really, the prospect from your point of view is not very brilliant. Pray, what do you think of our national literature?"

"Simply, that a national literature is not the growth of a day. Centuries must contribute their dew and sunshine to it. Our own is growing slowly but surely, striking its roots downward, and its branches upward, as is natural; and I do not wish, for the sake of what some people call originality, to invert it, and try to make it grow with its roots in the air. And as for having it so savage and wild as you want it, I have only to say, that all literature, as well as all art, is the result of culture and intellectual refinement."

" Ah! we do not want art and refinement; we want genius, — untutored, wild, original, free."

" But, if this genius is to find any expression, it must employ art, for art is the external expression of our thoughts. Many have genius, but, wanting art, are forever dumb. The two must go together to form the great poet, painter, or sculptor."

" In that sense, very well."

" I was about to say also that I thought our literature would finally not be wanting in a kind of universality. As the blood of all nations is mingling with our own, so will their thoughts and feelings finally mingle in our literature. We shall draw from the Germans, tenderness; from the Spaniards, passion; from the French, vivacity, — to mingle more and more with our English solid sense. And this will give us universality, so much to be desired."

" If that is your way of thinking," interrupted the visitor, " you will like the work I am now engaged upon."

" What is it? "

" A great national drama, the scene of which is laid in New Mexico. It is entitled Don Serafin, or the Marquis of the Seven Churches. The principal characters are Don Serafin, an old Spanish hidalgo, his daughter Deseada, and Fra Serapion, the Curate. The play opens with Fra Serapion at breakfast; on the table a game-cock, tied by the leg, sharing his master's meal. Then follows a scene at the cockpit, where the Marquis stakes the remnant of his fortune — his herds and hacienda — on a favorite cock, and loses."

" But what do you know about cock-fighting?" demanded, rather than asked, the astonished and half-laughing schoolmaster.

" I am not very well informed on that subject, and I was going to ask you if you could not recommend some work."

" The only work I am acquainted with," replied Mr. Churchill, " is the Reverend Mr. Pegge's Essay on Cock-fighting among the Ancients, and I hardly see how you could apply that to the Mexicans."

" Why, they are a kind of ancients, you know. I certainly will hunt up the essay you mention, and see what I can do with it."

" And all I know about the matter itself," continued Mr. Churchill, " is, that Mark Antony was a patron of the pit, and that his cocks were always beaten by Cæsar's; and that, when Themistocles the Athenian general was marching against the Persians, he halted his army to see a cock-fight, and made a speech to his soldiery, to the effect, that those animals fought, not for the gods of their country, nor for the monuments of their ancestors, nor for glory, nor for freedom, nor for their children, but only for the sake of victory. On his return to Athens, he established cock-fights in that capital. But how this is to help you in Mexico I do not see, unless you introduce Santa Anna, and compare him to Cæsar and Themistocles."

" That is it; I will do so. It will give historic interest to the play. I thank you for the suggestion."

" The subject is certainly very original, but it does not strike me as particularly national."

"Prospective, you see!" said Mr. Hathaway, with a penetrating look.

"Ah, yes; I perceive you fish with a heavy sinker, — down, far down in the future, — among posterity, as it were."

"You have seized the idea. Besides, I obviate your objection, by introducing an American circus company from the United States, which enables me to bring horses on the stage and produce great scenic effect."

"That is a bold design. The critics will be out upon you without fail."

"Never fear that. I know the critics root and branch, — out and out, — have summered them, and wintered them, — in fact, am one of them myself. Very good fellows are the critics, are they not?"

"Oh, yes; only they have such a pleasant way of talking down upon authors."

"If they did not talk down upon them, they would show no superiority; and, of course, that would never do."

"Nor is it to be wondered at, that authors are sometimes a little irritable. I often recall the poet in the Spanish fable, whose manuscripts were devoured by mice, till at length he put some corrosive sublimate into his ink, and was never troubled again."

"Why don't you try it yourself?" said Mr. Hathaway, rather sharply.

"Oh," answered Mr. Churchill, with a smile of humility, "I and my writings are too insignificant. They may gnaw and welcome. I do not

like to have poison about, even for such pur-
poses."

"By the way, Mr. Churchill," said the visitor,
adroitly changing the subject, "do you know
Honeywell?"

"No, I do not. Who is he?"

"Honeywell the poet, I mean."

"No, I never even heard of him. There are so
many poets nowadays!"

"That is very strange indeed! Why, I con-
sider Honeywell one of the finest writers in the
country, — quite in the front rank of American
authors. He is a real poet, and no mistake. Na-
ture made him with her shirt-sleeves rolled up."

"What has he published?"

"He has not published anything yet, except in
the newspapers. But, this autumn, he is going to
bring out a volume of poems. I could not help
having my joke with him about it. I told him he
had better print it on cartridge-paper."

"Why so?"

"Why, to make it go off better; don't you
understand?"

"Oh, yes, now that you explain it. Very good."

"Honeywell is going to write for the Magazine;
he is to furnish a poem for every number; and as
he succeeds equally well in the plaintive and
didactic style of Wordsworth, and the more vehe-
ment and impassioned style of Byron, I think we
shall do very well."

"And what do you mean to call the new Maga-
zine?" inquired Mr. Churchill.

"We think of calling it The Niagara."

" Why, that is the name of our fire-engine!
Why not call it the Extinguisher?"

" That is also a good name; but I prefer The
Niagara, as more national. And I hope, Mr.
Churchill, you will let us count upon you. We
should like to have an article from your pen for
every number."

" Do you mean to pay your contributors?"

" Not the first year, I am sorry to say. But
after that, if the work succeeds, we shall pay
handsomely. And, of course, it will succeed, for
we mean it shall; and we never say fail. There
is no such word in our dictionary. Before the
year is out, we mean to print fifty thousand copies;
and fifty thousand copies will give us, at least, one
hundred and fifty thousand readers; and, with
such an audience, any author might be satisfied."

He had touched at length the right strings in
Mr. Churchill's bosom; and they vibrated to the
touch with pleasant harmonies. Literary vanity!
— literary ambition! The editor perceived it;
and so cunningly did he play upon these chords,
that, before he departed, Mr. Churchill had prom-
ised to write for him a series of papers on Ob-
scure Martyrs, — a kind of tragic history of the
unrecorded and life-long sufferings of women,
which hitherto had found no historian, save now
and then a novelist.

Notwithstanding the certainty of success, — not-
withstanding the fifty thousand subscribers and the
one hundred and fifty thousand readers, — the
Magazine never went into operation. Still the
dream was enough to occupy Mr. Churchill's

thoughts, and to withdraw them entirely from his Romance for many weeks together.

XXI.

Every State, and almost every county, of New England, has its Roaring Brook, — a mountain streamlet, overhung by woods, impeded by a mill, encumbered by fallen trees, but ever racing, rushing, roaring down through gurgling gullies, and filling the forest with its delicious sound and freshness ; the drinking-place of home-returning herds ; the mysterious haunt of squirrels and blue-jays ; the sylvan retreat of school-girls, who frequent it on summer holidays, and mingle their restless thoughts, their overflowing fancies, their fair imaginings, with its restless, exuberant, and rejoicing stream.

Fairmeadow had no Roaring Brook. As its name indicates, it was too level a land for that. But the neighboring town of Westwood, lying more inland, and among the hills, had one of the fairest and fullest of all the brooks that roar. It was the boast of the neighborhood. Not to have seen it was to have seen no brook, no waterfall, no mountain ravine. And, consequently, to behold it and admire was Kavanagh taken by Mr. Churchill as soon as the summer vacation gave leisure and opportunity. The party consisted of Mr. and Mrs. Churchill, and Alfred, in a one-horse chaise ; and Cecilia, Alice, and Kavanagh, in a carryall, — the fourth seat in which was occupied by a large basket, containing what the Squire of the Grove, in Don

Quixote, called his "fiambreras," — that magnilo-
quent Castilian word for cold collation. Over warm
uplands, smelling of clover and mint ; through
cool glades, still wet with the rain of yesterday ;
along the river ; across the rattling and tilting
planks of wooden bridges ; by orchards ; by the
gates of fields, with the tall mullen growing at the
bars ; by stone walls overrun with privet and bar-
berries ; in sun and heat, in shadow and coolness,
— forward drove the happy party on that pleasant
summer morning.

At length they reached the Roaring Brook.
From a gorge in the mountains, through a long,
winding gallery of birch, and beech, and pine,
leaped the bright, brown waters of the jubilant
streamlet ; out of the woods, across the plain,
under the rude bridge of logs, into the woods
again, — a day between two nights. With it went
a song that made the heart sing likewise — a song
of joy, and exultation, and freedom ; a continuous
and unbroken song of life, and pleasure, and per-
petual youth. Like the old Icelandic Scald, the
streamlet seemed to say, —

"I am possessed of songs such as neither the
spouse of a king, or any son of man, can repeat ;
one of them is called the Helper ; it will help
thee at thy need, in sickness, grief, and all adver-
sity."

The little party left their carriages at a farm-
house by the bridge, and followed the rough road
on foot along the brook ; now close upon it, now
shut out by intervening trees. Mr. Churchill,
bearing the basket on his arm, walked in front

with his wife and Alfred. Kavanagh came behind with Cecilia and Alice. The music of the brook silenced all conversation; only occasional exclamations of delight were uttered, — the irrepressible applause of fresh and sensitive natures, in a scene so lovely. Presently, turning off from the road, which led directly to the mill, and was rough with the tracks of heavy wheels, they went down to the margin of the brook.

"How indescribably beautiful this brown water is!" exclaimed Kavanagh. "It is like wine, or the nectar of the gods of Olympus; as if the falling Hebe had poured it from her goblet."

"More like the mead or metheglin of the northern gods," said Mr. Churchill, "spilled from the drinking-horns of Valhalla."

But all the ladies thought Kavanagh's comparison the better of the two, and in fact the best that could be made; and Mr. Churchill was obliged to retract and apologize for his allusion to the celestial ale-house of Odin.

Erelong they were forced to cross the brook, stepping from stone to stone, over the little rapids and cascades. All crossed lightly, easily, safely; even "the sumpter mule," as Mr. Churchill called himself, on account of the pannier. Only Cecilia lingered behind, as if afraid to cross. Cecilia, who had crossed at that same place a hundred times before, — Cecilia, who had the surest foot, and the firmest nerves, of all the village maidens, — she now stood irresolute, seized with a sudden tremor; blushing, and laughing at her own timidity, and yet unable to advance. Kavanagh saw

her embarrassment and hastened back to help her.
Her hand trembled in his ; she thanked him with
a gentle look and word. His whole soul was
softened within him. His attitude, his counte-
nance, his voice, were alike submissive and sub-
dued. He was as one penetrated with tenderest
emotions.

It is difficult to know at what moment love be-
gins ; it is less difficult to know that it has begun.
A thousand heralds proclaim it to the listening
air ; a thousand ministers and messengers betray
it to the eye. Tone, act, attitude and look, — the
signals upon the countenance, — the electric tel-
egraph of touch ; all these betray the yielding cit-
adel before the word itself is uttered, which, like
the key surrendered, opens every avenue and gate
of entrance, and makes retreat impossible !

The day passed delightfully with all. They sat
upon the stones and the roots of trees. Cecilia
read, from a volume she had brought with her,
poems that rhymed with the running water. The
others listened and commented. Little Alfred
waded in the stream, with his bare white feet, and
launched boats over the falls. Noon had been
fixed upon for dining, but they anticipated it by
at least an hour. The great basket was opened ;
endless sandwiches were drawn forth, and a cold
pastry, as large as that of the Squire of the Grove.
During the repast, Mr. Churchill slipped into the
brook, while in the act of handing a sandwich to
his wife, which caused unbounded mirth ; and
Kavanagh sat down on a mossy trunk, that gave
way beneath him, and crumbled into powder. This,
also, was received with great merriment.

After dinner, they ascended the brook still farther, — indeed, quite to the mill, which was not going. It had been stopped in the midst of its work. The saw still held its hungry teeth fixed in the heart of a pine. Mr. Churchill took occasion to make known to the company his long cherished purpose of writing a poem called " The Song of the Saw-Mill," and enlarged on the beautiful associations of flood and forest connected with the theme. He delighted himself and his audience with the fine fancies he meant to weave into his poem, and wondered nobody had thought of the subject before. Kavanagh said it had been thought of before ; and cited Kerner's little poem, so charmingly translated by Bryant. Mr. Churchill had not seen it. Kavanagh looked into his pocket-book for it, but it was not to be found ; still he was sure that there was such a poem. Mr. Churchill abandoned his design. He had spoken, — and the treasure, just as he had touched it with his hand, was gone forever.

The party returned home as it came, all tired and happy, excepting little Alfred, who was tired and cross, and sat sleepy and sagging on his father's knee, with his hat cocked rather fiercely over his eyes.

XXII.

The brown autumn came. Out of doors, it brought to the fields the prodigality of the golden harvest, — to the forest, revelations of light, — and to the sky, the sharp air, the morning mist,

the red clouds at evening. Within doors, the
sense of seclusion, the stillness of closed and cur-
tained windows, musings by the fireside, books,
friends, conversation, and the long, meditative
evenings. To the farmer, it brought surcease of
toil, — to the scholar, that sweet delirium of the
brain which changes toil to pleasure. It brought
the wild duck back to the reedy marshes of the
south ; it brought the wild song back to the fervid
brain of the poet. Without, the village street was
paved with gold ; the river ran red with the re-
flection of the leaves. Within, the faces of
friends brightened the gloomy walls ; the return-
ing footsteps of the long-absent gladdened the
threshold ; and all the sweet amenities of social
life again resumed their interrupted reign.

Kavanagh preached a sermon on the coming of
autumn. He chose his text from Isaiah, " Who
is this that cometh from Edom, with dyed gar-
ments from Bozrah ? this that is glorious in his ap-
parel, travelling in the greatness of his strength ?
Wherefore art thou red in thine apparel, and thy
garments like him that treadeth in the wine-vat ? "

To Mr. Churchill, this beloved season — this
Joseph with his coat of many colors, as he was
fond of calling it — brought an unexpected guest,
the forlorn, forsaken Lucy. The surmises of the
family were too true. She had wandered away
with the Briareus of boots. She returned alone,
in destitution and despair ; and often, in the grief
of a broken heart and a bewildered brain, was
heard to say, —

" Oh, how I wish I were a Christian ! If I were

only a Christian, I would not live any longer; I
would kill myself! I am too wretched ! "

A few days afterwards, a gloomy-looking man
rode through the town on horseback, stopping at
every corner, and crying into every street, with a
loud and solemn voice, —

" Prepare! prepare ! prepare to meet the living
God ! "

It was one of that fanatical sect who believed
the end of the world was imminent, and had pre-
pared their ascension robes to be lifted up in clouds
of glory, while the worn-out, weary world was to
burn with fire beneath them, and a new and fairer
earth to be prepared for their inheritance. The
appearance of this forerunner of the end of the
world was followed by numerous camp-meetings,
held in the woods near the village, to whose white
tents and leafy chapels many went for consolation
and found despair.

XXIII.

Again the two crumbly old women sat and
talked together in the little parlor of the gloomy
house under the poplars, and the two girls sat
above, holding each other by the hand, thoughtful,
and speaking only at intervals.

Alice was unusually sad and silent. The mists
were already gathering over her vision, — those
mists that were to deepen and darken as the sea-
son advanced, until the external world should be
shrouded and finally shut from her view. Already
the landscape began to wear a pale and sickly hue,

as if the sun were withdrawing farther and farther, and were soon wholly to disappear, as in a northern winter. But to brighten this northern winter there now arose within her a soft, auroral light. Yes, the auroral light of love, blushing through the whole heaven of her thoughts. She had not breathed that word to herself, nor did she recognize any thrill of passion in the new emotion she experienced. But love it was; and it lifted her soul into a region which she at once felt was native to it, — into a subtler ether, which seemed its natural element.

This feeling, however, was not all exhilaration. It brought with it its own peculiar languor and sadness, its fluctuations and swift vicissitudes of excitement and depression. To this the trivial circumstances of life contributed. Kavanagh had met her in the street, and had passed her without recognition ; and, in the bitterness of the moment, she forgot that she wore a thick veil, which entirely concealed her face. At an evening party at Mr. Churchill's, by a kind of fatality, Kavanagh had stood very near her for a long time. but with his back turned, conversing with Miss Hawkins, from whose toils, he was, in fact, though vainly, struggling to extricate himself ; and, in the irritation of supposed neglect, Alice had said to herself, —

"This is the kind of woman which most fascinates men ! "

But these cruel moments of pain were few and short, while those of delight were many and lasting. In a life so lonely, and with so little to enliven and embellish it as hers, the guest in disguise was

welcomed with ardor, and entertained without fear
or suspicion. Had he been feared or suspected, he
would have been no longer dangerous. He came
as friendship, where friendship was most needed;
he came as devotion, where her holy ministrations
were always welcome.

Somewhat differently had the same passion come
to the heart of Cecilia; for as the heart is, so is
love to the heart. It partakes of its strength or
weakness, its health or disease. In Cecilia, it but
heightened the keen sensation of life. To all eyes,
she became more beautiful, more radiant, more
lovely, though they knew not why. When she
and Kavanagh first met, it was hardly as strangers
meet, but rather as friends long separated. When
they first spoke to each other, it seemed but as the
renewal of some previous interrupted conversation.
Their souls flowed together at once, without tur-
bulence or agitation, like waters on the same level.
As they found each other without seeking, so their
intercourse was without affectation and without
embarrassment.

Thus, while Alice, unconsciously to herself, de-
sired the love of Kavanagh, Cecilia, as uncon-
sciously, assumed it as already her own. Alice
keenly felt her own unworthiness; Cecilia made
no comparison of merit. When Kavanagh was
present, Alice was happy, but embarrassed; Cecilia,
joyous and natural. The former feared she might
displease; the latter divined from the first that
she already pleased. In both, this was the intuition
of the heart.

So sat the friends together, as they had done so

many times before. But now, for the first time, each cherished a secret, which she did not confide to the other. Daily, for many weeks, the feathered courier had come and gone from window to window, but this secret had never been intrusted to his keeping. Almost daily the friends had met and talked together, but this secret had not been told. That could not be confided to another, which had not been confided to themselves ; that could not be fashioned into words, which was not yet fashioned into thoughts, but was still floating, vague and formless, through the mind. Nay, had it been stated in words, each, perhaps, would have denied it. The distinct apparition of this fair spirit, in a visible form, would have startled them ; though, while it haunted all the chambers of their souls as an invisible presence, it gave them only solace and delight.

"How very feverish your hand is, dearest ! " said Cecilia. "What is the matter ? Are you unwell ? "

"Those are the very words my mother said to me this morning," replied Alice. "I feel rather languid and tired, that is all. I could not sleep last night ; I never can, when it rains."

"Did it rain last night ? I did not hear it."

"Yes ; about midnight, quite hard. I listened to it for hours. I love to lie awake, and hear the drops fall on the roof, and on the leaves. It throws me into a delicious, dreamy state, which I like much better than sleep."

Cecilia looked tenderly at her pale face. Her eyes were very bright, and on each cheek was a

crimson signal, the sight of which would have given her mother so much anguish, that, perhaps, it was better for her to be blind than to see.

" When you enter the land of dreams, Alice, you come into my peculiar realm. I am the queen of that country, you know. But, of late, I have thought of resigning my throne. These endless reveries are really a great waste of time and strength."

" Do you think so ? "

" Yes ; and Mr. Kavanagh thinks so, too. We talked about it the other evening ; and afterwards, upon reflection, I thought he was right."

And the friends resolved, half in jest and half in earnest, that, from that day forth, the gate of their day-dreams should be closed. And closed it was, erelong ; — for one, by the Angel of Life ; for the other, by the Angel of Death !

XXIV.

The project of the new Magazine being heard of no more, and Mr. Churchill being consequently deprived of his one hundred and fifty thousand readers, he laid aside the few notes he had made for his papers on the Obscure Martyrs, and turned his thoughts again to the great Romance. A whole leisure Saturday afternoon was before him, — pure gold, without alloy. Ere beginning his task, he stepped forth into his garden to inhale the sunny air, and let his thoughts recede a little, in order to leap farther. When he returned, glowing and radiant with poetic fancies, he found, to his

unspeakable dismay, an unknown damsel sitting in his arm-chair. She was rather gayly yet elegantly dressed, and wore a veil, which she raised as Mr. Churchill entered, fixing upon him the full, liquid orbs of her large eyes.

"Mr. Churchill, I suppose?" said she, rising, and stepping forward.

"The same," replied the schoolmaster, with dignified courtesy.

"And will you permit me," she continued, not without a certain serene self-possession, "to introduce myself, for want of a better person to do it for me? My name is Cartwright, — Clarissa Cartwright."

This announcement did not produce that powerful and instantaneous effect on Mr. Churchill which the speaker seemed to anticipate, or at least to hope. His eye did not brighten with any quick recognition, nor did he suddenly exclaim, —

"What! Are you Miss Cartwright, the poetess, whose delightful effusions I have seen in all the magazines?"

On the contrary, he looked rather blank and expectant, and only said, —

"I am very glad to see you; pray sit down."

So that the young lady herself was obliged to communicate the literary intelligence above alluded to, which she did very gracefully, and then added, —

"I have come to ask a great favor of you, Mr. Churchill, which I hope you will not deny me. By the advice of some friends, I have collected my poems together," — and here she drew forth from

a paper a large, thin manuscript, bound in crimson velvet, — "and think of publishing them in a volume. Now, would you do me the favor to look them over, and give me your candid opinion, whether they are worth publishing? I should value your advice so highly!"

This simultaneous appeal to his vanity and his gallantry from a fair young girl, standing on the verge of that broad, dangerous ocean, in which so many have perished, and looking wistfully over its flashing waters to the shores of the green Isle of Palms, — such an appeal, from such a person, it was impossible for Mr. Churchill to resist. He made, however, a faint show of resistance, — a feeble grasping after some excuse for refusal, — and then yielded. He received from Clarissa's delicate, trembling hand the precious volume, and from her eyes a still more precious look of thanks, and then said, —

"What name do you propose to give the volume?"

"Symphonies of the Soul, and other Poems," said the young lady; "and, if you like them, and it would not be asking too much, I should be delighted to have you write a Preface, to introduce the work to the public. The publisher says it would increase the sale very considerably."

"Ah, the publisher! yes, but that is not very complimentary to yourself," suggested Mr. Churchill. "I can already see your Poems rebelling against the intrusion of my Preface, and rising like so many nuns in a convent to expel the audacious foot that has dared to invade their sacred precincts."

But it was all in vain, this pale effort at pleasantry. Objection was useless, and the soft-hearted schoolmaster a second time yielded gracefully to his fate, and promised the Preface. The young lady took her leave with a profusion of thanks and blushes, and the dainty manuscript, with its delicate chirography and crimson cover, remained in the hands of Mr. Churchill, who gazed at it less as a Paradise of Dainty Devices than as a deed or mortgage of so many precious hours of his own scanty inheritance of time.

Afterwards, when he complained a little of this to his wife, — who, during the interview, had peeped in at the door, and, seeing how he was occupied, had immediately withdrawn, — she said that nobody was to blame but himself; that he should learn to say "No!" and not do just as every romantic girl from the Academy wanted him to do; adding, as a final aggravation and climax of reproof, that she really believed he never would, and never meant to, begin his Romance!

XXV.

Not long afterwards, Kavanagh and Mr. Churchill took a stroll together across the fields, and down green lanes, walking all the bright, brief afternoon. From the summit of the hill, beside the old windmill, they saw the sun set, and, opposite, the full moon rise, dewy, large, and red. As they descended, they felt the heavy dampness of the air, like water, rising to meet them, — bathing with coolness first their feet, then their hands, then

their faces, till they were submerged in that sea of dew. As they skirted the woodland on their homeward way, trampling the golden leaves underfoot, they heard voices at a distance, singing; and then saw the lights of the camp-meeting gleaming through the trees, and, drawing nearer, distinguished a portion of the hymn: —

> Don't you hear the Lord a-coming
> To the old churchyards,
> With a band of music,
> With a band of music,
> With a band of music,
> Sounding through the air?

These words, at once awful and ludicrous, rose on the still twilight air from a hundred voices, thrilling with emotion, and from as many beating, fluttering, struggling hearts. High above them all was heard one voice, clear and musical as a clarion.

"I know that voice," said Mr. Churchill; "it is Elder Evans's."

"Ah!" exclaimed Kavanagh, — for only the impression of awe was upon him, — "he never acted in a deeper tragedy than this! How terrible it is! Let us pass on."

They hurried away, Kavanagh trembling in every fibre. Silently they walked, the music fading into softest vibrations behind them.

"How strange is this fanaticism!" at length said Mr. Churchill, rather as a relief to his own thoughts, than for the purpose of reviving the conversation. "These people really believe that the end of the world is close at hand."

"And to thousands," answered Kavanagh, "this

is no fiction, — no illusion of an over-heated imagination. To-day, to-morrow, every day, to thousands, the end of the world is close at hand. And why should we fear it? We walk here as it were in the crypts of life; at times, from the great cathedral above us, we can hear the organ and the chanting of the choir; we see the light stream through the open door, when some friend goes up before us; and shall we fear to mount the narrow staircase of the grave, that leads us out of this uncertain twilight into the serene mansions of the life eternal?"

They reached the wooden bridge over the river, which the moonlight converted into a river of light. Their footsteps sounded on the planks; they passed without perceiving a female figure that stood in the shadow below on the brink of the stream, watching wistfully the steady flow of the current. It was Lucy! Her bonnet and shawl were lying at her feet; and when they had passed, she waded far out into the shallow stream, laid herself gently down in its deeper waves, and floated slowly away into the moonlight, among the golden leaves that were faded and fallen like herself, — among the water-lilies, whose fragrant white blossoms had been broken off and polluted long ago. Without a struggle, without a sigh, without a sound, she floated downward, downward, and silently sank into the silent river. Far off, faint, and indistinct, was heard the startling hymn, with its wild and peculiar melody, —

Oh, there will be mourning, mourning, mourning, mourning, —
Oh, there will be mourning, at the judgment-seat of Christ!

Kavanagh's heart was full of sadness. He left Mr. Churchill at his door, and proceeded homeward. On passing his church, he could not resist the temptation to go in. He climbed to his chamber in the tower, lighted by the moon. He sat for a long time gazing from the window, and watching a distant and feeble candle, whose rays scarcely reached him across the brilliant moon-lighted air. Gentler thoughts stole over him; an invisible presence soothed him; an invisible hand was laid upon his head, and the trouble and unrest of his spirit were changed to peace.

"Answer me, thou mysterious future!" exclaimed he; "tell me, — shall these things be according to my desires?"

And the mysterious future, interpreted by those desires, replied, —

"Soon thou shalt know all. It shall be well with thee!"

XXVI.

On the following morning, Kavanagh sat as usual in his study in the tower. No traces were left of the heaviness and sadness of the preceding night. It was a bright, warm morning; and the window, open towards the south, let in the genial sunshine. The odor of decaying leaves scented the air; far off flashed the hazy river.

Kavanagh's heart, however, was not at rest. At times he rose from his books, and paced up and down his little study; then took up his hat as if to go out; then laid it down again, and again re-

sumed his books. At length he arose, and, leaning on the window sill, gazed for a long time on the scene before him. Some thought was laboring in his bosom, some doubt or fear, which alternated with hope, but thwarted any fixed resolve.

Ah, how pleasantly that fair autumnal landscape smiled upon him! The great golden elms that marked the line of the village street, and under whose shadows no beggars sat; the air of comfort and plenty, of neatness, thrift, and equality, visible everywhere; and from far-off farms the sound of flails, beating the triumphal march of Ceres through the land; — these were the sights and sounds that greeted him as he looked. Silently the yellow leaves fell upon the graves in the churchyard, and the dew glistened in the grass, which was still long and green.

Presently his attention was arrested by a dove, pursued by a little king-bird, who constantly endeavored to soar above it, in order to attack it at greater advantage. The flight of the birds, thus shooting through the air at arrowy speed, was beautiful. When they were opposite the tower, the dove suddenly wheeled, and darted in at the open window, while the pursuer held on his way with a long sweep, and was out of sight in a moment.

At the first glance, Kavanagh recognized the dove, which lay panting on the floor. It was the same he had seen Cecilia buy of the little man in gray. He took it in his hands. Its heart was beating violently. About its neck was a silken

band; beneath its wing a billet, upon which was a
single word, "Cecilia." The bird, then, was on its
way to Cecilia Vaughan. He hailed the omen as
auspicious, and, immediately closing the window,
seated himself at his table, and wrote a few hur-
ried words, which, being carefully folded and
sealed, he fastened to the band, and then hastily,
as if afraid his purpose might be changed by de-
lay, opened the window and set the bird at liberty.
It sailed once or twice round the tower, apparently
uncertain and bewildered, or still in fear of its
pursuer. Then, instead of holding its way over
the fields to Cecilia Vaughan, it darted over the
roofs of the village, and alighted at the window
of Alice Archer.

Having written that morning to Cecilia some-
thing urgent and confidential, she was already
waiting the answer; and, not doubting that the
bird had brought it, she hastily untied the silken
band, and, without looking at the superscription,
opened the first note that fell on the table. It
was very brief — only a few lines, and not a name
mentioned in it; an impulse, an ejaculation of
love; every line quivering with electric fire, —
every word a pulsation of the writer's heart. It
was signed "Arthur Kavanagh."

Overwhelmed by the suddenness and violence of
her emotions, Alice sat for a long time motionless,
holding the open letter in her hand. Then she
read it again, and then relapsed into her dream of
joy and wonder. It would be difficult to say
which of the two emotions was the greater, —
her joy that her prayer for love should be an-

swered, and so answered, — her wonder that
Kavanagh should have selected her! In the
tumult of her sensations, and hardly conscious of
what she was doing, she folded the note and re-
placed it in its envelope. Then, for the first time,
her eye fell on the superscription. It was "Cecilia
Vaughan." Alice fainted.

On recovering her senses, her first act was one
of heroism. She sealed the note, attached it to
the neck of the pigeon, and sent the messenger
rejoicing on his journey. Then her feelings had
way, and she wept long and bitterly. Then, with
a desperate calmness, she reproved her own weak-
ness and selfishness, and felt that she ought to re-
joice in the happiness of her friend, and sacrifice
her affection, even her life, to her. Her heart ex-
culpated Kavanagh from all blame. He had not
deluded her; she had deluded herself. She alone
was in fault; and in deep humiliation, with
wounded pride and wounded love, and utter self-
abasement, she bowed her head and prayed for
consolation and fortitude.

One consolation she already had. The secret
was her own. She had not revealed it even to
Cecilia. Kavanagh did not suspect it. Public
curiosity, public pity, she would not have to
undergo.

She was resigned. She made the heroic sacri-
fice of self, leaving her sorrow to the great physi-
cian, Time, — the nurse of care, the healer of all
smarts, the soother and consoler of all sorrows.
And, thenceforward, she became unto Kavanagh
what the moon is to the sun, forever following,
forever separated, forever sad!

As a traveller, about to start upon his journey, resolved and yet irresolute, watches the clouds, and notes the struggle between the sunshine and the showers, and says, " It will be fair; I will go," — and again says, " Ah, no, not yet; the rain is not yet over," — so at this same hour sat Cecilia Vaughan, resolved and yet irresolute, longing to depart upon the fair journey before her, and yet lingering on the paternal threshold, as if she wished both to stay and to go, seeing the sky was not without its clouds, nor the road without its dangers.

It was a beautiful picture, as she sat there with sweet perplexity in her face, and above it an immortal radiance streaming from her brow.　She was like Guercino's Sibyl, with the scroll of fate and the uplifted pen; and the scroll she held contained but three words, — three words that controlled the destiny of a man, and, by their soft impulsion, directed forevermore the current of his thoughts.　They were, —

" Come to me! "

The magic syllables brought Kavanagh to her side.　The full soul is silent.　Only the rising and falling tides rush murmuring through their channels.　So sat the lovers, hand in hand; but for a long time neither spake, — neither had need of speech!

XXVII.

In the afternoon, Cecilia went to communicate the news to Alice with her own lips, thinking it

too important to be intrusted to the wings of the carrier-pigeon. As she entered the door, the cheerful doctor was coming out; but this was no unusual apparition, and excited no alarm. Mrs. Archer, too, according to custom, was sitting in the little parlor with her decrepit old neighbor, who seemed almost to have taken up her abode under that roof, so many hours of every day did she pass there.

With a light, elastic step, Cecilia bounded up to Alice's room. She found her reclining in her large chair, flushed and excited. Sitting down by her side, and taking both her hands, she said, with great emotion in the tones of her voice, —

" Dearest Alice, I have brought you some news that I am sure will make you well. For my sake, you will be no longer ill when you hear it. I am engaged to Mr. Kavanagh ! "

Alice feigned no surprise at this announcement. She returned the warm pressure of Cecilia's hand, and, looking affectionately in her face, said very calmly, —

" I knew it would be so. I knew that he loved you, and that you would love him."

" How could I help it ? " said Cecilia, her eyes beaming with dewy light; " could any one help loving him ? "

" No," answered Alice, throwing her arms around Cecilia's neck, and laying her head upon her shoulder ; " at least, no one whom he loved. But when did this happen ? Tell me all about it, dearest ! "

Cecilia was surprised, and perhaps a little hurt,

at the quiet, almost impassive manner in which
her friend received this great intelligence. She
had expected exclamations of wonder and delight,
and such a glow of excitement as that with which
she was sure she should have hailed the announce-
ment of Alice's engagement. But this momentary
annoyance was soon swept away by the tide of
her own joyous sensations, as she proceeded to re-
call to the recollection of her friend the thousand
little circumstances that had marked the progress
of her love and Kavanagh's; things which she
must have noticed, which she could not have for-
gotten; with questions interspersed at intervals,
such as, " Do you recollect when? " and " I am
sure you have not forgotten, have you? " and
dreamy little pauses of silence, and intercalated
sighs. She related to her, also, the perilous ad-
venture of the carrier-pigeon; how it had been
pursued by the cruel king-bird; how it had taken
refuge in Kavanagh's tower, and had been the
bearer of his letter, as well as her own. When
she had finished, she felt her bosom wet with the
tears of Alice, who was suffering martyrdom on
that soft breast, so full of happiness. Tears of
bitterness, — tears of blood! And Cecilia, in the
exultant temper of her soul at the moment, thought
them tears of joy, and pressed Alice closer to her
heart, and kissed and caressed her.

" Ah, how very happy you are, Cecilia! " at
length sighed the poor sufferer, in that slightly
querulous tone to which Cecilia was not unaccus-
tomed; " how very happy you are, and how very
wretched am I! You have all the joy of life, I all

its loneliness. How little you will think of me
now! How little you will need me! I shall be
nothing to you, — you will forget me."

" Never, dearest ! " exclaimed Cecilia, with much
warmth and sincerity. " I shall love you only the
more. We shall both love you. You will now
have two friends instead of one."

" Yes ; but both will not be equal to the one I
lose. No, Cecilia ; let us not make to ourselves
any illusions. I do not. You cannot now be with
me so much and so often as you have been. Even
if you were, your thoughts would be elsewhere.
Ah, I have lost my friend, when most I needed
her ! "

Cecilia protested ardently and earnestly, and
dilated with eagerness on her little plan of life, in
which their romantic friendship was to gain only
new strength and beauty from the more romantic
love. She was interrupted by a knock at the
street door; on hearing which, she paused a mo-
ment, and then said, —

" It is Arthur. He was to call for me."

Ah, what glimpses of home, and fireside, and a
whole life of happiness for Cecilia, were revealed
by that one word of love and intimacy, " Arthur "!
and for Alice, what a sentence of doom! what sor-
row without a name! what an endless struggle of
love and friendship, of duty and inclination ! A
little quiver of the eyelids and the hands, a hasty
motion to raise her head from Cecilia's shoulder, —
these were the only outward signs of emotion. But
a terrible pang went to her heart ; her blood rushed
eddying to her brain ; and when Cecilia had taken

leave of her with the triumphant look of love beaming upon her brow, and an elevation in her whole attitude and bearing, as if borne up by attendant angels, she sank back into her chair, exhausted, fainting, fearing, longing, hoping to die.

And below sat the two old women, talking of moths, and cheap furniture, and what was the best remedy for rheumatism ; and from the door went forth two happy hearts, beating side by side with the pulse of youth and hope and joy, and within them and around them was a new heaven and a new earth !

Only those who have lived in a small town can really know how great an event therein is a new engagement. From tongue to tongue passes the swift countersign ; from eye to eye flashes the illumination of joy, or the bale-fire of alarm ; the streets and houses ring with it, as with the penetrating, all-pervading sound of the village bell ; the whole community feels a thrill of sympathy, and seems to congratulate itself that all the great events are by no means confined to the great towns. As Cecilia and Kavanagh passed arm in arm through the village, many curious eyes watched them from the windows, many hearts grown cold or careless rekindled their household fires of love from the golden altar of God, borne through the streets by those pure and holy hands !

The intelligence of the engagement, however, was received very differently by different persons. Mrs. Wilmerdings wondered, for her part, why anybody wanted to get married at all. The little taxidermist said he knew it would be so from the

very first day they had met at his aviary. Miss
Hawkins lost suddenly much of her piety and all
her patience, and laughed rather hysterically. Mr.
Hawkins said it was impossible, but went in secret
to consult a friend, an old bachelor, on the best
remedy for love ; and the old bachelor, as one well
versed in such affairs, gravely advised him to think
of the lady as a beautiful statue !

Once more the indefatigable school-girl took up
her pen, and wrote to her foreign correspondent
a letter that might rival the famous epistle of
Madame de Sévigné to her daughter, announcing
the engagement of Mademoiselle Montpensier.
Through the whole of the first page, she told her
to guess who the lady was ; through the whole of
the second, who the gentleman was ; the third was
devoted to what was said about it in the village ;
and on the fourth there were two postscripts, one
at the top and the other at the bottom, the first
stating that they were to be married in the Spring,
and to go to Italy immediately afterwards, and
the last, that Alice Archer was dangerously ill with
a fever.

As for the Churchills, they could find no words
powerful enough to express their delight, but gave
vent to it in a banquet on Thanksgiving-day, in
which the wife had all the trouble and the husband
all the pleasure. In order that the entertainment
might be worthy of the occasion, Mr. Churchill
wrote to the city for the best cookery-book ; and
the bookseller, executing the order in all its ampli-
tude, sent him the Practical Guide to the Culinary
Art in all its Branches, by Frascatelli, pupil of the

celebrated Carême, and Chief Cook to Her Majesty
the Queen, — a ponderous volume, illustrated with
numerous engravings, and furnished with bills of
fare for every month in the year, and any number
of persons. This great work was duly studied,
evening after evening; and Mr. Churchill confessed
to his wife, that, although at first startled by the
size of the book, he had really enjoyed it very
highly, and had been much pleased to be present
in imagination at so many grand entertainments,
and to sit opposite the Queen without having to
change his dress or the general style of his con-
versation.

The dinner hour, as well as the dinner itself,
was duly debated. Mr. Churchill was in favor
of the usual hour of one ; but his wife thought
it should be an hour later. Whereupon he re-
marked, —

"King Henry the Eighth dined at ten o'clock
and supped at four. His queen's maids of honor
had a gallon of ale and a chine of beef for their
breakfast."

To which his wife answered, —

" I hope we shall have something a little more
refined than that."

The day on which the banquet should take place
was next discussed, and both agreed that no day
could be so appropriate as Thanksgiving - day ;
for, as Mrs. Churchill very truly remarked, it was
really a day of thanksgiving to Kavanagh. She
then said, —

" How very solemnly he read the Governor's
Proclamation yesterday ! particularly the words

'God save the Commonwealth of Massachusetts!'
And what a Proclamation it was! When he spread
it out on the pulpit, it looked like a table-cloth!"

Mr. Churchill then asked,

"What day of the week is the first of December? Let me see, —

> 'At Dover dwells George Brown, Esquire,
> Good Christopher Finch and Daniel Friar!'

Thursday."

"I could have told you that," said his wife, "by
a shorter process than your old rhyme. Thanksgiving-day always comes on Thursday."

These preliminaries being duly settled, the dinner was given.

There being only six guests, and the dinner being modelled upon one for twenty-four persons,
Russian style in November, it was very abundant.
It began with a Colbert soup, and ended with a
Nesselrode pudding; but as no allusion was made
in the course of the repast to the French names of
the dishes, and the mutton, and turnips, and pancakes were all called by their English patronymics,
the dinner appeared less magnificent in reality
than in the bill of fare, and the guests did not
fully appreciate how superb a banquet they were
enjoying. The hilarity of the occasion was not
marred by any untoward accident; though once or
twice Mr. Churchill was much annoyed, and the
company much amused, by Master Alfred, who
was allowed to be present at the festivities, and
audibly proclaimed what was coming, long before
it made its appearance. When the dinner was
over, several of the guests remembered brilliant

and appropriate things they might have said, and wondered they were so dull as not to think of them in season; and when they were all gone, Mr. Churchill remarked to his wife that he had enjoyed himself very much, and that he should like to ask his friends to just such a dinner every week!

XXVIII.

The first snow came. How beautiful it was, falling so silently, all day long, all night long, on the mountains, on the meadows, on the roofs of the living, on the graves of the dead! All white save the river, that marked its course by a winding black line across the landscape; and the leafless trees, that against the leaden sky now revealed more fully the wonderful beauty and intricacy of their branches!

What silence, too, came with the snow, and what seclusion! Every sound was muffled, every noise changed to something soft and musical. No more trampling hoofs, — no more rattling wheels! Only the chiming sleigh-bells, beating as swift and merrily as the hearts of children.

All day long, all night long, the snow fell on the village and on the churchyard; on the happy home of Cecilia Vaughan, on the lonely grave of Alice Archer! Yes; for before the winter came she had gone to that land where winter never comes. Her long domestic tragedy was ended. She was dead; and with her had died her secret sorrow and her secret love. Kavanagh never knew what wealth

of affection for him faded from the world when
she departed ; Cecilia never knew what fidelity
of friendship, what delicate regard, what gentle
magnanimity, what angelic patience, had gone
with her into the grave ; Mr. Churchill never
knew, that, while he was exploring the Past for
records of obscure and unknown martyrs, in his
own village, near his own door, before his own
eyes, one of that silent sisterhood had passed away
into oblivion, unnoticed and unknown.

How often, ah, how often, between the desire
of the heart and its fulfilment, lies only the brief-
est space of time and distance, and yet the desire
remains forever unfulfilled ! It is so near that
we can touch it with the hand, and yet so far
away that the eye cannot perceive it. What Mr.
Churchill most desired was before him. The
Romance he was longing to find and record had
really occurred in his neighborhood, among his own
friends. It had been set like a picture into the
frame-work of his life, enclosed within his own
experience. But he could not see it as an object
apart from himself ; and as he was gazing at what
was remote and strange and indistinct, the nearer
incidents of aspiration, love, and death, escaped
him. They were too near to be clothed by the im-
agination with the golden vapors of romance ; for
the familiar seems trivial, and only the distant and
unknown completely fill and satisfy the mind.

The winter did not pass without its peculiar de-
lights and recreations. The singing of the great
wood fires ; the blowing of the wind over the chim-
ney-tops, as if they were organ pipes ; the splendor

of the spotless snow; the purple wall built round the horizon at sunset; the sea-suggesting pines, with the moan of the billows in their branches, on which the snows were furled like sails; the northern lights; the stars of steel; the transcendent moonlight, and the lovely shadows of the leafless trees upon the snow; — these things did not pass unnoticed nor unremembered. Every one of them made its record upon the heart of Mr. Churchill.

His twilight walks, his long Saturday afternoon rambles, had again become solitary; for Kavanagh was lost to him for such purposes, and his wife was one of those women who never walk. Sometimes he went down to the banks of the frozen river, and saw the farmers crossing it with their heavy-laden sleds, and the Fairmeadow schooner imbedded in the ice; and thought of Lapland sledges, and the song of Kulnasatz, and the dismantled, ice-locked vessels of the explorers in the Arctic Ocean. Sometimes he went to the neighboring lake, and saw the skaters wheeling round their fire, and speeding away before the wind; and in his imagination arose images of the Norwegian Skate-Runners, bearing the tidings of King Charles's death from Frederickshall to Drontheim, and of the retreating Swedish army, frozen to death in its fireless tents among the mountains. And then he would watch the cutting of the ice with ploughs, and the horses dragging the huge blocks to the storehouses, and contrast them with the Grecian mules, bearing the snows of Mount Parnassus to the markets of Athens, in panniers,

protected from the sun by boughs of oleander and rhododendron.

The rest of his leisure hours were employed in anything and everything save in writing his Romance. A great deal of time was daily consumed in reading the newspapers, because it was necessary, he said, to keep up with the times ; and a great deal more in writing a Lyceum Lecture, on "What Lady Macbeth might have been, had her energies been properly directed." He also made some little progress in a poetical arithmetic, founded on Bhascara's, but relinquished it, because the school committee thought it was not practical enough, and more than hinted that he had better adhere to the old system. And still the vision of the great Romance moved before his mind, august and glorious, a beautiful mirage of the desert.

XXIX.

The wedding did not take place till spring. And then Kavanagh and his Cecilia departed on their journey to Italy and the East, — a sacred mission, a visit like the Apostle's to the Seven Churches, nay, to all the Churches of Christendom ; he hoping by some means to sow in many devout hearts the desire and prophecy that filled his own, — the union of all sects into one universal Church of Christ. They intended to be absent one year only ; they were gone three. It seemed to their friends that they never would return. But at length they came, — the long absent, the long looked for, the long desired, — bearing with them

that delicious perfume of travel, that genial, sunny atmosphere, and soft, Ausonian air, which returning travellers always bring about them.

It was night when they reached the village, and they could not see what changes had taken place in it during their absence. How it had dilated and magnified itself, — how it had puffed itself up, and bedizened itself with flaunting, ostentatious signs, — how it stood, rotund and rubicund with brick, like a portly man, with his back to the fire and both hands in his pockets, warm, expansive, apoplectic, and entertaining a very favorable opinion of himself, — all this they did not see, for the darkness; but Kavanagh beheld it all, and more, when he went forth on the following morning.

How Cecilia's heart beat as they drove up the avenue to the old house! The piny odors in the night air, the solitary light at her father's window, the familiar bark of the dog Major at the sound of the wheels, awakened feelings at once new and old. A sweet perplexity of thought, a strange familiarity, a no less pleasing strangeness! The lifting of the heavy brass latch, and the jarring of the heavy brass knocker as the door closed, were echoes from her childhood. Mr. Vaughan they found, as usual, among his papers in the study; — the same bland, white-haired man, hardly a day older than when they left him there. To Cecilia the whole long absence in Italy became a dream, and vanished away. Even Kavanagh was for the moment forgotten. She was a daughter, not a wife; — she had not been married, she had not been in Italy!

In the morning, Kavanagh sallied forth to find the Fairmeadow of his memory, but found it not. The railroad had completely transformed it. The simple village had become a very precocious town. New shops, with new names over the doors ; new streets, with new forms and faces in them ; the whole town seemed to have been taken and occupied by a besieging army of strangers. Nothing was permanent but the workhouse, standing alone in the pasture by the river ; and, at the end of the street, the school-house, that other workhouse, where in childhood we twist and untwist the cordage of the brain, that, later in life, we may not be obliged to pull to pieces the more material cordage of old ships.

Kavanagh soon turned in despair from the main street into a little green lane, where there were few houses, and where the barberry still nodded over the old stone wall ; — a place he had much loved in the olden time for its silence and seclusion. He seemed to have entered his ancient realm of dreams again, and was walking with his hat drawn a little over his eyes. He had not proceeded far, when he was startled by a woman's voice, quite sharp and loud, crying from the opposite side of the lane. Looking up, he beheld a small cottage, against the wall of which rested a ladder, and on this ladder stood the woman from whom the voice came. Her face was nearly concealed by a spacious gingham sun-bonnet, and in her right hand she held extended a large brush, with which she was painting the front of her cottage, when interrupted by the approach of Kava-

nagh, who, thinking she was calling to him, but
not understanding what she said, made haste to
cross over to. her assistance. At this movement
her tone became louder and more peremptory, and
he could now understand that her cry was rather a
warning than an invitation.

"Go away!" she said, flourishing her brush.
"Go away! What are you coming down here for,
when I am on the ladder, painting my house? If
you don't go right about your business, I will come
down and" —

"Why, Miss Manchester!" exclaimed Kava-
nagh; "how could I know that you would be
going up the ladder just as I came down the
lane?"

"Well, I declare! If it is not Mr. Kav-
anagh!"

And she scrambled down the ladder backwards
with as much grace as the circumstances permit-
ted. She, too, like the rest of his friends in the
village, showed symptoms of growing older. The
passing years had drunk a portion of the light
from her eyes, and left their traces on her cheeks,
as birds that drink at lakes leave their footprints
on the margin. But the pleasant smile remained,
and reminded him of the bygone days, when she
used to open for him the door of the gloomy house
under the poplars.

Many things had she to ask, and many to tell;
and for full half an hour Kavanagh stood leaning
over the paling, while she remained among the
hollyhocks, as stately and red as the plants them-
selves. At parting, she gave him one of the flow-

ers for his wife; and, when he was fairly out of
sight, again climbed the perilous ladder, and re-
sumed her fresco painting.

Through all the vicissitudes of these later years,
Sally had remained true to her principles and reso-
lution. At Mrs. Archer's death, which occurred
soon after Kavanagh's wedding, she had retired to
this little cottage, bought and paid for by her own
savings. Though often urged by Mr. Vaughan's
man, Silas, who breathed his soul out upon the air
of summer evenings through a keyed bugle, she
resolutely refused to marry. In vain did he send
her letters written with his own blood, — going
barefooted into the brook to be bitten by leeches,
and then using his feet as inkstands: she refused
again and again. Was it that in some blue cham-
ber, or some little warm back parlor, of her heart,
the portrait of the inconstant dentist was still hang-
ing? Alas, no! But as to some hearts it is given
in youth to blossom with the fragrant blooms of
young desire, so others are doomed by a mysterious
destiny to be checked in Spring by chill winds,
blowing over the bleak common of the world. So
had it been with her desires and thoughts of love.
Fear now predominated over hope; and to die un-
married had become to her a fatality which she
dared not resist.

In the course of his long conversation with Miss
Manchester, Kavanagh learned many things about
the inhabitants of the town. Mrs. Wilmerdings
was still carrying on her labors in the " Dunstable
and eleven-braid, open-work and colored straws."
Her husband had taken to the tavern, and often

came home very late, " with a brick in his hat," as
Sally expressed it. Their son and heir was far
away in the Pacific, on board a whale-ship. Miss
Amelia Hawkins remained unmarried, though pos-
sessing a talent for matrimony which amounted
almost to genius. Her brother, the poet, was no
more. Finding it impossible to follow the old
bachelor's advice, and look upon Miss Vaughan as
a beautiful statue, he made one or two attempts,
but in vain, to throw himself away on unworthy
objects, and then died. At this event, two elderly
maidens went into mourning simultaneously, each
thinking herself engaged to him; and suddenly
went out of it again, mutually indignant with each
other, and mortified with themselves. The little
taxidermist was still hopping about in his aviary,
looking more than ever like his gray African par-
rot. Mrs. Archer's house was uninhabited.

XXX.

Kavanagh continued his walk in the direction
of Mr. Churchill's residence. This, at least, was
unchanged, — quite unchanged. The same white
front, the same brass knocker, the same old
wooden gate, with its chain and ball, the same
damask roses under the windows, the same sun-
shine without and within. The outer door and
study door were both open, as usual in the warm
weather, and at the table sat Mr. Churchill, writ-
ing. Over each ear was a black and inky stump
of a pen, which, like the two ravens perched on
Odin's shoulders, seemed to whisper to him all that

passed in heaven and on earth. On this occasion, their revelations were of the earth. He was correcting school exercises.

The joyful welcome of Mr. Churchill, as Kavanagh entered, and the cheerful sound of their voices, soon brought Mrs. Churchill to the study, — her eyes bluer than ever, her cheeks fairer, her form more round and full. The children came in also, — Alfred grown to boy's estate and exalted into a jacket, and the baby, that was less than two years behind him, and catching all his falling mantles, and all his tricks and maladies.

Kavanagh found Mr. Churchill precisely where he left him. He had not advanced one step, — not one. The same dreams, the same longings, the same aspirations, the same indecision. A thousand things had been planned, and none completed. His imagination seemed still to exhaust itself in running, before it tried to leap the ditch. While he mused, the fire burned in other brains. Other hands wrote the books he dreamed about. He freely used his good ideas in conversation, and in letters, and they were straightway wrought into the texture of other men's books, and so lost to him forever. His work on Obscure Martyrs was anticipated by Mr. Hathaway, who, catching the idea from him, wrote and published a series of papers on Unknown Saints, before Mr. Churchill had fairly arranged his materials. Before he had written a chapter of his great Romance, another friend and novelist had published one on the same subject.

Poor Mr. Churchill! So far as fame and ex-

ternal success were concerned, his life certainly was a failure. He was, perhaps, too deeply freighted, too much laden by the head, to ride the waves gracefully. Every sea broke over him, — he was half the time under water !

All his defects and mortifications he attributed to the outward circumstances of his life, the exigencies of his profession, the accidents of chance. But, in reality, they lay much deeper than this. They were within himself. He wanted the all-controlling, all-subduing will. He wanted the fixed purpose that sways and bends all circumstances to its uses, as the wind bends the reeds and rushes beneath it.

In a few minutes, and in that broad style of handling in which nothing is distinctly defined, but everything clearly suggested, Kavanagh sketched to his friends his three years' life in Italy and the East. And then, turning to Mr. Churchill, he said, —

" And you, my friend, — what have you been doing all this while ? You have written to me so rarely that I have hardly kept pace with you. But I have thought of you constantly. In all the old cathedrals ; in all the lovely landscapes, among the Alps and Apennines ; in looking down on Duomo d'Ossola ; at the Inn of Baveno ; at Gaeta ; at Naples ; in old and mouldy Rome ; in older Egypt ; in the Holy Land ; in all galleries and churches and ruins ; in our rural retirement at Fiesoli ; — whenever I have seen anything beautiful, I have thought of you, and of how much you would have enjoyed it ! "

Mr. Churchill sighed ; and then, as if, with a touch as masterly, he would draw a picture that should define nothing, but suggest everything, he said, —

"You have no children, Kavanagh ; we have five."

"Ah, so many already ! " exclaimed Kavanagh, " A living Pentateuch ! A beautiful Pentapylon, or five-gated temple of Life ! A charming number ! "

" Yes," answered Mr. Churchill, " a beautiful number, Juno's own ; the wedding of the first even and first uneven numbers ; the number sacred to marriage, but having no reference, direct or indirect, to the Pythagorean novitiate of five years of silence."

" No ; it certainly is not the vocation of children to be silent," said Kavanagh, laughing. " That would be out of nature ; saving always the children of the brain, which do not often make so much noise in the world as we desire. I hope a still larger family of these has grown up around you during my absence."

" Quite otherwise," answered the schoolmaster, sadly. " My brain has been almost barren of songs. I have only been trifling, and I am afraid, that, if I play any longer with Apollo, the untoward winds will blow the discus of the god against my forehead, and strike me dead with it, as they did Hyacinth of old."

" And your Romance, — have you been more successful with that ? I hope it is finished, or nearly finished ? "

" Not yet begun," said Mr. Churchill. " The plan and characters still remain vague and indefinite in my mind. I have not even found a name for it."

" That you can determine after the book is written," suggested Kavanagh. " You can name it, for instance, as the old Heimskringla was named, from the initial word of the first chapter."

" Ah! that was very well in the olden time, and in Iceland, when there were no quarterly reviews. It would be called affectation now."

" I see you still stand a little in awe of opinion. Never fear that. The strength of criticism lies only in the weakness of the thing criticised."

" That is the truth, Kavanagh; and I am more afraid of deserving criticism than of receiving it. I stand in awe of my own opinion. The secret demerits of which we alone, perhaps, are conscious, are often more difficult to bear than those which have been publicly censured in us, and thus in some degree atoned for."

" I will not say," replied Kavanagh, " that humility is the only road to excellence, but I am sure that it is one road."

" Yes, humility, but not humiliation," sighed Mr. Churchill, despondingly. " As for excellence, I can only desire it and dream of it; I cannot attain to it, it lies too far from me; I cannot reach it. These very books about me here, that once stimulated me to action, have now become my accusers. They are my Eumenides, and drive me to despair."

" My friend," said Kavanagh, after a short

pause, during which he had taken note of Mr. Churchill's sadness, " that is not always excellent which lies far away from us. What is remote and difficult of access we are apt to overrate; what is really best for us lies always within our reach, though often overlooked. To speak frankly, I am afraid this is the case with your Romance. You are evidently grasping at something which lies beyond the confines of your own experience, and which, consequently, is only a play of shadows in the realm of fancy. The figures have no vitality; they are only outward shows, wanting inward life. We can give to others only what we have."

" And if we have nothing worth giving ? " interrupted Mr. Churchill.

" No man is so poor as that. As well might the mountain streamlets say they have nothing worth giving to the sea, because they are not rivers. Give what you have. To some one, it may be better than you dare to think. If you had looked nearer for the materials of your Romance, and had set about it in earnest, it would now have been finished."

" And burned, perhaps," interposed Mr. Churchill; " or sunk with the books of Simon Magus to the bottom of the Dead Sea."

" At all events, you would have had the pleasure of writing it. I remember one of the old traditions of Art, from which you may perhaps draw a moral. When Raphael desired to paint his Holy Family, for a long time he strove in vain to express the idea that filled and possessed his soul. One morning, as he walked beyond the city gates, meditat-

ing the sacred theme, he beheld, sitting beneath a
vine at her cottage door, a peasant woman, holding
a boy in her arms, while another leaned upon her
knee, and gazed at the approaching stranger. The
painter found here, in real life, what he had so
long sought for in vain in the realms of his imag-
ination; and quickly, with his chalk pencil, he
sketched, upon the head of a wine-cask that stood
near them, the lovely group, which afterwards,
when brought into full perfection, became the
transcendent Madonna della Seggiola."

"All this is true," replied Mr. Churchill, "but
it gives me no consolation. I now despair of writ-
ing anything excellent. I have no time to devote
to meditation and study. My life is given to
others, and to this destiny I submit without a
murmur; for I have the satisfaction of having
labored faithfully in my calling, and of having
perhaps trained and incited others to do what I
shall never do. Life is still precious to me for its
many uses, of which the writing of books is but
one. I do not complain, but accept this destiny,
and say, with that pleasant author, Marcus An-
toninus, ' Whatever is agreeable to thee shall be
agreeable to me, O graceful Universe! nothing
shall be to me too early or too late, which is sea-
sonable to thee! Whatever thy seasons bear shall
be joyful fruit to me, O Nature! from thee are all
things; in thee they subsist; to thee they return.
Could one say, Thou dearly beloved city of
Cecrops? and wilt thou not say, Thou dearly be-
loved city of God?' "

"Amen!" said Kavanagh. "And, to follow

your quotation with another, ' The gale that blows from God we must endure, toiling but not repining.' "

Here Mrs. Churchill, who had something of Martha in her, as well as of Mary, and had left the room when the conversation took a literary turn, came back to announce that dinner was ready, and Kavanagh, though warmly urged to stay, took his leave, having first obtained from the Churchills the promise of a visit to Cecilia during the evening.

" Nothing done! nothing done! " exclaimed he, as he wended his way homeward, musing and meditating. " And shall all these lofty aspirations end in nothing? Shall the arms be thus stretched forth to encircle the universe, and come back empty against a bleeding, aching breast? "

And the words of the poet came into his mind, and he thought them worthy to be written in letters of gold, and placed above every door in every house, as a warning, a suggestion, an incitement: —

> Stay, stay the present instant!
> Imprint the marks of wisdom on its wings!
> Oh, let it not elude thy grasp, but like
> The good old patriarch upon record,
> Hold the fleet angel fast until he bless thee!

www.ingramcontent.com/pod-product-compliance
Lightning Source LLC
Chambersburg PA
CBHW032314280326
41932CB00009B/805